# THE
# CHOSEN
# FEW

# THE CHOSEN FEW

A COMPANY OF PARATROOPERS AND
ITS HEROIC STRUGGLE TO SURVIVE IN
THE MOUNTAINS OF AFGHANISTAN

## GREGG ZOROYA

DA CAPO PRESS

First Da Capo Press edition 2017

Library of Congress Control Number: 2016954213
ISBN 978-0-306-82483-8 (hardcover)
ISBN 978-0-306-82484-5 (ebook)

Published by Da Capo Press, an imprint of Perseus Books, LLC,
a subsidiary of Hachette Book Group, Inc.
www.dacapopress.com

Da Capo Press books are available at special discounts for bulk purchases in the U.S. by corporations, institutions, and other organizations. For more information, please contact the Special Markets De-partment at Perseus Books, 2300 Chestnut Street, Suite 200, Philadelphia, PA 19103, or call (800) 810-4145, ext. 5000, or e-mail special.markets@perseusbooks.com.

Editorial production by Christine Marra, Marrathon Production Services.
www.marrathon.net

Book design by Jane Raese
Set in 13-point Seria

10 9 8 7 6 5 4 3 2 1

TO THE CHOSEN FEW.
They lived it.


AND TO MY SONS,
Jackson and Noah Zoroya,
for their humanity, their love, and their affirmation of life.

# >>> CONTENTS

# > > > MAPS

I assumed command of a joint special operations unit in June 2008. As I sought to gain understanding and appreciation for the fight our elements were engaged in, I quickly learned that the remote mountains of Kunar and Nuristan Provinces in northeast Afghanistan provided a nearly impenetrable sanctuary for several international terrorist groups. Within a month of my taking command, the Battle of Wanat occurred. This battle served to draw international attention to this area. It also served to highlight the tough fight being waged by "the Rock"—the 2nd Battalion, 503rd Parachute Infantry Regiment, 173rd Airborne Brigade.

This was a twenty-first-century war against terrorist insurgents. The young US Army paratroopers stationed there were locked in close-quarters combat not unlike the infantry experience of Vietnam, Korea, and World War II. They faced determined enemies who more often than not controlled the high ground—and with certainty, it was an enemy who sought to fight the Americans. At that time, there were not the resources we had later in the Afghanistan fight. There was not enough air support, MEDEVAC, or ground support. Not enough troops for the front lines.

While the world's attention was consumed with the broadening conflict in Iraq, the Rock fought desperate engagements, often outnumbered, with only their training, determination, and acts of valor helping them to prevail.

There had been some media attention for the battalion's Battle Company, whose exploits in the infamous Korengal Valley became the focus of the well-received documentary *Restrepo* and the book *WAR*. But in a valley just north of the Korengal, fighting in relative obscurity, were two platoons and a headquarters unit of one of Battle's sister companies—Chosen.

Those paratroopers liked to call themselves the Chosen Few. They were, in fact, seemingly chosen by fate to experience some of the most brutal aspects of war. In three major engagements and several small skirmishes, they fought off successive, coordinated efforts by an enemy determined to wipe them out.

After fifteen months of combat, nearly two-thirds of the Chosen Few would be Purple Heart recipients. Two would be awarded the Medal of Honor, two more would receive a Distinguished Service Cross; more than a dozen Silver Stars and more than two dozen Bronze Stars for valor would be awarded to this company. Rarely in the annals of modern war have fighting men displayed such teamwork, courage, and fighting heart as the Chosen Few.

People often look back with awe upon early generations of American combat troops, up to and including the famous Greatest Generation of World War II, as if to conclude that that kind of warrior has come and gone and we will never see their like again. But that is just not true.

If there is any lesson that the Chosen Few teaches us, it is that the kind of spirit and sense of sacrifice borne out in the young men and women who fill the ranks of the US military are as strong today as they ever were. Special operators, conventional forces, active or reserve—our nation should be grateful to have the troops we do. Paratroopers like the Chosen Few demonstrate what our country has come to expect of our warriors—commitment, selflessness, and grit. This is an American story that rivals any in our history for valor, heroism, and sacrifice.

William H. McRaven
Admiral (US Navy, Retired)

I feel how weak and fruitless must be any words
of mine which should attempt to beguile you
from the grief of a loss so overwhelming.

  —ABRAHAM LINCOLN,
    from an 1864 letter to a grieving mother of sons killed in battle

*So this would be the end.*

Ryan Pitts lay covered in his own blood, the paratrooper's twenty-two-year-old body so riddled with shards of metal from exploding grenades that his legs were all but useless. His friends were dead all around him. Others had fled. Pitts propped himself against a dirt wall inside a sand-bagged observation post in an obscure valley of a mountainous province of eastern Afghanistan, seven thousand miles from his home in New Hampshire. He pulled a rifle into his lap and sat tucked into a corner of one fighting position facing the direction from where the enemy had been attacking.

*I want to kill at least two or three of them before they finally kill me.*

Even over the din of gunfire and explosions, he could hear enemy fighters just yards away yelling back and forth at one another in Pashtun or Dari or one of those obscure Nuristani dialects that were impossible even for the Army's Afghan interpreters to understand. Oddly, the pain from his wounds was not so bad. Ryan's nervous system was still in shock from the explosions that had tossed him like a rag doll and engulfed him in a cloud of steel parts. Blood ran down his face from where the skin of his forehead had been filleted open. The shroud of shrapnel was so condensed that several small pieces had nearly punched holes through two narrow, black memorial bracelets that Ryan wore, each engraved with the names of Chosen Few soldiers who had died during the fourteen months he and the others of his paratrooper company had been fighting in this valley of sheer cliffs and breath-robbing altitude.

→ ←

They all cherished that nickname for their company, the Chosen Few. It was a play on the unit designation: C Company, or Chosen Company, of the 2nd Battalion—"the Rock"—503rd Parachute Infantry Regiment, 173rd Airborne Brigade. "Sky Soldiers." Paratroopers.

The "Chosen Few" nickname carried plenty of meaning for these men in their late teens and early twenties. Made them feel special. Prized. Maybe because so many of them came from places or families where they had grown up feeling anything but special. Where fathers died or disappeared. Where parents never married or drifted apart. Where a mother lost herself to drugs, leaving a son in despair and desperate for a family. Grandparents had taken charge when some of these men were boys, raising them to adulthood. For others it was just a matter of biding time until they were old enough to break away and start defining life on their terms, which would ultimately mean joining the Army.

Growing up, Ryan never knew his dad. His parents never married and broke up within a year after he was born. He spent much of his childhood moving between New Hampshire and Vermont, living with his mother and a younger half-brother in a string of rented apartments, switching schools every couple of years. His mother worked as a secretary—married, divorced, and married again—and his family struggled with finances and lived modestly.

When he flew to basic training at Fort Sill, Oklahoma, in 2003 at eighteen, it was his first time on an airplane. The structure, the clarity of purpose in the Army—all of it made sense to Ryan when he enlisted. A roof over your head, food, health care. No worries with any of it. And the men he trained with or jumped with out of airplanes or fought beside—he'd come to know they would never abandon him as others had.

More than that, he realized they would actually lay down their lives for this child of a broken home.

Some of his paratrooper buddies—now lying near him, dead or wounded—were quiet and kept to themselves. Others were brash and played fast and loose with Army rules and regulations. A couple of them had incredible comic timing and a gift for mimicry that left everyone in stitches. More than a few could sometimes be a real pain in the ass.

But it was family, Ryan realized. Like sharing the same blood. More than that, it was a family each man had chosen. Not one issued at birth, no questions asked. Ryan had even passed on a chance for a promotion to staff sergeant just so he could stay with 2nd Platoon and Chosen Company. And if their worst nightmare came to pass—as it did in the stifling heat of this predawn Sunday in July 2008—the brothers would place themselves between Ryan and whatever was trying to kill him. They would move—and the sight of this was riveting—toward the gunfire.

The rest of the world simply had no idea.

Since May of the previous year Chosen Company paratroopers had been fighting against annihilation in a series of battles and stand-offs in the Waigal Valley with far larger numbers of fierce, mountain warriors augmented by highly trained terrorist groups made up of Afghans, Pakistanis, Arabs, Chechens, and Uzbeks. The American public might as well have been on a different planet.

Back home people were waiting in long lines to drop $500 on the first iPhones, or clamoring to get their hands on J. K. Rowling's last Harry Potter installment, or gaping at suggestive Vanity Fair photos of fifteen-year-old Disney star Miley Cyrus. They were arguing about whether Barry Bonds and his 756 home runs deserved asterisks because of a steroid scandal or whether Tony Soprano actually died in that diner in the last episode of the HBO series. Home mortgages were collapsing; Barack Obama's presidential prospects were rising, and George W. Bush was rushing twenty thousand troops to Iraq with his "surge" to save a foundering war effort.

That last event had direct bearing on these paratroopers' fortunes, not that anyone back home had a clue. Shifting America's military focus to Iraq left the US war effort in Afghanistan with what uniformed leaders euphemistically described as an "economy of force" campaign. Everyone had to do more with less—fewer aircraft, fewer surveillance drones, fewer soldiers. Within this world of rationed military resources, arguably the most obscure battlefield was the Waigal Valley, a serpentine scar trailing northward between towering escarpments inhabited by a hardy, warlike subculture separate from the Pashtuns, Tajiks, or Hazaras who populated the rest of Afghanistan.

The land was brutally inhospitable. When the paratroopers first entered the valley in May of 2007 aboard helicopters straining against thin air to reach their most remote base, they disembarked at an outpost called Ranch House built on the side of a mountain at more than seven thousand feet. Some of them vomited from the effects of altitude just hiking up to their barracks for the first time.

They would fight for their lives on that mountain. And later again along the cliffs of a narrow canyon near the Waigal Valley and still later in this place where a bleeding Ryan Pitts now lay ready to kill as many of the enemy as possible before they could kill him. Fighting through the spring, summer, and fall of 2007 in the Waigal and then through the winter, spring, and summer of 2008 would change the meaning of life for those of the Chosen Few. It would draw some of them closer to God and cause others to lose their faith entirely. But nearly all, to a man, would discover something they never expected: love. It was a seismic revelation, particularly for those who came from difficult childhoods where they were starved for affection, where they knew nothing about unconditional acceptance and sacrifice.

Some of those same people would be cut down with Ryan this day as the first rays of daylight filled the skies over the valley with a rich sapphire blue and the surrounding hillsides suddenly exploded with an earsplitting thunderclap of unleashed violence. Rocket-propelled grenades, Soviet-designed PK machine guns, Kalashnikov rifles all fired at once at the rudimentary combat base the paratroopers had only started to build five days earlier on the valley floor. The enemy focused their torrent of gunfire not only on the new combat base but also higher up, on a series of terraced fields, into the sand-bagged observation post the soldiers called "Topside," where Ryan was the forward observer.

The Chosen Few were plunged into what would become the bloodiest battle of possibly the bloodiest combat tour any US troops had endured since jet planes flew into the Twin Towers in New York, the Pentagon in Washington, and a furrowed field outside Shanksville, Pennsylvania.

→  ←

When the shooting started early that morning there were forty-nine Americans manning the base and the Topside observation post. There were another twenty-four Afghan soldiers split between a traffic-control bunker south of 1st Squad's position and dug-in positions along the north edge of the base. Potentially three times that many or more attacked—a force of fighters from terror organizations such as Al Qaeda, Army of Mohammed, or Army of the Righteous. Assisted by the local police and the people of Wanat, they had crept in the darkness up to the paratroopers' defenses, setting up their weapons in buildings, hedgerows, and even tree tops in a rough encirclement of the partially finished base and nearby Topside.

About a half hour into the fight Ryan was now the last one alive at Topside. He could peer around the side of a sand-bagged wall and see his friends' bodies.

Only minutes before, a wounded Sergeant Matt Gobble had yelled out from the other end of their maze of fighting positions: "Is there anyone alive?" Gobble was a sergeant assigned to the observation post. He too could see the bodies of his soldiers everywhere. Gobble had been stunned by a rocket-propelled grenade blast and peppered with countless small pieces of metal. He was having a hard time shaking off the effects of the explosion. It felt like he couldn't gather his thoughts. Right beside him, still alive, was Specialist Tyler Stafford, covered with penetrating shrapnel wounds and looking like he had blood oozing from every square inch of his body.

When Gobble heard nothing after his shout-out, he and Stafford half-crawled, half-stumbled their way across a single strand of razor wire that was Topside's outer perimeter. They moved along one of the terraces and then down toward the nearest American fighting position fifty yards away. The terraces had stood for generations, offering slices of tillable land for mountain farmers. Gobble and Stafford scrambled down each embankment to flee Topside. And when Gobble learned later that he had left his buddy behind, it gave rise to a guilt that would torment him for years to come, bringing him to tears of shame over the memory of it: "I should have known." But how could he? Neither he nor Stafford heard an answer from Ryan when Gobble called out. The enemy was very close, possibly just on the other side of the sand-bags across from where Pitts lay. Some were certainly over by a huge boulder that anchored one corner of Topside. That meant enemy fighters were actually inside the wire. One of them had reached around the rock with an AK47 and taken a shot at Gobble as he and Stafford slipped away.

Ryan feared the enemy would simply point their rifles over the edge of the sandbags and finish him off. And all at once he was alone, terri-fied. He reached for a radio handset and whispered into the mouthpiece to Chosen Company commander Matt Myer, who was down below in the besieged compound trying desperately to manage the battle from a makeshift headquarters.

"I'm the only one left alive," Pitts said in a hushed voice. "Everyone else here is either gone or dead."

Myer's heart fell. But he had his own burden of dying and wounded paratroopers around him at the command post. The West Point gradu-ate calmly told Ryan the truth: there was no one to send.

The valley continued to reverberate with the noise of competing walls of gunfire. Insurgent fighters in positions up and down the ridges, from immediately outside the perimeter of the rudimentary combat base to high up in the rocks of the canyon walls, poured fire down on the Americans. They could see every fortified position where the paratroopers were pinned down—it was laid out before them like a neat series of targets.

The paratroopers, fighting with a few Army engineers and Marine advisers for the Afghan troops who were also present, pushed back against the volume of incoming bullets and propelled grenades with their own counter-fire, shooting at muzzle flashes or rustling branches or the vague outline of a human figure in a darkened window or behind foliage. A thick haze of dust and smoke was building up over the battlefield, fed by burning piles of large, flat, folded layers of fabric liner the Americans used for constructing fortifications. In the center, rising skyward, was an inky column of smoke from the flaming remains of an Army Humvee. The vehicle had contained the best defensive weapon the Americans had that day, a wire-guided missile system so precise and lethal in its effect that Islamist terrorist fighters called it the "Finger of God." It was one of the first things they targeted that morning with the opening barrage, and they destroyed it almost immediately with rocket-propelled grenades.

The militants had used machine gun fire to drive the paratroopers out of their only fortified mortar position on the base, forcing them to abandon a 120mm mortar that could have wreaked havoc on the enemy positions. The same barrage of bullets disabled one of only two .50-caliber heavy machine guns the paratroopers were using to defend themselves.

Now all the soldiers were hunkered down in four isolated islands of sandbagged foxholes, each braced on one side with an armored Humvee. Two dozen Afghan Army troops assigned to Chosen Company fought from their own built-up defensive positions close within the unfinished fort.

At Topside Ryan Pitts absorbed the news from Myer. Either send someone, or Topside will fall, he told his commander in a hush, and he signed off.

"Nine-two out."

What else to do, Pitts thought. He had a grenade launcher slung under the barrel of the M4 rifle he held in his hands. Pitts loaded a 40mm, brass-covered grenade into the launcher, pointed the weapon skyward, almost straight up, and fired. It arced upward and for a second he thought it might fall right back down on top of him. But it landed instead in the direction from where the enemy had been attacking. He launched more grenades. He used the radio to reach the closest group of paratroopers hunkered down in a fighting position at the base of the terraced hillside about fifty yards away. His buddy, Sergeant Brian Hissong, picked up the mic and heard Pitts give directions to fire over Topside, lay down an umbrella of bullets to maybe keep the enemy from overwhelming him. Hissong obliged, opening fire with his M4, aiming right over the Topside defensive walls.

As Pitts worked to wreak some havoc on the militants before they could launch their final assault, he realized he was no longer afraid. In fact, a sense of calm swept over him. There was nothing more he could do now but wait for the attack.

He held the rifle in his lap and could hear voices.

They're coming.

# 1

## >>> FALLING FROM THE SKIES

*There's a definite pucker factor* when the door opens on a C130 jump plane at 1,250 feet. The sudden roar of the outside airstream has a way of instantly focusing the mind, sending tremors through the nervous system right down to the balls of the feet. The amygdala of every young paratrooper-in-training is lighting up with the same neon-blinking message: your destiny is a raging void of air and sky. Just outside the open doorway of the airplane that is bucking up and down in the turbulence is a small ledge bordered with a white stripe marking the last footfall before thin air.

Paratroopers never forget the first jump.

Jeddah Deloria, who used to catch rattlesnakes for fun while growing up in Rancho Cucamonga, California, had a palpable case of the jitters when he stepped onto that ledge. Like so many who would become part of the Chosen Few, he hated heights yet was compelled to push the limits of that fear by volunteering for the US Army Airborne. When the moment finally came and the Philippine-born Deloria stood second in line approaching the door, the patchwork pattern of the earth below looked almost artificial. And when he jumped, it wasn't at all the way he thought it would be. The warm, loud airstream sucked him up and away so that a fraction of a second later he was floating under a canopy in utterly peaceful silence. That stutter step of terror followed by absolute serenity was thrilling.

Only a three-week course at Fort Benning, Georgia, separated earth-bound soldiers—"dirty legs," paratroopers called them—from the ones in the sky. The Fort Benning "black hats," trainers who cruised the instruction lanes in their black T-shirts and baseball caps to turn service members into paratroopers, cranked out fourteen thousand of them a year. Fort Benning had been making paratroopers since 1940.

The Chosen Few trickled through airborne school at different times, depending on when each entered the Army. In a few cases they went through side by side. The hulking wrestling champion, Pruitt Rainey of Haw River, North Carolina, wound up rooming with beefy Iowa-native Jonathan Albert, and they became lifelong friends, both destined for Chosen.

It was literally a ground-up training program. The first week was devoted to parachute orientation—what it looks like, how it fits, the way it's worn. Jumping during that first week was limited to stepping off a two-foot-high platform and practicing how to hit the ground. They learned the up-36-out-36 drill, jumping up three feet and out three feet to acquire some distance and separation once they squirted out of the metal monster that would be traveling well over one hundred miles per hour.

During the second week trainees entered an area of Fort Benning that looked like something out of a Universal Studios theme park where there were 12-foot stands with swing harnesses and 34-foot platforms with zip lines attached—all to recreate the feel of descending under a canopy at 16 feet per second—and there were soaring 250-foot towers dominating the skyline. From these a soldier dangling from a parachute was lifted high into the air and dropped. A definite white-knuckler. The point was to teach the trainee how to control the parachute's descent by tugging down on risers—the straps connecting him to the canopy—in the face of a wind.

Then in the third week they did it all for real. Each had to successfully complete five parachute jumps to pass the course.

When Jon Albert, who enlisted at age twenty after getting a cold call from an Army recruiter, woke up in the barracks on the morning of his first jump, the reality of what he was about to do hit him in the face like a bucket of cold water.

*What the hell did I get myself into? I'm deathly afraid of heights ...*

His stomach churned as he waited with the other trainees on wooden benches inside a warehouse-size staging area, each of them trussed up tightly into a harness with a parachute on their backs and a reserve chute tucked against their bellies. They sat staring at a plaque tacked up on the wall for inspiration. It was shaped like the jump wings they would earn if they graduated. Then came the single-file hike onto the aircraft, and soon they were airborne and ten minutes from the drop zone. Heart rates quickened, and they stood up in unison, hooking up their static lines and checking the harness, helmet, and straps of the soldier in front of them, sounding off if everything was okay. Then the door was opened.

Any refusal to proceed at this point meant automatically failing the course, something that only happened about once every six months.

When Jacob Sones, an eighteen-year-old Texan, was walking out to the plane for his first jump, a trainer nearby trying to put the fear of God in him yelled out, "Shit, Airborne, there's something wrong with your parachute!" Sones fired right back, "Fuck it, Sergeant Airborne. I've got a reserve." The trainer laughed, but Sones couldn't help but keep asking anyone standing nearby if his parachute looked okay.

Planes always made the same approach to the drop zone during training. Flying over the Chattahoochee River, they were one minute out. Over a paved road, they were thirty seconds away. And then there would be the green light, a tap on the rump by a jump master, and blue sky.

For Alaska-raised Kyle Silvernale, who would later become a Chosen Company squad leader, the shock of the airstream sucking him away in the midst of his up-36-out-36 felt like divine retribution.

Like getting smacked out of the sky by God. That's the only way I could describe it.

Jason Baldwin, who turned eighteen one week before basic training, closed his eyes during that first jump—exactly what they tell you not to do.

Oh my God, I'm going to die.

It was straight out of the paratrooper joke guide, the one that says everybody does a night jump the first time because they always do it with their eyes closed. Every one of them found the experience when the chute popped open and they floated soundlessly down to earth exhilarating.

When Mike Denton, the Florida son of a paramedic, first launched himself out of an airplane, his chute popped opened and he was terrified to find that his risers were twisted above his head. He somehow managed to follow protocol and start bicycling his legs like crazy to spin himself out of it.

Scarier than hell.

New Jersey native Chris McKaig, son of a mail carrier, thought his heart was pounding its way out of his chest when they opened the aircraft door and he could hear the rush of air. When they all rose to their feet to hook up static lines, his legs were shaking. And when he jumped, McKaig actually skimmed the side of the aircraft. He wasn't hurt, but when the chute popped open, there was so much adrenalin coursing through his veins, McKaig couldn't help but yell, "THIS IS FUCKING AWESOME!" so loud that the black hats could hear him down on the ground.

"Shut up, Airborne!" one of the hats hollered into the sky through a bullhorn. "Quit screaming up there!"

When McKaig touched down, he desperately needed to relieve himself and did so soon afterward, the birth of a ritual. From then on he would christen every drop zone.

It was only about sixty seconds from chute-opening to ground, and trainees quickly found that not everyone was created equal when it came to falling out of the sky. Truly, the bigger they were, the harder they fell. Mike Denton, at six-feet-one, 190 pounds, dropped like a rock.

Almost like a B-movie script for a vintage war film, the troopers who would fill the ranks of Chosen Company hailed from literally every corner of the country. Jason Bogar, the son of a Baptist minister, was raised in Seattle, Washington; Sergio Abad, whose mother abused heroin, grew up in Miami. Jonathan Ayers was from Georgia and vacationed with his family on the Atlantic at Hilton Head, South Carolina; and Matt Ferrara from Southern California and Jonathan Brostrom from Hawaii were Pacific surfers.

For twenty-nine-year-old Chuck Bell, a country-born child of the Ozarks, the first airplane he ever flew on in his life was the commercial flight the Army paid for to take him to boot camp in Georgia. The second airplane he ever rode on he jumped out of.

Every one of them had volunteered, their portal into the military usually a local recruiting office tucked into a strip mall with other competing office space taken up by the Marines, Air Force, or Navy. Often what sealed the deal were the videos a recruitment officer would slip into a VCR—"Here, son, take a look at this"—of soldiers jumping out of airplanes or crawling through mud, looking aggressive and heroic.

It was surprising how many of them signed up after simply driving past a recruiting station and pulling into the parking lot on a whim just to see what the military was all about. That's exactly what Justin Kalenits did. Living on the outskirts of Cleveland at twenty-one, he wound up joining the Army almost as an afterthought. Life after high school had turned aimless, and the idea of a sudden and dramatic shift into the Army had strong appeal.

*I need to get out of here. My life isn't going anywhere. I'm kind of a punk. I need discipline.*

He was twenty-two when he joined Chosen Company. At five-feet-six and 140 pounds, he wound up being one of Chosen's smallest, even while carrying one of its biggest guns, the squad automatic weapon

(SAW). His big, loopy grin and ears that stuck out like jug handles gave him an impish look, like he was always up to mischief.

Tyler Stafford was working as a waiter and bartender at a Champps Sports Bar in Denver in 2005 when he got drunk one night at his buddy's birthday party and the two suddenly made a pact to join the Army "before we miss the war." Stafford was the youngest of three children to middle-income-earning parents living in suburban Parker, Colorado. He'd lettered in basketball, football, baseball, and track at Ponderosa High School, and his dream was to fly aircraft. But he blew out his knee playing pick-up basketball shortly before starting basic training for a Marine ROTC flight program, and after that his life lost some direction. The Army offered a course correction. He enlisted at twenty-one.

For many of the Chosen Few, signing up was a chance to exorcise, once and for all, that feeling that they had become perennial disappointments to their parents.

"I know very well that I haven't turned out to be the man you might have wanted me to be," Joseph Lancour wrote to his mother, explaining his decision to quit his job at a Burger King and join the Army. He penned the letter from boot camp in Fort Benning in early 2006. "I always allowed myself to accept second place. But that's not going to be good enough anymore. I'm not going to settle for first loser anymore. . . . I won't let you down."

Joe was the only son of Rob and Starla Lancour, a native of Michigan who grew up near Lake Michigan. His parents divorced when he was five, and Joe spent a childhood shifting back and forth between households during the week.

Joe was five-feet-nine with a narrow build, olive-colored skin, and dark brown eyes. It was after graduating from high school and living in Flint, Michigan, working the grill at a Burger King, that Joe felt the need to turn things around by enlisting in the Army. His father was stunned by the transformation after Joe graduated from boot camp. He seemed confident and mature, and loved the structure, discipline, and camaraderie of the Army. After finishing paratrooper training, Joe Lancour was sent to the 173rd Airborne Brigade.

During the fall and winter of 2006 and the spring of 2007 Chosen prepared for war in eastern Afghanistan with a stew of seasoned combat veterans and brand-new recruits. The roughly 150-man company was, like much of the Army infantry, predominantly young and white. The largest minority was Latino, a little more than 10 percent. There were about ten African Americans; two members of Chosen were born in the Philippines; one was half-Thai, half African American; and one was a full-blooded Native American.

No one stayed with Chosen Company forever. The new company commander in 2006, West Point graduate Matthew Myer, could be expected to remain in charge for the one combat rotation of 2007–2008 before moving on to another assignment and a likely promotion to major. Chosen Company platoon lieutenants like Matthew Ferrara and Devon George could very easily follow the same pattern. Senior enlisted officers like Company First Sergeant Scott Beeson or Platoon Sergeant Matt Kahler and Shane Stockard were probably "lifers" for whom the Army would be a career, but even they would be expected to rotate out of Chosen.

Further down the ranks squad leaders like Staff Sergeant David Dzwik from Michigan or six-feet-three Kyle Silvernale might be just as likely to make the Army a career as go back to civilian life. That was even more true for sergeants who led teams within the squads—because they had even less time in the Army and might be more uncertain about their futures.

But most of the GIs who made up the Chosen Few were young men barely out of their teens. For them the Army was just one doorway on a life path still in search of a destination. Most of them joined for reasons that had nothing to do with a career.

Ryan Pitts just kind of drifted into it. It was early 2003, the nation was at war, Iraq was about to be invaded. Serving his country would be a good thing, Pitts thought, though he was certain all the real fighting would be over by the time he got into uniform.

He was only seventeen, and Pitts's mother had to approve, and he knew she would never agree to him joining the infantry. The Army recruiter had an idea. He suggested Pitts ask his parents to let him become a forward observer who calls in artillery and air support.

*Hey, it wasn't infantry.*

She agreed to sign.

Mike Denton was resolved to serve just as his grandfather and older brother had served before him. These were the wars of his generation, Denton believed, and it was time to step up.

Others, like Chris McKaig, were lured for the reasons a lot of young boys become enthralled with the military, playing at it for hours in the hills and forests of their childhoods and developing a growing fascination with guns and shooting.

Still more were like Jon Albert, who found himself living at home in Cedar Rapids after graduating from high school with no plans for his future as his dad, Dave, prodded him about where he saw his life heading. Jon was ripe for some direction when that cold call came from an intrepid Army recruiter. A video of soldiers in action against a hard-charging musical score did the trick.

A large number of the Chosen Few came from broken homes and arrived in the Army without a father figure or at least none who had been around full-time. Some were like lost boys searching without realizing it for a surrogate family after a childhood of abuse or neglect.

Jacob Sones was one of them. He was born in Waco, Texas, and had one sibling, a younger brother who died in infancy. The tragedy strained the marriage of Phillip and Teri Sones. The couple divorced when Jacob was just a young boy, and he went to live with his mother.

Teri was a free-spirited woman, a new-age parent who taught her son to question authority and encouraged him to read contemporary literature. His father was the opposite—practical and clear-eyed, believing that only sacrifice and hard work led to success. When his mom remarried and moved to Connecticut, Jacob shuttled back and forth between there and Texas. He dropped out of high school in the tenth grade and did a poor job of trying to make it on his own. He was drifting. At his father's urging, Jacob joined the Army after obtaining his high school degree equivalency certificate and chose Airborne. He was eighteen.

→ ←

After Fort Benning, troopers in Chosen Company were sent to Italy for additional training before their deployment.

When he reached Camp Ederle near Vicenza, Italy, in mid-2006, for the first time in his life Sones felt really safe—like he had finally caught up on a pathway that had meaning and he was no longer a screw-up. It was an achievement and he could be proud. And Sones loved Italy, in no small part because the Italian drinking age was eighteen. This fed his reckless streak and before long, Sones earned a reputation for acquiring more punishments for misbehavior—Article 15s—than any other soldier in Chosen Company: missing formation, showing up drunk in formation, having military police escort him back to the base. It usually meant a loss of rank and pay as well as extra duty. By the time they later deployed to Afghanistan, Sones was still a private first class. His profligacy lead to one of the more famous bits of Chosen Company lore when he passed out on the grounds of Camp Ederle after a night of drinking. He could feel someone prodding him with a boot and instinctively rolled over and reacted.

"Fuck you."

It was Lieutenant Colonel William Brian Ostlund. And it was another Article 15.

The officer standing over Sones would lead him and the 2nd Battalion into combat in May of 2007. Ostlund had taken command of 2/503 (2nd Battalion, 503rd Infantry Regiment) the previous June at the age of forty. He was a focused, fiercely driven officer as comfortable—when at war—at raining fire and death down on the enemy as he was laboring to strike an accord with recalcitrant tribesmen over cups of sweet tea. He was also a child of divorce, born in Park Rapids and raised in Detroit Lakes, a vacation area about fifty miles due east of Fargo, North Dakota. As someone of Native American descent, he was fascinated with the local Indian community; he built friendships there and fought beside them with his fists when white boys threw insults. His was a childhood spent outdoors camping and playing hockey; he earned his spending money recovering golf balls and cleaning fish for vacationers. The family moved to Omaha, Nebraska, when Ostlund was fourteen, and by then he was determined to become a Marine infantryman. When a hapless Marine recruiter put him off, the Army won him on the re-bound, and by age eighteen, Ostlund had earned a spot with the prestigious First Ranger Battalion, turning nineteen in the Army's arduous Ranger course. He served more than four years before shifting into the Nebraska National Guard and attending ROTC at the University of Nebraska at Omaha to become an officer.

Ostlund was a platoon leader in the 101st Airborne when he deployed to Desert Storm in 1990. The battalion he was part of was eventually commanded by then-Lieutenant Colonel David Petraeus. It was during a live-fire exercise with Ostlund's platoon in 1991 that a soldier tripped and fell and accidentally shot Petraeus through the chest with an M16. Then Brigadier General Jack Keane, the deputy commanding general of the division, was standing next to Petraeus when he went down. When Ostlund ran up, Keane said, "Hey, Lieutenant, your battalion commander has been shot. Treat him, medevac him, and get this range opened back up. Great live-fire."

Ostlund had to cut off Petraeus's gear and called over some infantrymen who had upper-level medical training to give aid, with Petraeus muttering all the while, "This is great fucking training."

In the intervening fifteen years before Ostlund was named commander of the 2nd Battalion, he earned a master's degree and taught American political and international security studies at West Point. He served a tour in Iraq after 9/11 as an operations officer for the 173rd Airborne Division.

He saw the 2nd Battalion as a jewel of a unit to lead and was thrilled when he was finally named commander.

→ ←

The US Army is built on tradition, carefully enshrining what happened in the past for the purpose of enabling and inspiring what happens in the future.

Units of any size can boast a nickname freighted with symbolism: the "All Americans" for the paratroopers of the 82nd Airborne Division, or 1st Infantry Division as the "Big Red One." The 101st Division "Screaming Eagles" are composed of brigades with such nicknames as "Bastogne" in honor of that unit's heroism during World War II or the "Rakassans," the word the Japanese used in wartime dispatches to describe the unit as it fought in the Pacific Theater—it roughly translates to "falling down umbrella man."

When freshly minted paratroopers arrived in Italy, they found themselves part of a fighting group with its own fabled past. The 173rd Airborne Brigade activated in 1963 took as its nickname the words Nationalist Chinese paratroopers used to describe the unit: *tien bien*, or "Sky Soldiers." The brigade was assembled from battalions such as the 2/503, which had its own proud history as one of America's original parachute infantry units formed in 1941 when that war-fighting concept was still in its infancy. The next year the battalion conducted the first combat parachute jump in US military history into Algeria. In 1943 the paratroopers made the first US combat jump in the Pacific theater of war, dropping into New Guinea. They later fought in the Philippines, earning their moniker, "The Rock," by recapturing the Philippine fortress island of Corregidor that carried the same name.

The Rock was where US soldiers in 1942 had held out against a Japanese siege for nearly five months after Pearl Harbor. The 2/503 parachuted onto the two-square-mile island on February 16, 1945, and spearheaded taking it back. The victory earned the battalion a Presidential Unit Citation, the equivalent of awarding each soldier in the unit a Distinguished Service Cross, the second-highest award for valor.

Twenty years later the unit was part of the 173rd Airborne Brigade, which became the first Army combat unit committed to the war in Vietnam. The paratroopers fought in some of the bloodiest battles of that conflict and conducted the only major combat parachute jump. The battalion earned a second Presidential Unit Citation for the Battle of Dak To and the assault on Hill 875 in November of 1967. The 173rd Airborne Brigade was deactivated after Vietnam and then reactivated in 2000.

A third Presidential Unit Citation would be waiting for a new generation of Rock paratroopers in the mountains of eastern Afghanistan. Rock Battalion contained six companies: Able, Battle, Chosen, Destined, Fusion, and, lastly, Black Sheep, the headquarters unit.

Chosen paratroopers came up with their own mascot, the Punisher, from a Marvel comic character first created in the 1970s and whose trademark was a skull. The comic-book Punisher was a former Marine turned vigilante who, unlike other superheroes who refrained from taking lives, was not afraid to kill his enemies. The skull emblem found its way onto uniforms and gear, and a five-feet-high plywood version would be posted to the company headquarters building in Afghanistan.

The Chosen Company that prepared for war in Italy had a mixture of experienced soldiers and rookies; many were veterans who had deployed with Chosen to Afghanistan in 2005–2006, including a small number who had been with the unit since its first combat tour to Iraq in 2003. But the majority who went to war during the fateful combat tour of 2007–2008 arrived as new recruits in 2006. And then there were a few who joined Chosen in Afghanistan as necessary replacements as that violent combat tour unfolded.

Pruitt Rainey and Jon Albert had gone through basic training together at Fort Benning. They were roommates during airborne school, and both got tapped to go to Italy and join the 173rd. They had become fast friends, and when they stood together in a formation of new recruits on a parking lot at the Army Garrison in Vicenza and an officer began to arbitrarily assign each soldier to one of the two battalions, Albert took matters into his own hands.

Rainey got picked for the Rock Battalion and Albert for its sister unit, 1st Battalion. So as the crowd of recruits began to split up to form two lines, Albert just eased over to the Rock line and nobody seemed to notice. He got to stay with Rainey and they wound up in Chosen Company together. It was a small violation of the rules, but it profoundly changed the arc of Albert's life.

Young paratroopers fresh out of airborne school like Kyle White, Tyler Hanson, and Scott Derry were utterly intimidated by the veteran members of Chosen Company after arriving in Vicenza in 2006. Chosen Company had just returned from twelve months of combat in Afghanistan, and the recruits had been nowhere near a battlefield yet. They were in awe of platoon sergeants like Shane Stockard and Matt Kahler, who had already been to war twice—the first time jumping into Iraq and the second time fighting in Afghanistan. And the company sergeant, Scott Beeson, seemed almost larger than life.

The rangy, six-feet-three first sergeant actually had two stars on his jump wings, almost unheard of among conventional forces. He had parachuted with the 82nd Airborne into Panama in 1989, and he had jumped into Iraq with the Rock Battalion in 2003.

A native of Indiana who grew up in the small town of Greenfield about twenty miles east of Indianapolis, Beeson was the second of four children. He had barely finished airborne school when he jumped into Panama and then did an uneventful combat tour during the Persian Gulf War. He left the Army and for a time worked on a factory assembly line making fenders and hoods for Ford while serving in the Indiana National Guard. In 1994 he went back to the regular Army and became one of the original Chosen Few when the company was activated in

2001. By the time he parachuted into Iraq, he had forged this reputation as the apotheosis of a combat warrior. The new recruits idolized him, even though the reputation surprised Beeson himself.

*Everybody thinks I'm this super-crazy war monger.*

It helped that he was blunt, profane, and refused to suffer fools but had a psychotherapist's instincts for when to push people and when to acknowledge their pain. Matt Myer and his senior noncommissioned advisor were polar opposites in almost every way. Where Beeson was loud and volatile, Myer was contemplative and careful in thought and action. But the two men somehow made their relationship work and became extremely close, if not always in agreement as the deployment wore on.

First-timers to the Army base in Vicenza found one of the most distinctive US military installations in the world. Because of the land mass required to operate tank or troop formations, most US Army bases were relegated to rural, distant areas. But Camp Ederle was a small, 145-acre military installation located on the edge of the city. It was named for an Italian Army major and World War I hero.

Camp Ederle was more like a campus. There was one indoor gun range. Parachute drops were done at Aviano Air Base two hours away. At the center of Camp Ederle was a statue of the archangel Saint Michael, leader of all angels in the fight against Satan and the designated patron saint of the Airborne.

For some paratroopers who had barely traveled outside the confines of their midwestern hometowns, Italy was a culture shock. Many never fully appreciated the artistic gems only a few minutes' stroll from the base, preferring instead to enjoy the legal drinking age of eighteen or take in the swanky strip bars on the city's west side where Eastern European beauties arrived to dance and flirt with American soldiers. They were, after all, young men with plenty of disposable income from thousands of dollars in bonuses earned for enlisting—or re-enlisting.

Many other paratroopers took on Europe as an adventure. Venice was only forty minutes by train, Rome just four hours away. There were low-cost airline flights that could take them anywhere on the continent. Soldiers loved spending a weekend at the Italian seaside resort of Rimimi on the coast of the Adriatic Sea where there were broad beaches, volleyball, alcohol, and night life. The guys who hung out with Jake Walker had the benefit of a translator. Walker, a Mormon who grew up in southeastern Washington, had spent time in Italy as a missionary and knew the language. He helped buddies like Tyler Stafford, Matthew Phillips, Pruitt Rainey, and John Hayes navigate Italian backwaters where English wasn't readily spoken.

Even better, Chosen soldiers could immerse themselves in the Italian way of life by renting homes in nearby neighborhoods or villages and "living off the economy." Officers and married soldiers could use their government subsidies to rent flats in quaint seventeenth-century buildings. It was a charmed life for young, single officers. Matt Ferrara, who arrived in 2006 to become leader of Chosen Company's 1st Platoon, found a two-bedroom, third-floor flat in an ancient building overlooking the piazza in Vicenza with a spectacular view of a thirteenth-century cathedral just outside his balcony.

The five-feet-five officer bore a square-jawed resemblance to a young Bobby Kennedy and held a dual citizenship for the United States and New Zealand. He was only twenty-two when he showed up in Italy in 2006 after graduating from the US Army Military Academy at West Point, where he studied Chinese and economics and finished in the top ten of his class.

Matt Ferrara was born and raised in Torrance, California, the third of five children, including four boys who would all serve in the US military, three of them West Point graduates. Friends called him Matty. He relished living in Europe, buying a Spanish Seat Ibiza supermini car for $2,000 and traveling to Spain to see the running of the bulls in Pamplona, scuba diving in the Mediterranean, skiing the Alps, prowling a Roman emperor's summer palace in Croatia, and spending weekends in Paris.

For Israel Garcia and his wife, Lesly, traveling to Europe and living in Vicenza was like a dream come true. Sergeant Garcia was born in the Pacific coastal state of Nayarit in Mexico and became a naturalized citizen before enlisting in 2002 out of high school in Long Beach, California. He and Lesly had first met while bowling at the Polynesian-themed Java Lanes and, after a lengthy engagement, married in 2006. They were both twenty-two.

Garcia saw combat in the embattled city of Fallujah while serving with the 82nd Airborne, and when he re-enlisted in 2006, he got the chance to take his new bride to Italy. They were both ecstatic. She had always dreamed of traveling. Now they were going to Venice every weekend, riding the gondolas, tasting gelato, and munching on genuine Italian pizza. Lesly never wanted to go home.

Newlywed couple Sean and Jessica Langevin had married the previous January. They turned their hundred-year-old Italian apartment into a crash pad for some of the single guys from 1st Platoon who had to live on the base. Sean was a native of Walnut Creek, California, just outside of San Francisco. His heritage was a rich mixture of French on his father's side, Japanese and Portuguese on his mother's. He was five-feet-seven and stocky, and had long eyelashes that girls in high school thought were hot. Sean was an Eagle Scout who skateboarded, Rollerbladed, and loved to snowboard. He started to lose his hair as a young man and kept his head shaved.

He and Jessica met at a pizza restaurant where she was a waitress and he delivered pies. Sean felt strongly about serving his country and also thought it was a good way to provide for a new family. Despite Jessica's protests that he stay off the frontlines, he chose to become a paratrooper and was sent to Vicenza.

Jessica loved Italy—the way everything closed down for afternoon siestas, how tending gardens was a daily ritual, and you bought fresh food every day from the markets and cooked it up for dinner at night. That May she got pregnant.

Langevin had a quick, self-deprecating sense of humor and rapidly became one of the most popular soldiers in 1st Platoon. A growing number would come to call him one of their best friends. He and Jessica filled their living room with mattresses, comforters, and pillows so buddies like Chuck Bell, Justin Kalenits, Kyle White (whom they all called Whitey), and Jon Albert had a place to sleep after a night of heavy drinking. Sergeant James Takes, a team leader, and even Lieutenant Matt Ferrara would come by occasionally.

The Langevins weren't the only ones to succumb to the charms of Vicenza. Gabriel Green fell madly in love. A twenty-five-year-old native of Puerto Rico, he grew up in the Bronx after his parents divorced, got vocational training in food services, and worked as a kitchen manager before enlisting in 2005. He chose Airborne and the job of forward observer, directing artillery fire and close air support. But his life truly changed on a bus in Vicenza when he noticed a dark-haired beauty sitting in the back. He couldn't take his eyes off of her. When her phone rang with a ringtone from a song by the Puerto Rican reggaeton duo Wisin & Yandel, he struck up a conversation. She was half-Italian, half-Columbian, and her name was Addy. It wasn't much longer before the six-foot-one paratrooper with the chiseled jaw and dimpled chin had won a lunch date.

It was love at first sight, and within a few months they decided to tie the knot. The day for the civil ceremony in her hometown of Verona unfortunately fell on the day before the platoon was heading to Germany for their last round of field training before deployment. Commanders refused to give him the day off, and Green was frantic. He turned to his platoon leader, First Lieutenant Matthew Ferrara, who managed to fix things. Not only did Green make it to the courthouse on time, but his forward observer teammates were able to show up in their dress uniforms, guys like Kain Schilling and Jason Eller. Lieutenant Brad Mercier was there too. He led the forward observers for Chosen Company, and one of the senior NCOs, Ryan Pitts, attended. Everyone posed for pictures at the courthouse with the beaming new bride. Green didn't have to report back until the following day.

Matthew Phillips was another of the Chosen Few who got married before heading off to war. The twenty-five-year-old Army specialist from the suburbs of Atlanta, who had enlisted the year prior after living and scuba diving in Central America, had proposed to a school teacher, Eve, he met back in Georgia. He and Eve planned on a wedding in December 2006. Eve didn't want him spending his bachelor party at one of Vicenza's famed strip joints, so he, Jacob Walker, and some of the other paratroopers settled on a pub crawl through the city, but not before visiting a dress shop and buying a used white wedding dress that Phillips wore for the duration of the evening. It was a snug fit.

Throughout that spring and summer of 2006 new recruits or transfers filtered into the 173rd, were assigned to the Rock Battalion, and finally divided up between the companies—Able, Battle, Chosen, Destined, and Fusion—and the platoons.

Paratroopers living on base were assigned two to a room, and sometimes apples mixed with oranges. Jeddah Deloria could tolerate a certain chaos in his quarters, but his roommate, Kyle White, was obsessively neat and would follow Deloria around with a broom, making sure everything was ready for any spot inspection.

Life here took some adjusting. When Scott Derry showed up at age twenty-one—the son of an Airborne veteran from Riverside, California, who grew up believing in the creed America First—he woke up the first morning covered in bedbug bites. Without asking permission, he cleared out his barracks room and sprayed some insecticide, an initiative that did not sit well with the Chosen Company sergeant on duty, Jeff Mersman, a big, broad-shouldered Kansan who "smoked" him—made him do push-ups until it ached.

Mike Denton, who arrived in Italy on June 6, 2006, the anniversary of D-Day, quickly broke the code for fitting into an organization top-heavy with battle-hardened veterans: keep your mouth shut, speak when spoken to, bust your backside at every task, and admit mistakes. He breezed into Chosen Company. Denton was born in Pontiac, Michigan, and spent his young adolescence in the suburbs of Detroit after his parents divorced when he was seven. He took the break-up hard, and when his rebellious teenage years began, he was sent to live with his father, a paramedic in Florida. The six-feet-one, 190-pound Denton felt a duty to serve his country and was inspired to be a paratrooper in part by reading about how the 173rd Airborne parachuted into Iraq in 2003. His mind made up, Denton graduated a semester early from high school and was at basic training within four weeks of turning eighteen.

Denton and the other recruits found a culture in Vicenza that was different from many other military installations. It was a tight-knit community where the social formalities of rank among the enlisted soldiers were suspended during downtime. The Army normally frowned on junior and senior enlisted soldiers spending social time with one another—that was fraternizing. But the policy was more relaxed in Vicenza for several reasons. The language barrier with Italians made the Americans feel more isolated. Camp Ederle was a relatively small, more intimate base—you could walk across it in ten minutes. The men tended to venture out in groups, and it was just easier if they could enjoy themselves without the burden of avoiding someone because he was a team leader or a squad leader. During the day it was "Yes, Sergeant" or "No, Sergeant" or "Roger, Sergeant," but after hours it became "Hey, dude, you wanna go grab a drink?"

For Staff Sergeant Erich Phillips, that breach of protocol took some getting used to. He had come from the 82nd Airborne, where sergeants didn't share a drink with privates or squad leaders with team leaders. These were the men they had to be tough on during training, to "smoke" for something done improperly. In Vicenza, Phillips watched how they would shed the divisions of rank at night or on the weekends, only to resume when soldiering began all over again in the morning. It seemed to work seamlessly. He was amazed.

"This ain't the 82nd, dude," said Stephen Simmons, an old buddy Phillips met up with again in Vicenza. "You're good to go, man. Just relax."

The informality was unorthodox, but the end result appeared to be that squads or platoons grew even more comfortable and at ease with one another. They could trust that someone in the group would stay sober enough to make sure everybody got home safely or count on one another in a tight spot if tempers flared at a local bar.

Their trust in one another would be essential in the months ahead.

# 2

> > > **EAGER FOR WAR**

*Twilight gathered across the live-fire training range* in Germany as Chosen Company prepared for war. Paratroopers fired their weapons in a simulated combat exercise. A bank of fog rolled in out of nowhere, obscuring what they could see. Matt Myer watched as the pall drifted over the training range.

The paratroopers sensed that the drill would be ending because the weather had turned bad. But Myer instructed them to keep going. *This is important training.* The enemy they would face in Afghanistan could attack at any time, any place. The soldiers would not have the luxury of choosing the weather or the terrain where they would fight. So they couldn't let it matter now.

*You fight where you have to, and the paratroopers must learn to adapt.*

As the training for combat progressed, the new captain leading Chosen Company, twenty-eight-year-old Matt Myer, felt lucky. The virtue of serving in the 173rd Brigade meant that commanders virtually had their pick of leading West Point graduates and experienced noncommissioned officers. One of his new lieutenants, Matt Ferrara, had graduated near the top of his class. His company sergeant, Scott Beeson, had jumped into Panama in 1989 and then did a second combat jump during the US-led invasion of Iraq in 2003.

The reality was that Myer felt spoiled as Chosen's company commander. Every sergeant first class leading a platoon in his company had earned a coveted Ranger tab. A lot of his sergeants and specialists already had combat experience. In fact, probably half of Chosen Company had been to combat at least once before this deployment. As a result Myer felt like he commanded a high-caliber group of soldiers going into the vital training cycle. Myer himself had seen combat while leading a platoon for the 4th Infantry Division in Iraq. He and his men were working the fringes of an operation that led to the capture of the fugitive Iraqi president, Saddam Hussein, near Tikrit, Iraq, in December of 2003—one of the high points for a war that within a year or two would begin spinning out of control.

But Myer's personal journey into the Army was different from a lot of his peers. In some ways the slender six-foot Army brat was kind of an accidental soldier, although he certainly had the pedigree as the child of an Army colonel, grandson of an Army general who served in Vietnam, and great-grandson of an Army 1st sergeant who fought in World War I. Matt's father and grandfather were both West Point Military Academy graduates. Matt was born in an Army hospital at Fort Bragg, North Carolina.

But for all the lineage, Myer was never passionate about the Army as a child. He neither dreamed of joining nor felt pressure to carry on any kind of military family tradition, although that heritage certainly shaped his formative years. He and his two older sisters and younger brother moved frequently with their father's changing Army duties, living in North Carolina, California, New York, Missouri, and Virginia. Like other Army children, he learned to easily make and shed friends.

Lacrosse was his favorite sport in high school, where Matt earned B-pluses and A-minuses and was a pretty easygoing adolescent. He entered his sophomore year largely clueless about where his life might go until his father gently suggested West Point.

For Matt it seemed like something to try, and it was, after all, a world he had known since childhood. But it proved to be an academic stretch at first because of his less-than stellar SAT scores. Matt was placed on a waiting list, using an Army scholarship to attend a Virginia state school for a year before starting his four full years at the Academy. The vaunted institution overlooking the Hudson River pulsed with an intensity and rigor that challenged the young cadet who was by nature restrained and nonconfrontational. And the legendary setting where the likes of Grant, Patton, and Eisenhower had studied was lost on the freshman—Matt didn't really care about any of that.

But he adjusted, built a coterie of friends, grew more disciplined in his studies, and saw his performance improve. Just as importantly, he appreciated how his future was being shaped, his career guaranteed. He took solace in the knowledge that top-of-the-class excellence didn't always equate to good leadership. Some of the Army's biggest stars, Grant and Patton among them, struggled at the Academy. Matt left in spring of 2001 with an academic rating in the bottom two-thirds of his class.

When he arrived in Vicenza with his wife, Laura, who was four months pregnant, he accepted a job as operations officer for the battalion. Within three months he was in command of Chosen Company.

Myer was a quiet, unflappable leader. There would be times in the months of deployment ahead when his effort to radiate toughness wore thin for some of the soldiers. But the Chosen Few largely grew to respect him as their company commander, and he would prove fearless in combat.

In the waning months of 2006, Chosen Company focused on basic principles of infantry—fire and maneuver. Putting out a wall of steel toward the enemy to keep them pinned down and occupied as paratroopers advanced on the battlefield.

The concept of "bounding" was a vital part of infantry tactics. A group of three or four soldiers lays down relentless fire as a second group of roughly the same size maneuvers—bounds—forward to gain advantage. The rushing element then takes up position to unleash more accurate fire so the first group can move. The first one bounds forward, then the other. Back and forth. Each fueling the other's advance, feeding off the other's aggression until they close in and destroy the enemy.

The battalion would pile into a convoy of buses for the long trip through Austria and into Germany and four weeks of live-fire training at the Joint Multinational Training Command in Grafenwöhr, Germany, northwest of Nuremburg, where they would fire at pop-up silhouette targets while they negotiated different courses. Or they would do four weeks of training exercises against other soldiers playing the role of enemy forces at an old Nazi military training site in Hohenfels southwest of Nuremberg. On the way up to Germany the troops would always stop at a world-famous McDonald's in the Austrian Alps with a spectacular view.

The trips were during the fall and winter of 2006–2007, and during the first two training periods at Grafenwöhr, when they were preparing to go to the more urban Iraq, the training largely revolved around operating and fighting out of armored Humvees or practicing how to clear enemy forces out of buildings. They would do drills on procedures if a convoy of trucks came under attack. They'd call in helicopters and learn to coordinate air support with vehicles on the ground. It was military operations in city terrain.

Bill Ostlund put a high premium on live-fire training—drills conducted with live ammunition. He and his command sergeant major, Bradley Meyers, constantly critiqued technique and compared unit performances. Matt Myer pushed the live-fire drills even further with Chosen Company. Through the winter of 2006–2007 he had his men train from early morning into the night every day, six days a week.

Myer wanted the weapon that each man carried to eventually feel like a natural extension of the body, as if muscle and sinew flowed directly into the rifle so that wielding it came as easily and naturally as a handshake. He wanted the firing of a gun to be done without a shred of hesitation.

In the fight that lay ahead an enemy could not be permitted to gain advantage in the moments before aircraft or artillery support arrived.

The enemy must immediately pay a price, be set back on their heels. It meant meeting enemy gunfire and rocket-propelled grenades with American gunfire and grenade launchers, standing and fighting as a group, rapidly pouring out a deadly volume of controlled fire in the first "mad minute" after being attacked. Matt Myer talked about creating a "lane of violence," quickly drawing blood for blood.

Ostlund likewise demanded company commanders instill this concept in their men.

*We have to make the men very comfortable shooting their weapon very quickly. Your job is to know when to pull the trigger. Your job is to bring violence upon the enemy.*

So Myer and Beeson prowled the assault lanes during the live-fire exercises at Grafenwoehr using handheld controls to trigger pop-up targets so they could assess each soldier's split-second decisions. Myer would scribble his assessments down in a personal journal: 2nd Platoon's 1st Squad, "Look at what you are shooting"; 2nd Platoon's 2nd Squad, "Shoot, don't talk"; 2nd Platoon's 1st Squad again, "Bounds too long."

He did the same with platoon leaders: 2nd Platoon's Lieutenant Devon George: "Good insert . . . cover! . . . take control"; 1st Platoon's Lieutenant Matt Ferrara: "Practice more initiative . . . provide your platoon energy/be proactive . . . build platoon cohesion, always 'we,' not 'you guys.'"

Parachute training was carried out at NATO's Aviano Air Base about ninety miles northwest of Vicenza. The paratroopers were also trained in battlefield medicine that was a notch higher than rank-and-file US Infantry soldiers. Not only were they instructed in assessing wounds, applying field dressings, and using tourniquets, but they also learned how to administer intravenous fluids and, in fact, carried needles and IV fluids with them at all times in a small field medical kit. Always the crucial lesson was to control bleeding and replenish lost fluids, the two keys to keeping a wounded soldier alive long enough to be medevacked to a field hospital.

Even after returning to Vicenza from Germany, lessons continued without the guns. Staff Sergeant Kyle Silvernale would take 1st Platoon's 1st Squad down to the athletic field on the base in Vicenza, a place they called the North Forty, popular for tackle football games. They would do walk-throughs, reacting to enemy contact. The focus was always on laying down suppressive fire immediately. Silvernale became impressed with how willing and focused his soldiers were about the lessons, sergeants like James Takes or privates like Justin Kalenits, Scott Derry, Joe Lancour, or Ananthachai Nantakul. Nantakul, twenty-two, was half African American, half Thai, and spoke fluent German; the soldiers called him "Nanny" or "Nancy" for short. Silvernale was proud to see that some of his men—Takes, Kalenits, and Lancour—were proving to be excellent marksmen.

Kyle Silvernale was born in Spokane, Washington, but when he was in junior high, the family moved to Alaska, which proved to be a land of adventure for a teenager. He joined the Army in part as a patriotic response to the 9/11 attacks, chose Airborne, and then was sent to South Korea, where he served with the only US Army platoon working inside the Demilitarized Zone between North and South Korea. When he re-enlisted and couldn't get assigned to Fort Richardson in Alaska near his family, he chose the 173rd Airborne. Silvernale was a big man, at six-feet-three, 210 pounds, and his squad members loved him.

Physical conditioning was another area of intense focus, pushing soldiers to the brink of exhaustion, a real "ass whoopin'," as Scott Beeson would say. In Vicenza they ran twenty-five miles a week, taking various routes through the city to the top of Mount Berico, where the Blessed Virgin Mary appeared to a peasant six centuries before. On the summit there was a magnificent Baroque chapel more than three hundred years old.

To keep disruption of the Italian neighborhood streets to a minimum, the paratroopers would head out in small running groups beginning around six in the morning. Scott Derry, for all of his prowess on the baseball field in high school, was never much of a long-distance runner and would fall back as 1st Squad headed out for a run. It could make him a prime target for an angry harangue from a team leader. But that was never Sergeant James Takes's style; instead, Takes would begin running side-by-side with Derry, the team sergeant pounding along with this five-feet-eight protégé, making conversation about anything, about life in general. It was as if the problem wasn't lack of stamina for Derry but rather some other issue on the private's mind. All they had to do was talk it out and he'd run better.

James Takes was another one of Chosen Company's lost boys. Like so many others, he came from a broken home and struggled as a teenager growing up in Danville, Virginia, never finishing high school. When the Marines told him they had filled their monthly quota of applicants who had only a high school graduation equivalency certificate, Takes walked into an Army recruiting office and signed up. A trim six feet tall and handsome, with a strong score on his military entrance exam, Takes was accepted into the Old Guard, the Army's 3rd Infantry Regiment based outside Washington, DC, most notably tasked with guarding the Tomb of the Unknowns at Arlington National Cemetery, providing military funeral escorts, and serving as the official ceremonial unit and escort for the president. Takes was one of the soldiers who conducted the rifle-fire salutes during the funeral proceedings. He remembers being severely hung over during the George W. Bush inauguration when he and other members of the regiment were called on to sit in their dress blue uniforms directly behind the Bush family during the swearing-in ceremony. Sweat was pouring off Takes, and he was just praying no one would notice.

But Takes loved the Army and found it to be a world where he could excel. He took every course and strived for every badge he could find. He earned the Old Guard's black and tan buff strap, went to Airborne school, sniper school, and even barber school. The one thing he hadn't earned was combat duty. He was serving on a burial detail for soldiers who had died in combat and felt it was his time to experience war. After three years in the Old Guard he transferred to the 173rd Airborne Brigade and Chosen Company in 2006 as a sergeant.

As the time to go to war grew near, commanders found themselves wrestling with issues that were never a factor for the generations of warfighters who came before them.

Company First Sergeant Scott Beeson was shocked to find out perhaps half of Chosen Company was on antidepressants or anti-anxiety drugs, often prescribed for depression or posttraumatic stress disorder. He was particularly upset that he didn't know this.

There were advances in technology that had never before been a factor for commanders. The new iPhone would go on the market in June. Digital cameras and editing software made it easy for soldiers to create videos. When it became clear that paratroopers were embracing all of this technology, their commander, Bill Ostlund, at first tried to tamp it down. But he finally gave up. The result was that soldiers would be able to assemble footage of anything they pleased with their digital cameras and laptops. There would be hundreds of videos that captured Chosen Company at war.

→ ←

When word arrived during training in Germany that their deployment was unexpectedly shifting from Iraq to Afghanistan, Ostlund switched up the training that very night in an effort to replicate conditions in Afghanistan, ordering a battalion-wide assault on three objectives.

A lot of them hadn't been too crazy about going to Iraq anyway. Too many roadside bombs in that country were taking off legs and arms or worse, and that was just for driving down the road. A good many of them had already been to Afghanistan, and a sense of confidence rippled through the ranks of the veterans that essentially said, "We got this."

One of those who felt good about going to Afghanistan was Staff Sergeant David Dzwik, a stocky twenty-nine-year-old from Traverse City, Michigan, who grew up deer hunting with his father. Dzwik had been with Chosen Company during the last tour in Afghanistan and didn't mind going back.

The only hesitation came when their battalion commander gave them a PowerPoint presentation. Some of the slides were images of mountainous terrain the men hadn't seen before in Afghanistan. One picture showed a combat outpost called Ranch House during the winter, covered in snow. At more than seven thousand feet, it was possibly the highest US base in Afghanistan, and some of Chosen's men would have to defend it, Ostlund told them.

Dzwik leaned over to his platoon sergeant, Shane Stockard, during the presentation and whispered, "Wow, I hope that's not me."

→  ←

One of the last to join Chosen before the paratroopers completed training and prepared to head overseas was a soldier whose reputation preceded him. By the time Erich Phillips showed up in Vicenza he had already achieved more than most soldiers accomplish in a lifetime.

He had earned the coveted black and yellow Ranger tab by successfully completing a punishing nine weeks of mental and physical torture in one of the US military's most grueling training courses. He had already been to war three times, twice to Iraq and once to Afghanistan. In Iraq he led an attack by a scout team against insurgents who had been intimidating voters during one of Iraq's first elections. Phillips had quickly risen to the rank of staff sergeant, the equivalent of a squad leader.

All this, and when he showed up at Chosen, he had just turned twenty-three.

Chosen's paratroopers would come to look upon the boyishly handsome Phillips as the closest thing to a true warrior they'd ever seen.

Brian Hissong would describe Phillips—Phil to his friends—as something that belonged behind glass with a hammer and a sign that read, "Break in the Event of War."

All of five-feet-seven and 180 pounds, Phillips seemed to always carry this aura into combat. The men just knew that Phillips—like the light-imbued Colonel Kilgore in the film *Apocalypse Now*—"wasn't gonna get so much as a scratch." Some primordial set of instincts could always be counted on to drive his physical movements—where he stepped or how he turned and fired his weapon—or the split-second decisions he made in the heat of the moment to frustrate foes trying to kill him or to help comrades desperately in need of assistance.

Phillips was a mortar man by training and assigned to the 82nd Airborne out of Fort Bragg, North Carolina, when one of his buddies, Stephen Simmons, called from Afghanistan. Simmons was part of Chosen Company, and the call home came during a 2005–2006 combat tour. Simmons sounded stressed by some of the tough fighting the unit had been through in Afghanistan's southwest province of Zabul. Phillips was worried about his friend. So, facing the end of an enlistment period, he promptly paid a visit to a re-enlistment officer and told him he'd stay in the Army but only if they sent him to the 173rd in Italy.

There was a slot open for a mortar section staff sergeant. Phillips was on his way.

Army life, especially during war, had a way of working out for Erich Phillips like that, balancing the scales for a young man who had such a disadvantaged past. "Shit," was how Erich summarized his boyhood. If there were truly lost boys for whom the Army and, particularly, Chosen Company became the family they never had, Erich Phillips was first in line. It began the night he was born in Salem, New Jersey, when his father, exhausted after standing vigil over a long labor, evidently nodded off on his way home and slammed into a telephone pole. His death led to a childhood for Erich of second-hand clothes, food stamps, and nomadic shifting from one low-income neighborhood to another across four states. Erich got in fights, was expelled, and fell into trouble with the police—once ending up with a felony arrest in high school when he was with a friend who was stealing a speaker.

An epiphany came when he was seventeen, bagging groceries at a Fry's in Tucson, Arizona, and trying to date a girl named Stephanie, whose retired military father sat Erich down and told him in no uncertain terms that he wasn't good enough for his daughter. Had he ever considered the military?

A few days later Erich was at a strip mall recruiting office where the Marines rejected him for the felony arrest but the Army didn't care. His basic-training performance and math scores earned him an assignment as a mortar man, mastering azimuth, deflection, tracking the latitude and longitude of targets, setting a base plate, and handling 60- and 120mm rounds. Even his disapproving stepfather was proud. He turned nineteen in Ranger school and headed the next year to Afghanistan for the first of three deployments. By late September 2006 he was in Italy with the Rock Battalion, running the mortars team for Chosen Company.

To keep Chosen Company, the Rock Battalion, and the entire 173rd Airborne Brigade at full strength, commanders ordered an involuntary extension of some of the soldiers' service under their enlistment contracts, a process that became famously known as stop-loss. The extensions affected at least a handful of soldiers in the company, Ryan Pitts among them. He shrugged it off, in large part because he felt such a deep connection with the other soldiers of Chosen that it seemed right that they should remain together in the fighting that lay ahead.

But stop-loss was a problem for Mike Santiago. He grew up in South Florida and joined the Army with some buddies after he got tired of changing tires in the auto shop at a Sam's Club warehouse in Port Charlotte, Florida. He had been with Chosen Company since 2004, fought in Afghanistan during the 2005–2006 tour, and was slated to get out of the Army in August 2007, just two months after the company was to arrive in Afghanistan. Under stop-loss he had to remain in the Army for more than a year until the deployment ended. He wasn't happy about it and had a tough time explaining it to his wife, Ella.

In the months and weeks leading up to their deployment scheduled for late May, there was a mix of excitement and apprehension among the paratroopers. Some of them thought long and hard about what should be done in the event they didn't come home alive.

Twenty-year-old Joe Lancour gave considerable thought to his own funeral and planned the arrangements with exquisite detail. When the deployment grew near, Joe explained to his mother exactly what he wanted done in the event he was killed. He wanted a wooden casket with a white silk lining, he listed the photographs to be placed inside the casket, and he wanted a white rose to be placed in his hands.

Sergeant Israel Garcia had been to war twice before and was, by any standard, a hardened combat veteran. But for some reason he worried about this deployment. Garcia found himself oddly moved to tears on occasion and struggled to interpret the feelings.

"You don't understand," the twenty-three-year-old soldier told his wife, Lesly. "This is my third deployment. I'm messing with fire, and you never know. I might get burned."

He began discussing where he might be buried, assuring his wife that she could take the liberty of interring him anywhere that was convenient for her. He didn't need to be buried in the vaunted Arlington National Cemetery a continent away from their home in Long Beach.

Lesly hated this kind of talk. It frightened her, and each time he brought it up, she told him to stop it. Several weeks before he left for Afghanistan, Lesly was cooking in the kitchen and could hear Israel crying in the living room. She rushed out and found him writing a letter, something to be opened in the event of his death.

"I can't leave without writing something."

She went back to the kitchen, but they both lost their appetites that night.

→  ←

For many if not most of the Chosen Few, the upcoming deployment was an adventure to meet head on. Many were eager to finally experience combat. All had trained hard for this moment. They acquired deadly skills that were about to be put into play. They were young, healthy, and full of piss and vinegar.

One freezing night in Vicenza, Sean and Jessica Langevin, James Takes, Chuck Bell, and Jon Albert were walking back to the Langevin crash pad after a night of drinking. Per custom, they stopped at a Greek restaurant down the street. Everybody was starving, and they wolfed down gyro sandwiches. Then someone suggested that Sean wouldn't have the guts to run naked back to the apartment.

That was all it took. In seconds Langevin, Takes, and Bell were stripped to their socks, reduced to three white figures streaking down a darkened Italian avenue. Jessica trotted after them, her arms burdened with clothing and shoes. They paused long enough in the cold for someone to take a photo, ultimately to be posted on the Internet—three alabaster backsides for all the world to see.

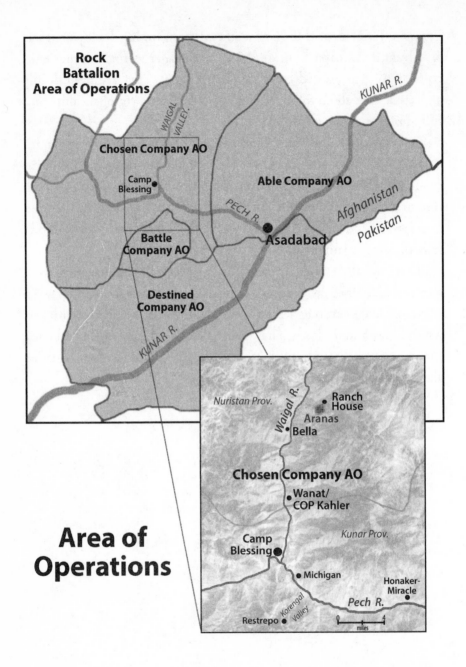

Rock
Battalion
Area of Operations

Chosen Company AO

Camp
Blessing

Battle
Company AO

Destined
Company AO

Able Company AO

Asadabad

Afghanistan

Pakistan

KUNAR R.

PECH R.

KUNAR R.

WAIGAL VALLEY.

**Area of
Operations**

Nuristan Prov.

Ranch
House

Aranas
Bella

Chosen Company AO

Wanat/
COP Kahler

Kunar Prov.

Camp
Blessing

Michigan

Honaker-
Miracle

Pech R.

Restrepo

Korengal Valley

Waigal R.

0        4
miles

# 3

## >>> GOOD MORNING, AFGHANISTAN

*The mountains took you and held you,* even if you were high in the air above in a helicopter and not struggling for footing on the broken rock and shale of the unforgiving slopes. The walls of the canyons rose up on every side and closed in for a Blackhawk carrying paratroopers deafened by the pounding of rotating blades digging into an ever-thinning atmosphere.

The sharply etched terrain left the impression that this was not a welcoming land. The rippling valleys falling off into folds of darkness seemed to hold violent secrets better left untouched, much less reckoned with face to face. The topography stretching to the horizon with peaks as high as twenty thousand feet belonged to the Hindu Kush mountain range that flowed northwest into the Himalayas and the roof of the world.

The destination of Chosen Company's 1st Platoon as it arrived on May 23, 2007, was the combat outpost called Ranch House, which they had seen in Matt Myer's presentation. Splayed out on a broad ridge two-thirds of the way up an eighty-four-hundred-foot mountain, it was arguably the most remote US combat outpost in Afghanistan.

The base rested high up the north flank of an east-west-running gorge, an offshoot of a larger valley to the west called the Waigal. The Waigal Valley was a major southern gateway into the vast and fiercely ungovernable Nuristan Province, a place roughly the size of Connecticut but with fewer people than Pasadena, California, with maybe one paved road. It shared a long, unrestricted border with Pakistan.

Nuristan and neighboring Kunar Province to the south together formed a historical smuggling route known colloquially as the Muj Highway. The Mujahedeen were Muslim fighters who drove the Soviets from Afghanistan in 1989 after launching a die-hard resistance precisely from these valleys. The Muj Highway extended from Pakistan's western frontier to the Afghan capital of Kabul and, with the US-led invasion after 9/11, became a crucial infiltration route for the insurgency.

Jihadist radicals, mercenaries, and rank-and-file gunmen for some of the most violent terrorist organizations on the planet streamed back and forth through this corridor, forming lasting bonds with the mountain residents, marrying into their families, and finding pockets of sanctuary in their remote valleys.

The organizations were a rogue's gallery of international mayhem carefully tracked by the US National Counterterrorism Center created just a few years earlier. The most infamous was Al Qaeda, its operatives usually well financed. There might be a few Afghan Taliban, although their territory typically ran farther to the south.

More importantly, there were vicious organized groups that were quickly earning international reputations. Chief among them was Lashkar-e-Tayyiba—LET, or the Army of the Righteous—created in the 1990s to battle the Indians over the disputed states of Jammu and Kashmir. They were savage fighters who, in 2008, would shock the world with brazen, coordinated attacks on several sites in Mumbai, India, including a luxury hotel, a historic rail station, and a Jewish outreach center, leaving more than 160 dead. Lashkar-e-Tayyiba members were skilled at training local fighters in tactical skills, including zeroing in mortar fire and ambush organization.

There was also Jaish-e-Mohammed—known as JEM, or the Army of Mohammed—equally dedicated to expelling not only Indians from Kashmir but also foreign troops from Afghanistan. JEM had openly declared war on the United States, and a member was involved in the abduction and murder of *Wall Street Journal* reporter Daniel Pearl in 2002.

Hezb-e-Islami Gulbuddin, known by its initials HIG, was dedicated to transforming Afghanistan into an Islamic State and would, in years to come, prove sophisticated in using car bombs against Americans in Kabul.

Other groups included Tehrik-e Taliban, or the Pakistan Taliban, that in 2012 would try to kill fifteen-year-old education activist and future Nobel Laureate Malala Yousafzai, and the Islamic Movement of Uzbekistan, which had allied itself with Al Qaeda and the Taliban and would ultimately pledge allegiance to the Islamic State.

These were the elements operating in eastern Afghanistan when Chosen Company arrived in May of 2007. From where the paratroopers touched down at the Ranch House combat outpost, the canyon below wound westward four miles before intersecting with the Waigal Valley. At that crossroads rock walls formed a cavernous natural bowl hundreds of feet deep. At the bottom was a small Nuristani settlement called Bella, which was little more than a hotel, bazaar, and medical clinic. And next to that was a second US military combat outpost built in part to support the more far-flung Ranch House. This base was called Bella, and it too was accessible only by helicopter, on foot, or by small Toyota pickup trucks, which some local residents favored.

From Bella the Waigal ran straight south until crossing into Kunar Province and opening into a broader valley stretching east and west, known as the Pech. Forward Operating Base Blessing was located there, ten miles south of Bella. It was headquarters for Chosen Company and the entire Rock Battalion, a place of warm showers, hot meals, protective walls, and reinforced concrete barracks.

From there the pathway to civilization ran east another eighteen miles until the Pech River Valley, through which a paved highway was under construction when the Rock Battalion arrived, connected with the Kunar River Valley. At the confluence of the Pech and Kunar rivers was Asadabad, a city of fifty thousand that was the capital of Kunar

Province. The Kunar River Valley ran southeast from there along the Pakistan border before opening into a broad alluvial plain that held Afghanistan's fifth-largest city of Jalalabad, population two hundred thousand, astride Highway 1, the crucial eastern corridor of Afghanistan. The highway, which traced the course of the ancient Silk Route traversed by caravans going back two millennia, stretched from Jalalabad east through the Khyber Pass into Pakistan and west eighty miles to the Afghan capital of Kabul.

Far back up into the Hindu Kush Mountains where the two squads of Chosen Company's 1st Platoon paratroopers arrived on that day in May, the Ranch House outpost sat above the village of Aranas, where about six thousand locals lived. The largest of eight isolated communities in these deeply slotted valleys of Nuristan Province, it was different from any place these young Americans soldiers had ever seen.

There were no main streets, town squares, or commercial districts. Aranas existed as a vertical village—mud homes standing for generations nearly one on top of another, staircasing their way up the steep valley walls. To round a corner and see a town in this valley for the first time was to view it all at once, arrayed up and down like an abstract painting.

For the paratroopers, things horizontal were only a memory in these up-and-down Afghan wilds. Living here meant climbing up or climbing down. For a rifleman it meant burning thighs and breathless lungs under sixty-eight pounds of body armor, helmet, rifle, 270 rounds of 5.56mm ammo filling nine magazines, an assault pack, at least a half gallon of water in a Camelback pouch, frag grenades, smoke grenades, and sundry necessaries such as protective eyewear, gloves, knee pads, knife, weapon-cleaning kit, and a bottle of oil. If you were a grenadier, it meant a heavier weapon and more grenades, another twenty pounds if you were hauling an M249 squad automatic weapon or SAW, and thirty to forty-five pounds more if you were part of an M240 machine gun team.

It meant wearing out the ass of your fatigues or split and tattered combat boots from sliding down steep, broken shale, requiring you to

Internet shop and spend a few hundred dollars of your own money on a set of Garmont T8 Extremes or maybe even Danners. Not regulation wear, but commanders didn't seem to mind—after all, the men were ordering the boots themselves.

Erich Phillips watched the panorama of this challenging terrain unfold from the windows of a Blackhawk helicopter approaching Ranch House.

*This is going to suck.*

The landing zone, or LZ, was the roof of one of the few original structures on the base—a broad, low-slung mud and wood-beamed building that bore a passing resemblance to the ranch house on the 1960s *Ponderosa* television series. So soldiers of the 10th Mountain Division, who created the outpost the previous year, started calling it Ranch House—the irony of a name suggesting relaxation and leisure not lost on them.

The altitude here was about a mile and a half above sea level. Surrounding mountains towered to fourteen thousand feet, so arriving helicopters flew up valleys, *ascending* to where they would touch down. Blackhawk helicopter pilots only pretended to land. The Ranch House roof, though offering the only area flat and serviceable enough for a landing zone, couldn't hold the six tons of a helicopter at rest. So arriving or departing aircraft kept their engines spun up to maintain a margin of lift as human or other cargo was dropped off or taken aboard. Larger CH47 Chinook copters could only deliver supplies slung under their bellies.

From the landing zone the Ranch House combat outpost was all uphill, laid out across a large spur running downhill roughly from east to west. The spur was on the southward-facing side of the valley. Above the base the ground just kept rising ever higher. The Ranch House perimeter was a rough oval of razor wire laid out with stakes. The key defensive features were plywood and sandbag huts that served as guard posts or towers, each of them essentially firing platforms for machine guns or MK19 (pronounced "mark nineteen") 40mm automatic grenade

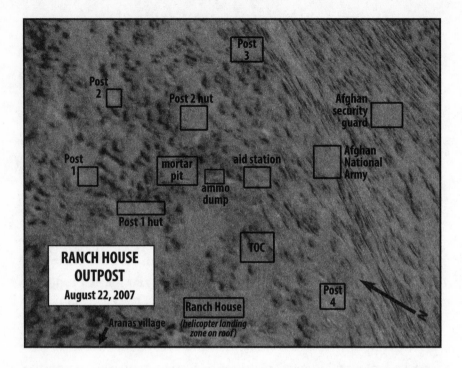

launchers. The plywood was fortified on the outside with layers of sand-bags, with more sandbags piled up on the roof. There were four of these small, fortress-like guard posts manned by US troops. They numbered, clockwise from the landing zone, one through four. A fifth fortified hut far on the eastern end of the base was assigned to local Afghans hired as security guards—fighting-age men issued fatigues and rifles with the hope of dissuading them from enlisting with the insurgency. Mud and wood cottages on that eastern end of the base served as living quarters for the Afghan National Army.

On the steep terrain, near vertical in some places, the combat out-posts looked like sand-bagged chalets perched on the mountain. Post Three was the highest point on the base, about three hundred yards up-hill from the landing zone and another three hundred feet of altitude.

A series of Claymore mines surrounded the perimeter, augment-ing defenses. They were curved, rectangular boxes that were eight and a half inches wide and three and a quarter inches high connected by several feet of wire to a hand "clacker." When detonated, the side of the box, printed with the words "Front Toward Enemy," unleashed seven hundred steel balls like a giant shotgun shell. Two 155mm howitzers at Blessing down in the Pech Valley and a 120mm mortar at Bella over in the Waigal were close enough to provide artillery support if necessary.

The angular terrain across the base was thick with tall grass, bushes, and twisting oak trees. It was like living in a slanted forest. Large rock outcroppings emerged at the margins of the camp. The entire base was riven with dirt pathways or steps made of stone or sandbags. Brown lizards skittered across boulders, and black scorpions and camel spiders lurked in dark, cool spaces.

Rope lines crisscrossed the base on the steepest sections so soldiers loaded with gear could pull their way higher. Even in the driest conditions their boots slipped and their ankles twisted on broken rocky surfaces. The stones shed a kind of glitter dust that found its way onto their clothes, into their huts, and caked on their computer laptops, resisting efforts to be wiped away.

To the southwest toward the valley the land dropped off so sharply that the village of Aranas and the stream down below were completely out of sight. The men felt as if they were as far on the edge of the world as possible.

But the view was spectacular.

The horizon was a panoply of intersecting ridge lines running as far as the eye could see. The air was crisp, and cool breezes on their skin, slick with sweat from exertion, air conditioned the body against the summer heat. A common refrain among soldiers here—usually framed around a sentence that began like, "If the Afghans could ever get their act together . . ."—was of the fortunes and pleasures to be had by creating ski resorts or river-rafting adventures in this land of lush valleys and frothing waters.

From Ranch House soldiers could watch storm clouds forming miles away, see vertical walls of advancing rain, and track how they broke apart and then reformed as they marched across the Hindu Kush. Weather might sweep in and settle below where the paratroopers were based, or clouds might envelop Ranch House, or a sudden downpour could turn every pathway into a running mountain stream. Snow stayed on the distant peaks well into summer.

Bad weather increased the sense of isolation because, for the duration, rotary aircraft could not reach them, even if the worst happened.

The heavens at night were a canopy of shimmering stars. And on the dry, bright days when soldiers climbed high into the mountains, the clouds seemed so close that it was as if a GI could reach up and snag a fistful of them like cotton candy. "Life among the clouds," David Dzwik said in a video he sent to his parents.

Except that the soldiers of the 10th Mountain Division who were waiting for the Chosen Few to replace them at Ranch House were more than finished with all of it. They were filthy from weeks without a decent shower and smelled worse. Erich Phillips could see the exhaustion in their faces.

*They are done. They don't want to be there no more.*

Small surprise.

→  ←

If the Ranch House base—and, three miles down the valley, the Bella combat outpost—were new settlements in hostile Indian territory, then the pioneers carving them out of wilderness were the men now heading home: the light infantry soldiers of the 1st Battalion, 32nd Infantry Regiment (1/32), 10th Mountain Division.

The 1/32 Battalion commander, Princeton graduate Chris Cavoli, had sent his Bravo Company deep into the Waigal Valley in July 2006, led by six-feet-four Michigan native Doug Sloan, who was the arm-wrestling champion of the brigade.

Lieutenant Colonel Chris Cavoli's battalion was part of a brigade led by Colonel John "Mick" Nicholson that arrived in these eastern provinces in early 2006 with the goal of extending the Afghan government's reach into these rugged areas that had barely seen any signs of the fledgling Afghan democracy. By establishing a government presence here, they hoped that a deeply entrenched insurgency could be defeated. Nicholson and Cavoli would figure out ways to accomplish this mission that would advance the understanding of counterinsurgency and capture the imagination of a leading guru in irregular warfare, David Kilcullen, then the chief strategist for counterterrorism in the Bush administration's State Department. Kilcullen later applied the lessons he learned in these eastern Afghan provinces to the surge of US troops in Iraq in 2007 and 2008, when he served as a senior counterinsurgency advisor to General David Petraeus, then commander of all coalition forces in Iraq.

In 2006 Nicholson introduced the theory of "separate, connect, and transform"—separate the population from the insurgency, connect the people with the government, and transform their lives with the services that only a functioning government could provide.

A fundamental way of achieving these goals was simply to build roads—paved highways that would link otherwise remote villages to each other and the outside world, promoting commerce and providing military forces a rapid means of ground maneuver. Such projects would take time and, thus, demonstrate long-term commitment. They would provide employment, and they would require a persistent security presence that could double as a means of safeguarding villages along the highway.

Key projects included a highway from Jalalabad to Asadabad through the Kunar River Valley and another through the Pech Valley, both part of the area of operations for Cavoli's battalion and, later, for Lieutenant Colonel William Ostlund and the Rock Battalion. Cavoli constructed a string of combat outposts through the more volatile Pech Valley designed to provide security "bubbles" that would allow road building to proceed unhindered and keep the insurgency from threatening or subverting local villages.

Most valley residents rallied to the plans. They clamored for even more government assistance to improve their lives—schools, wells, medical care, and flood control. Cavoli would later write in an unpublished memoir about how the road projects offered a means for establishing a bond with these remote villages: "It gives us something we both want more than anything else. It gives us something to do together. It gives the people a reason for us to fight."

And it also provided opportunities for fighting—and for killing. By seeding the highway routes with quickly assembled combat outposts manned by small numbers of US ground troops and a contingent of Afghan Army soldiers, the insurgency was compelled to respond. Each encampment was a thumb in the eye of the rebellion, an affront to Al Qaeda or other terrorist group efforts to influence villagers. Out of frustration, the only option was to attack, to send fighters up onto the nearest ridgeline and open fire on one of the new US outposts set outside the villages.

This set the conditions that allowed Cavoli and his men to kill insurgents. The 10th Mountain troopers could immediately fix the attackers in their ambush site with a fusillade of rifle and machine gun fire or shoulder-fired rockets and portable wire-guided missiles. Once they had them pinned down, the Americans could rain destruction down on them with a barrage of 120mm mortars or 155mm artillery. They would bring an apocalyptic mix of shells; white phosphorous that would boil the air over hunkered enemy gunmen to five thousand degrees, forcing them into the open; and high-explosive rounds with delayed fuses detonating in the air to crush anyone in the open. Apache attack helicopters could join in, as could F16 fighters, A10 Warthog attack jets, or big Special Operation AC130 Spectre gunships. A B1 bomber might be available to drop a precision-guided two-thousand-pound bomb that could annihilate every living creature across a four-hundred-yard expanse of open ground.

"The enemy is like a moth to light—he has to come fight you," Cavoli told Kilcullen in 2006. Those fights, in turn, "leave the enemy away from populated areas and subject to all our 'toys.'"

Kilcullen would later write from his observations in the Pech Valley that "it is now possible to see what an effective Afghanistan strategy probably looks like."

There was only one hitch: although this strategy denied insurgents a presence in the Pech Valley, they could continue to stage attacks from the more rugged capillary valleys north and south of the Pech. It would be in these more inaccessible areas that Cavoli and, later, Ostlund would learn the limits of "separate, connect, and transform." People up in these mountains had chosen isolation, and now it came with a price.

Running south from the Pech was the six-mile-long Korengal Valley. It was virtually a microstate all to itself, inhabited by a clan of ten thousand who spoke an obscure dialect for which there was no written form. The people were geographically isolated, although there were a handful of elders enriched by the illicit harvesting and exporting of prized Himalayan cedars in defiance of government regulations on this lumber trade. For decades the valley had offered sanctuary to some of the toughest anti-Soviet combatants to enter Afghanistan during that nine-year war that ended in 1989.

During this time the Korengalis were introduced to Wahhabism, a form of Islam that dictates a literal and conservative interpretation of the Koran and brands more moderate interpretations as blasphemous. The valley people embraced these teachings. Their willingness to resist the central government and welcome violent outsiders who shared their brand of Islam left the geographically isolated valley a waystation for international terror organizations slipping across the border from Pakistan.

It was Korengali fighters in late 2005 who killed all but one of a four-man SEAL sniper team and then shot down a rescue helicopter, killing sixteen more Americans, the battle made famous in the 2013 film *Lone Survivor*.

In the years to come, as journalists embedded with paratroopers under Ostlund's command in the Korengal, the valley would earn a reputation as the most dangerous place in Afghanistan, the Valley of Death, the Heart of Darkness. The well-received 2010 documentary *Restrepo*, directed by writer Sebastian Junger and cameraman Tim Hetherington, would immortalize the Korengal Valley as a place of unremitting violence committed by a determined insurgency.

Yet it would be ten miles to the north, on the other side of the Pech Valley in a capillary called the Waigal, a narrow fold running deep into Nuristan Province, where some of the most desperate fighting of the war would occur largely out of sight of the media and the world.

It would be where the Chosen Few waged war—or, more accurately, had it waged upon them.

Nicholson and Cavoli saw something sinister in the Waigal Valley, especially at its crucial focal point, the village of Aranas, which was located along an eastern tributary. They knew from intelligence reports that Al Qaeda, LET, JEM, and HIG, along with Uzbek terrorists, moved freely through Aranas.

A kind of mirror image of what the US Army worked to accomplish in the Pech Valley the terrorists had already achieved in Aranas and many of the nearby communities. The terror groups had formed strong bonds with much of the Aranas leadership, creating an oasis in the wilderness where insurgents could meet, plan, and strategize violence against the Americans and the Afghan government, whom they labeled the apostates or slaves of the Western cultures. From the Waigal Valley US Army leaders were convinced these enemy fighters were supporting attacks against US forces in the Korengal Valley to the south. And Nicholson and Cavoli worried that the threat might even be much larger, that this area around Aranas was becoming a nerve center for operations potentially beyond the borders of Afghanistan.

Aranas fell within Cavoli's area of operation, and Nicholson believed it had to be targeted, if only to curb the free reign these very dangerous international terrorist organizations enjoyed. In the summer of 2006 Nicholson ordered Cavoli to take control of Aranas, and Bravo Company, under Doug Sloan, was given the task. The area was too rugged for an air assault by helicopter, so the soldiers hiked in on foot and, after positioning themselves outside the village, opened negotiations with those Aranas leaders receptive to the benefits and money that might flow in from the Americans. Cavoli's soldiers began breaking ground on the Bella and Ranch House outposts.

There were divisions among the elders and the people of Aranas over whether the security promised by the new American outpost being built on the ridge above the village was really necessary. Some of the same infrastructure changes brought to the Pech Valley down below were also promised here—a new school, a small hydroelectric plant, and the possibility of a road linking the remote valley to the world. But the terror groups, particularly Lashkar-e-Tayyiba, had formed bonds with the people, taking wives and sharing a strict interpretation of Islamic beliefs. There were rumors of an LET training base in the Aranas area. Cavoli began to understand throughout the fall of 2006 that Aranas and the other villages of the Waigal region would not turn his way as readily as had the villages along the Pech Valley below.

Meanwhile establishing Ranch House was proving a logistical nightmare, without road access or even a landing zone for helicopters. Supplies had to be brought up by air drops, helicopter sling loads, and even on the backs of donkeys. A column of American soldiers along a cliff-side trail into Aranas was ambushed in August of 2006. Three were killed and three wounded; one of those who died earned a Silver Star for single-handedly holding off attackers with a light machine gun until a counterassault could be launched that killed a dozen of the enemy.

Attacks on US forces picked up in September. In an eighteen-day period there were fifteen attacks. Negotiations resumed the next month and seemed to make progress. But at the end of October Doug Sloan was killed with two of his soldiers in a roadside bomb attack outside Wanat that engulfed their Humvee in flames.

Cavoli and his men diligently reopened discussions with those village elders they believed remained receptive as they worked to build a helicopter landing zone at the Ranch House base.

They continued to work hard to win over the people of Aranas by following through on promises to build a small hydroelectric plant and a school. They gave jobs to local men as security guards or day laborers at the combat outpost. There were plans for a paved road from the Pech Valley as far as Bella and, perhaps one day, all the way to Aranas. Through the winter attacks on the soldiers dropped off, and they hoped that violent factions within the village had been pressured to leave.

By the time Ostlund and the Rock Battalion arrived to replace Cavoli and the 10th Mountain soldiers in May of 2007, the Waigal appeared to be more peaceful. Cavoli had left a network of outposts stretching from the Korengal clear up to Aranas. If it was far reaching and a challenge to maintain, Cavoli believed it was necessary. He was playing a game of Jenga to keep the insurgency and the terrorist groups at bay. Remove any part of the interdependent web of security and expanded government control, and you threatened too much of what had been achieved.

Except that when Ostlund arrived in the spring of 2007 he didn't quite see it that way. When Ostlund took over Cavoli's area of operations, he had his own ideas about how to fight the enemy. One of them concerned the Waigal Valley outposts: they didn't need to be there. Or at the very least they didn't need to be so far removed up the valley at Ranch House and Bella that their only lifeline was a resupply by air.

Ostlund came to that view weeks before his battalion arrived, when he traveled to Afghanistan to tour Cavoli's area of operation. By the time the battalions switched out on June 7, the decision had already been made to close Ranch House. And without Ranch House, Bella—which was farther down the valley but still in a precarious position accessible only by helicopter—would necessarily have to close as well.

Under Ostlund's analysis any effort to extend the Afghan government's reach into the Waigal and prevent insurgent attacks into the broader population centers of the Pech Valley could be done from the village of Wanat, located farther down, near the mouth of the valley and connected by road to Blessing, the battalion headquarters.

Ostlund's only problem as Rock Battalion operations got underway in the late spring of 2007 was when he would get permission to close Ranch House and Bella. Because the bases were so inaccessible, this would require air assets that were constantly in demand elsewhere. It would also require high command, working with Afghan leaders as far away as the government in Kabul, to approve what was technically a withdrawal.

Getting approval would lead to interminable—and fateful—delays.

→ ←

Meanwhile Ostlund was rapidly concluding that the Waigal Valley should not be the primary focus of his battalion's campaign. The officer was a data-driven guy, and as the deployment got underway, statistics plainly showed that the valley where Chosen Company was operating was unusually quiet.

The Rock Battalion command was constantly crunching figures, tracking the number of patrols, the number of artillery or mortar rounds fired, bombs dropped, rockets launched. Ostlund's staff built spreadsheets filled with data on TICs, or troops in contact—any episode of violent contact with the enemy, whether it be a few shots fired or a full-on battle. They'd turn the data into graphs on a briefing slide that tracked the ebb and flow of combat for all sectors of battalion operations. Always out front in the numbers was the Korengal Valley, where it seemed there was shooting going on almost every day. In the Waigal Valley, by sharp contrast, the first few months of the battalion's deployment registered almost no violence at all.

While other areas of the battalion operation were heating up, there were ongoing concerns about how remote and inaccessible Ranch House and Bella were. But so far as where the action was, Chosen Company was at the end of a long line of American war priorities, particularly when it came to resources and what mattered to commanders. Within the Rock Battalion the Waigal Valley operations lived in the shadow of

Ostlund's stubborn fight in the Korengal. Across eastern Afghanistan, where the 173rd Airborne Brigade was engaged, the Rock Battalion fight in Kunar and Nuristan provinces was a second-tier priority to protecting the more populated Nangarhar Province to the south, where the city of Jalalabad was located. For all of Afghanistan US military efforts in the east were less of a priority than the mission in the southern provinces, which were historic homelands for the Taliban. And globally the Afghanistan war was a bit player to the Bush administration's surge in Iraq.

Not only was Iraq siphoning off troops, aircraft, and spy drones, but it was also dominating the news cycles. Americans were barely aware there was still a war going on in Afghanistan.

"It seems like a common problem that there is no war news at home," 2nd Platoon sergeant Matt Kahler would write to his grandparents later in the year. "I have had lots of guys go on leave already. They talk about people not even knowing that we have troops in Afghanistan, or they believe that we're not really fighting here and that Iraq is much worse. . . . Iraq has more casualties cuz we only have 10 percent of the soldiers here, compared to what they have."

→  ←

Chosen Company commander Matt Myer eagerly endorsed Ostlund's decision to work toward closing down Ranch House and Bella. He felt that operating in this remote area was tactically a dead end. The people living up in those rookeries chose the inaccessible for a reason: they clearly wanted no part of the outside world. Myer understood there was some strategic significance to Aranas because leaders or members of global terror groups sometimes lived in or frequented the town, but he believed it would be nearly impossible to drag these mountain people of Aranas into the broader Afghan society.

*What is the purpose of our being here? I'm assuming risk for something I can't control and don't see has a lot of benefit.*

He knew he certainly didn't have the force for it. He'd already lost 3rd Platoon, which shifted over to Destined Company to help patrol a valley along the Pakistan border on the far side of the battalion's operational area. That left 1st Platoon under Lieutenant Matt Ferrara and 2nd Platoon led by Lieutenant Devon George. Chosen Company headquarters was next to the battalion command center at Forward Operating Base Blessing in the Pech Valley.

One of Myer's two remaining platoons would have to work out of Blessing with a double assignment—patrolling the far western reaches of the Pech Valley and north to the village of Wanat and serving as a quick-reaction force that could be sent at a moment's notice to any battalion hotspot.

That really only left Myer with one platoon, supplemented by battalion scouts and company mortar crews, to handle the Waigal Valley where there were at least eight villages or hamlets, including Aranas. He would also have a little more than a platoon of Afghan National Army soldiers and several dozen local men hired as security guards; their effectiveness in combat was always subject to question.

Nearly all the villages in the valley system were a day or more hike from either Bella or Ranch House. The idea of visiting and working with elders for each of these communities to achieve the separate-stabilize-and-transform strategy goals Ostlund outlined in his Power-Points seemed too much to ask.

Even before leaving Italy Myer had decided how to array his shrunken force. He would give 1st Platoon the tougher assignment of Bella and Ranch House. Staff Sergeant Erich Phillips, in charge of Chosen Company's mortar section, would go to Ranch House with two members of his team and a 60mm mortar tube. The rest of his mortar team would remain at Blessing, operating a 120mm mortar there. A second 120mm mortar was already set up at Bella, capable of reaching out to provide support for Ranch House if necessary.

Myer would be replacing roughly thirty to thirty-five soldiers from the 10th Mountain Division at Ranch House with only twenty to twenty-five of his own. It was all he could spare. He planned to alternate 1st and 2nd Platoons during the deployment, allowing soldiers to take advantage of Blessing's warm showers and hot meals.

The 1st Platoon commander, Lieutenant Matt Ferrara, would work out of Ranch House. He and his platoon sergeant, Shane Stockard, decided the mountain post would be manned by the two 1st Platoon squads that were led by staff sergeants who had combat experience from the previous deployment, David Dzwik and Conrad Begaye.

Begaye was a full-blooded Navajo Indian with a round face, mischievous eyes, and brows that danced up and down when he was prankish or pestering. He was born on a reservation in Shiprock, New Mexico, and spoke only Navajo until grade school. He grew up in Tucson and Phoenix, but he enjoyed most of his summers working with livestock on his grandparents' ranch back on the reservation, where he learned to ride on a quarter-horse name Cherry Coke. A lot of Begaye's family had served in the US military, and he would never forget his Uncle Rick, a veteran of Vietnam and the 173rd Airborne.

Begaye was the oldest of three. Both parents were employed by aerospace companies, and his father was a computer engineer. Conrad's first job out of high school was working the red-eye shift as a disc jockey for an Indian-owned country western radio station on the Navajo reservation. He loved it and even had his own on-air moniker, Mad Lad. That led to a better-paying job as a broadcast technician for a country western station in Phoenix.

It was after lunch one day at an Applebee's in Phoenix that Begaye strolled over to an Army recruiter's office and saw a video of soldiers jumping out of airplanes. He was hooked. He enlisted and qualified to join the elite 75th Army Ranger Regiment. Two years later, when it came time to re-enlist, Begaye sought an airborne assignment and was happily sent to Italy to join the 173rd, following in his uncle's footsteps.

By the time he arrived at Ranch House in May of 2007 he was thirty and had already deployed to war twice with Chosen Company, first to

Iraq and then Afghanistan. From childhood Begaye had been raised in the beliefs and ways of the Navajo. He carried with him at all times an arrowhead symbolizing the power of the warrior as well as a medicine pouch to give him an aura of protection in battle.

After each of his deployments Begaye participated in cleansing ceremonies on the Navajo reservation, days of fasting and sweat-lodge gatherings designed to restore his body and soul after the damage done by war. He believed in this process and felt it made a difference.

Stockard would set up at Bella with the platoon's third squad.

Chosen Company's 1st Platoon leader, Matt Ferrara, would be at Ranch House. He was twenty-three, fresh out of West Point, and headed into combat for the first time. His senior noncommissioned officer, Shane Stockard, was nine years older and beginning his third combat deployment. By any measure Stockard was far more experienced. Yet Ferrara was in charge. This was how the Army grew leaders: the young officer developing the skills of command with the assistance of a seasoned veteran. At its best the relationship is almost like a dance—in both behavior and language, one side respects rank while the other defers to experience. The officer gives the orders, but the senior sergeant can advise and urge in ways that shape the decision making. The commissioned leader, if smart, absorbs the lesson and improves as a commander. The noncommissioned counterpart can take credit for shaping and developing a fine new officer, an accomplishment that will burnish a résumé for advancement in the ranks. Both sides win.

When it came to Ferrara and Stockard running 1st Platoon, the dance seemed to work. Ferrara was smart, discerning, and a quick study; he respected what Stockard had to offer. The platoon sergeant, for his part, tried to guide Ferrara in his leadership decisions. Upper echelons in Chosen Company joked about them being the "tiny platoon," with Ferrara all of five-feet-five and Stockard two inches shorter.

The thirty-three-year-old platoon sergeant was born in Amarillo, Texas; his parents divorced when he was five. As a young man Shane took jobs managing restaurants, and joining the Army was the furthest thing from his mind. It was almost as an afterthought that he finally enlisted in 1999 at the age of twenty-four, something he figured might be an interesting new experience. He chose the 101st Airborne Division as his first assignment and signed up for grueling Ranger School as a private first-class. When he re-enlisted four years later, he asked for 173rd Airborne Brigade and jumped into Iraq in 2003. Stockard had an imposing personality and fiery red hair to match, though many of the men didn't know it because he always kept his head shaved. One of his team sergeants, James Takes, thought he'd never met such a "big little man." Younger soldiers like Jon Albert found Stockard to be one of those people he would never forget, someone who led by example.

Where Stockard's leadership was more instinctive—he was blunt in his methods and direct in his style—2nd Platoon sergeant Matthew Kahler's approach was more studied. He researched the concept of leadership, reading extensively about the lives of military leaders he admired and observing how those he knew personally conducted themselves. Kahler wanted to understand how they earned respect from the soldiers they led. He concluded that a loud, berating style was not a good way to go. He came to see his men as volunteers and professionals who had earned the right to be treated with dignity. His style was to frame orders in the form of a request, "Could you . . ." "Would you mind . . ."

Nobody else did that.

Kahler pored over his soldiers, wanting to know where they were from, what their interests were, how they saw their futures in the Army. When a replacement showed up, the platoon sergeant would seek him out and spend time getting to know him, asking thoughtful questions about the soldier's family, exploring how he might help him meet his goals, all the while scribbling notes.

For years Kahler had made a study of how soldiers should be treated, as if he were preparing a doctoral thesis. He had learned compassion as a boy growing up with a younger brother, Brian, who suffered from Down's syndrome, and was often the only one in the family who could calm him during emotional meltdowns.

When they were in Vicenza, Chosen Company commander Matt Myer had worried that Kahler was a little too easy on his men and might be seen as soft. But the captain came to reassess his 2nd platoon sergeant when they moved into the war zone. The strength of his leadership, Myer soon realized, was in the devotion he had to his men. They wanted to measure up to his expectations. They didn't want to let him down, and it was making them better soldiers.

Matt Kahler (pronounced KAY-lor) was born in Iowa, but his parents, both school teachers, moved to western Minnesota when he was a baby. They divorced when he was eight, and the breakup was tough on Matt. Growing up, the military was a lifelong dream, a way to be part of something greater than himself. He fell in love with his high school sweetheart, Vicki, and married her after he enlisted. He had gone through airborne training and then Ranger school before joining the 82nd. Four months before 9/11 he and Vicki moved to Italy after he transferred to the 173rd Airborne Brigade. They got an apartment in Grosse di Gazzo, a village east of Vicenza, and their next-door neighbor was Shane Stockard. Matt and Shane became best friends. They both jumped into Iraq in 2003, served in Afghanistan in 2006, and became platoon sergeants for Chosen Company before deploying in 2007.

Slender, five-feet-eleven, with sandy blond hair and striking green eyes, Kahler had an easygoing banter with his men. They teased him about his taste in music and how the hard-driving American Celtic punk band Dropkick Murphys really got his juices flowing. They needled him about his Minnesota roots with Fargo-isms like "Oh, yahh" or "Don'tcha know." They could hear him in his quarters at night reading Curious George or some other children's book into a tape recorder for his four-year-old daughter, Ally—not the sort of thing a GI usually expects from a tough platoon sergeant.

His men wanted nothing more than to earn Kahler's approval. When they fell short, his disappointment alone was enough to make them try harder. The implied message from Kahler was always very simple:

*You and I both know you're better than that.*

"You know, sometimes all you got to do is let people know that they let you down," he told Ryan Pitts once. "That's enough of a punishment."

→ ←

It was a warm, uneventful summer after Ferrara and his men moved into Ranch House, so slow that the West Point economics graduate, worried about how his men were handling their personal expenses, once gathered them together with an easel and a grease board for a lesson in finances.

They listened politely, even if their minds were elsewhere. Their time up in the mountains had been marked by periods of boredom broken only by the arrival of mail. The paratroopers could go days or weeks without receiving anything from home because of bad weather or other demands on the small fleet of Army helicopters. Between patrols and all-night stakeouts there was a lot of nervous energy to burn.

One day during the summer of 2007 Specialist Jason Baldwin came up with the idea of a zip line across the base's vertical terrain, using a webbed belt draped over a slung rope as something to hold onto at least temporarily until they were flung to the ground. The soldiers launched themselves amid hooting and hollering and actually managed to gather some speed before tumbling onto a surface of what was basically rock thinly veiled with a layer of dirt. Bruised and bleeding limbs and heads were the payoff, but no one seemed to care. Philippine-born Lester Roque, a senior medic, became a star of the event largely because of the little jig he danced while waiting for the pain in his tailbone to subside.

Kain Schilling emerged smiling but with blood streaming down the front of his left leg. He was one of Chosen's forward observers, the guys who call in the artillery and air support. Slender and with a shy smile, the twenty-year-old Schilling was born in the little Iowa town of Shueyville on the outskirts of Cedar Rapids. He first joined the Army National Guard and later the active-duty Army. Movies like Blackhawk Down and Saving Private Ryan made him want to experience everything a wartime Army could offer. And like a lot of them, Band of Brothers, the HBO series about a company of paratroopers fighting their way across World War II Europe, convinced him to join Airborne.

Up at Ranch House commanders would occasionally fly in steaks for the troopers to broil. But the same erratic helicopter flights that held up the mail held up the food too, so the basic food staple remained military meals ready to eat, or MREs, served cold unless a GI wanted to use a foul-smelling, chemically activated heating pouch to warm one up. The self-contained food rations were designed for durability and a shelf life of years. Somehow, though, the Chosen Few got a spoiled batch that summer, and many of them got violently ill.

For Baldwin, it was like a scene from the Exorcist, only out of both ends. It temporarily got him out of guard duty, much to the annoyance of his comrades. Baldwin was another of the Chosen Few from a broken home. Born in Santa Ana, California, he was nine months old when his parents divorced, and he grew up in Colorado and Nevada, shuttling between two households and barely graduating from high school. Band of Brothers made him want to jump out of airplanes, and he got his mother to sign the enlistment papers when he was seventeen.

Baldwin deployed to Zabul Province in Afghanistan with Chosen Company during the unit's first Afghanistan tour in 2005–2006. He was a mortar man and took quickly to the skills of rapid positioning, elevation, and right-and-left deflection. But there was also a restless, undisciplined streak running through him. Baldwin was a smartass. The edges on that attitude began to round off when a new mortars section leader arrived in the spring of 2007, Staff Sergeant Erich Phillips. Phillips had been told the Army specialist was a little wild, and when the two met,

Baldwin would never forget the look on Phillips's face when the staff sergeant fixed eyes on him and said, "Well, we're not going to have that problem, are we?" Baldwin could only stammer a response, "No, no, no, negative."

Baldwin had developed a healthy loathing for his previous section leader. But from the moment he met Phillips, something about the staff sergeant's bearing, confidence, and knowledge left the wild kid wanting nothing more than to earn his approval.

*I want to be his favorite soldier.*

Baldwin became the fastest mortar man in the battalion for the 60mm, able to adjust settings and fire a round quicker than anyone else. He had volunteered to accompany Phillips to Ranch House because all expectations were that this would be the tip of the spear for Chosen Company. And when nothing happened for weeks—while Able Company in the Pech Valley and Battle Company in Korengal were seeing action almost daily—some of the younger soldiers started getting pissed. They had trained hard for this and felt cheated; they wanted a taste of combat. But it wasn't only that: this was the enemy that had brought violence to American shores, and the paratroopers were ready for some payback. For Jason Baldwin, who had seen limited combat during the 2005–2006 deployment and was eager for more, it was that simple.

*I want to kill Haj.*

→  ←

They couldn't know it just then, but the boredom that Chosen Company troopers felt was misplaced. At some point during that summer a group of jihadist fighters had gathered under a tree high up on the mountain. One of them was Hazrat Omar, an Aranas native and a dedicated insurrectionist who intelligence suggested was an Al Qaeda devotee. A slender man with a calm and steady demeanor, Omar wore a full beard but left his upper lip shaved clean. He had a hand-drawn map spread out on a rock and, with a long pointer in his right hand, was guiding his listeners through the stages of a planned attack. The meeting was captured on a digital camera, and it was unclear whether it was an actual strategy session or a scene staged for a future propaganda film.

"This is the map of the American base in Aranas Village," Omar says in Pashto, as the other men in military fatigues and ammo vests follow along intently. "There were three groups of the enemies of Islam stationed in this base. The first group is the American soldiers. Second group is the apostate soldiers of the Afghan National Army. And the third group is the local militia."

The hand-drawn map is filled with symbols and scratchings that, assembled together, closely approximate the actual layout of Ranch House, showing American guard posts, living quarters, and the tactical operations center. "The commander lives there in the most secured place," Omar says, pointing to a spot on the map. He even indicates where the soldiers get on the Internet. "God willing, the Mujahedeen will conquer this base," he says. "With the help of God they will first subdue the militias." Then he explains, step by step, guard post by guard post, how the base must fall.

To Omar's left is a stocky, bearded man in dark sunglasses who says he prays they breach the defenses and reach the interior of the base. "With the help of God, it is not that difficult."

The Chosen Few would later brood over who betrayed them with detailed information about the base layout. Given the number of day laborers and locally hired security guards on the grounds, the list of suspects was substantial. Later in the year, when two enemy fighters were killed during an attack on Bella, the Chosen Few would recognize one of the bodies as that of a former Ranch House day worker, someone personable they'd grown to like and trust.

→ ←

Three weeks after the Chosen Few took over Ranch House Dzwik drafted a memorandum to his company commander with an assessment of weaknesses in the base defenses. On balance, the staff sergeant didn't see too many risks. Without roads, much less vehicles, there was no real threat of improvised explosive devices or IEDs, or roadside bombs. He felt certain the enemy would refrain from using indirect fire such as mortars or rockets to attack, primarily because the outpost was so close to Aranas and a wayward missile could kill villagers, angering and alienating the local population.

When 10th Mountain troops were posted there, the most common avenue of attack was from the west with rifles, machine guns, and rocket-propelled grenades. There was harassing fire usually directed at Posts One and Two, Dzwik noted. In that direction the ground fell sharply away from the base into a draw, and there were places, because of that geography, where the concertina wire was only thirty yards from the American guard posts. Dzwik believed that kind of threat still existed for Posts One and Two because enemy fighters could sneak up close to the base from the draw, fire at the Americans, and then escape.

Dzwik told Myer in his memo that he was toughening defenses in that sector with Claymore mines and early-warning trip flares in the low ground as well as more sandbags on the guard posts. Soldiers on duty there were told to peer down into the dead zone now and again to check for infiltrators.

On August 22, 2007, there were twenty-two Americans defending Ranch House, almost all of them Chosen Company paratroopers. A few Marines were on base acting as training advisors for twenty-two Afghan National Army soldiers assigned to the post. And finally, there were forty-five local men hired as security guards.

Dzwik wrote in his memorandum that with the precautions he had taken, the risks for Ranch House would be acceptable. Ferrara largely agreed. Always the optimist, he saw the defense of Ranch House as a ledger of pros and cons. It was good they were up so high because they had a spectacular vista laid out below. But Ferrara knew there was also a hazard in the dead spaces that were, in some cases, only yards from some of the guard posts where the ground dropped off in a way that could conceal an enemy fighter. The twisting oaks that populated the grounds blocked a lot of what they could see within the fort's perimeter. The villagers placed a high premium on the hardwood trees and demanded hefty compensation if even one of them was cut down, a lesson their predecessors, the 10th Mountain troops, had learned. "One tree is worth one cow," Ferrara had been told. So Chosen Company built a series of secondary positions made with walls of sandbags to further supplement the defenses. Ferrara believed the defenses were as good as could be expected.

Ranch House is the best fighting position in a bad place.

# 4

## >>> ENEMY INSIDE THE WIRE

*On that warm morning of August 22,* the sky was just beginning to brighten as Staff Sergeant Conrad Begaye stepped outside the tactical operations center to catch the sunrise over the mountains after a night of radio duty. He stretched. A single gunshot broke the stillness. He figured it was an accidental discharge. But then the rising slopes to the east erupted in volleys of machine gun, rifle, and rocket-propelled grenade fire.

*Wow. This is happening . . .*

War had finally come to Ranch House, and at this critical juncture, uppermost in Conrad Begaye's mind was that he was standing there in his flip-flops and PT shorts. His rifle, helmet, and body armor were back in the aid station where he bunked and left them.

He slipped back into the Tactical Operating Center (TOC), and five dozen or more enemy fighters began their assault on what was essentially the backside of the fort. Other gunmen were scattered along the fringes to the south and southwest, taking up positions between Ranch House and Aranas down the hill. It was still a half-hour before sunrise, and the sky was just bright enough to render night-vision goggles useless but too dark to see things clearly.

Jihadist gunmen had hiked far up onto the ridge so they could descend into Ranch House, following the arrows of approach drawn on the map Hazrat Omar displayed to his comrades. That gave them the advantage of what the military likes to call plunging fire—the ability to shoot down into defensive works or toss down grenades. To create even more havoc, a heavy, Soviet-made machine gun was set up across the valley about 650 yards to the west so a constant rain of suppressive fire could be directed into the American base to try to keep the paratroopers hunkered down behind their sandbags while the main body of insurgent fighters advanced.

A propaganda video posted later online shows the seconds before the insurgents launched the attack. A gaggle of bearded young men, rifles and grenade launchers in hand, their faces tense with anticipation, stand poised behind an abandoned stone cottage, or *bondeh*, high up above Ranch House and shrouded by trees.

Hazrat Omar leads a stitched-together band of fighters from Aranas and surrounding villages dressed in a mix of military fatigues and the familiar *shalwar kameez* shirt and pants that GIs liked to call "man dresses." On their heads are flat, woolen Pashtun caps or Arab kufiyah headdresses. They've strapped on ammunition harnesses or vests stuffed with magazines full of 7.62mm rounds for their AK47 rifles or elongated missiles for the grenade launching tubes balanced on their shoulders.

There were several attack routes. Chosen Company leaders would later estimate that sixty to eighty gunmen made up the assault force. One band of insurgents moved west toward four US troops manning Post Four and north toward the center of Ranch House with the base command headquarters. To the right of that advance were two other groups of fighters converging on an Afghan security guard compound where there was a single defender on duty at Post Five; other guards were conducting morning prayers. A fortified compound immediately to the west housed Afghan soldiers.

Finally, a fourth group of insurgents attacked downhill toward Post Three. The guard station was a tower reached by a wooden ladder and built on top of a small plywood barracks, the entire structure tucked into the rising slope of the mountain. The barracks walls were painted with a large, looping camouflage pattern, and a huge parachute was draped on the downhill side of the building.

In the actual fighting position on the roof of the barracks, layers of sandbags were stacked around a wood-frame guard post. There was an M240 machine gun and an MK19 automatic grenade launcher. The grenade launcher looked like a machine gun on steroids and fired 40mm grenades fed into the gun on a belt at a rate of one per second. The grenade launcher and the machine gun were oriented uphill to the east over a kill zone of about thirty or forty yards of scrub brush that ended at a tree line. Post Three was the highest point on the base, and soldiers reached it by climbing a steep staircase of sandbags that had a rope line to grab onto.

Four paratroopers were assigned here, but one of them, Specialist Wallace Tinnin, had flown out with his team's laundry for Camp Blessing. On this morning Private First Class Jeddah Deloria, who just turned twenty-one in June, was on guard in the rooftop post. Down below asleep in cramped quarters were Specialist Chuck Bell and Sergeant Carlos Gonzales-Rodriguez.

Deloria had been aching for his first taste of combat since the Chosen Few arrived nearly three months earlier. The stocky, round-faced Californian always seemed to be smiling, as if the muscles in his face, when relaxed, slipped naturally into a pleasant expression.

Jeddah Deloria was another of Chosen's lost boys. His father was a mechanical engineer and his mother a dietitian, both Filipinos who were living and working in Jeddah, Saudi Arabia, when he was conceived—thus his unusual first name. The paratroopers would later call him Delo because those were the letters they could read on his uniform name tag under the straps of his ammo harness.

He was born in Manila, and his parents immigrated to the desert east of Los Angeles six months later. His father, Joseph, was a strict disciplinarian who required his two sons to stand at attention for long periods. Jeddah, who was only five or six, didn't really seem to mind it. In the undeveloped stretches of San Bernardino County there were rattlesnakes to catch and targets to shoot at with his dad. But at thirteen, when his parents divorced, he grew distant from his father; he got into fights, dropped out of school, and drifted.

Driving past a recruiting station with his brother one day, Jeddah decided on an impulse to join the Army. He was nineteen. Inside of a year he was assigned to Chosen Company, where he would find another family.

At five-feet-eight and 180 pounds, Delo was the slowest runner in Chosen Company, but he could hump almost anything up the side of a mountain. "A lot of torque, no horsepower," he liked to say, and Delo's oxen qualities were harnessed as part of a three-man machine crew carrying the M240. Jeddah loved that weapon—the power of six hundred rounds per minute; precise targeting at up to twelve hundred yards; the way the gas hydraulics drove through grit, resisting the weapon getting jammed; how you could punt-fire rounds over a ridge and hit fleeing enemy fighters on the other side. Now, after three months of not firing a shot in Afghanistan, he just wanted a chance to *finally use it.*

It was warm this early morning, even high up on the mountain, and like Begaye down at the TOC, Delo was standing post in a T-shirt, shorts, and flip-flops, though he also had on his armored vest. Delo had just put his night-vision goggles away with the growing daylight when he heard a couple of gunshots. He thought they might be from down in the village, but when he turned to face uphill, rounds were tearing into the sandbags in front of him and there were muzzle flashes from the underbrush and treeline far up the hill.

He grabbed the radio to the base tactical operations command: "Ranch House, Post Three taking contact."

Begaye was on the receiving end. He had already rushed over and shaken Ferrara, who was bunked out nearby inside the headquarters. "I think we're under attack!" The lieutenant was half awake after hearing the first explosions. Radio reports were tumbling in from all four guard posts, a chorus of agitated voices against a background of gunfire, and Begaye was trying to make sense of it all, to tease out the direction and size of the assault. He was busy acknowledging each call-in and briefed what he knew to Ferrara. All the time Begaye was desperately missing his gear.

*I've got to get up to my crap. I need my helmet.*

Up at Post Three Delo had two weapons at his disposal, an automatic grenade launcher on his left and his beloved machine gun on the right. There was really no question which he would choose, and in seconds he was blasting away with the M240, making small circles with the rounds, "painting" the hillside above with bullets. He was finally in combat, firing his favorite weapon. Delo was so happy he actually started laughing out loud.

Several dozen yards to the south and east the base defenses were quickly crumbling. In the predawn gloom a battle-scape of twisting mountain oak and tall grass was erupting in the white flash and boom of exploding, rocket-propelled grenades (RPGs). Amid the billowing smoke and dust, the advancing enemy fighters looked like ghosts picking their way down heavily vegetated slopes and yelling "Allahu Akbar!" (God is greatest) as they moved toward the Afghan security guard positions. Only one security guard was on duty, and after the first volley of RPGs, the hired local Afghans abandoned their compound and ran west. Enemy fighters rushed in and started clearing abandoned buildings with grenades. The retreating guards reached a complex of sandbag towers and plywood huts where a platoon of Afghan National Army soldiers was bivouacked. Most of the Afghan soldiers simply joined the security guards in a panicked retreat.

But a few Afghan military stood and fought—the platoon commander, a sergeant, and two of their soldiers. They held on for about fifteen minutes before being driven back. One Afghan soldier and one security guard were killed, and two Afghan soldiers were wounded.

On the far left flank of the main enemy assault, at the lowest elevation on the base, a handful of Chosen Few paratroopers manning Post Four found themselves nearly enveloped in gunfire. They were taking rounds from a heavy machine gun the enemy had set up across the valley. The Afghan National Army compound was to their north, and as the jihadist assault slashed down into the Ranch House base from the northeast to the southwest, fighters were advancing along that flank and pouring AK47 fire and RPGs into Post Four. Like Post Three, this fighting position was built on top of a small barracks. The man in charge was a quiet, unassuming Montana native, Sergeant Mike Johnson, who was on the eve of his twenty-sixth birthday.

Johnson, who was married and the father of two, grew up thirty-four miles outside Glacier National Park in the town of Whitefish. He graduated from high school in a class of twelve.

Johnson worked as a diesel mechanic before joining the Army at twenty-two. He first served with the 82nd Airborne and then went to Italy, where he joined Chosen Company during its first deployment to Afghanistan in 2005–2006.

At Ranch House on this day he was in charge of Post Four and was up in the guard tower with one of his paratroopers, Specialist Robert Remmel. With Remmel on an M240 machine gun and Johnson armed with an M4 rifle mounted with a grenade launcher, they focused their fire on enemy gunmen trying to reach the Afghan National Army position. Johnson had his two other soldiers, Specialist Jeffrey Shaw and Private First Class Gregg Rauwolf, direct their fire and throw grenades down a draw to the southeast where fighters had made their way to within fifty feet of the outpost.

Ranch House Post One was on the far west end of the base, the opposite side from the main enemy attack. The living quarters there were separate from the guard post, set back about fifty feet. Jason Baldwin was inside. He had just fallen asleep after finishing a guard shift. Army Specialist Hector Chavez had replaced him at Post One. There were test firings during early hours on other days, and Baldwin woke up, pissed at what he figured was another dry run of testing. He checked his watch—4:55 A.M.

*What the hell are they doing?*

Then he heard Chavez open up at Post One with a light machine gun. Chavez just kept firing. This was no drill.

*Oh shit.*

Baldwin cracked open the door and could hear a continuous exchange of gunfire. He leaned over toward a sleeping Sergeant Jose Canales Jr. "Hey, we're being attacked." The noncommissioned officer was suddenly up and kept saying, "Oh shit. Oh shit. Oh shit. Oh, shit. Oh shit." He barked at Baldwin for turning on the light so they could get dressed. The room was plunged back into darkness, and Baldwin was left feeling around to find his clothes. He threw a shirt on over his shorts, pulled on his body armor and shoes, and was out the door. Private First Class Kyle White was right behind him.

→ ←

Inside the living quarters at Post Three Chuck Bell was deep asleep when AK47 fire startled him awake. "Sergeant Gonzales, I think we're taking fire." They heard Delo firing the M240 on the roof. Within seconds an RPG slammed into the building. Gonzales was on his feet, throwing on his vest and helmet. He didn't bother pulling pants over his long underwear or even putting on his boots. "Hope for the best," he told Bell, and headed outside, climbing up a rear ladder to the firing post on the roof.

Bell's heart felt like it was beating its way out of his chest.

*This is real. This is it.*

In the guard tower above, Delo's war had barely begun when it was suddenly over. An RPG exploded into the right-front corner of his fighting position, the force of it collapsing the roof and sending a wave of hot shrapnel slicing into the right side of his body from his head down to his knee. The flesh on his right shoulder was shredded, and a thick layer of tissue on his forearm was literally peeled back. Delo was flat on his back under the fallen roof of the guard tower. He was conscious and fascinated with how the exposed muscles in his right arm would flex when he moved his hand. He couldn't see out his right eye or hear out of his right ear. One piece of shrapnel about a quarter of an inch wide had burrowed through his skull. Delo didn't realize it yet, but the metal had lodged in a part of his brain controlling movement on the left side of his body.

The enemy continued to shoot into the wrecked fighting position, and bullets skipped off Delo's body armor, slamming into the collapsed wooden roof and pinning him to the floor. Wood splinters from the impacts hit him in the face. His stunned body for the moment felt no immediate pain.

*I was so happy just a second ago.*

Gonzales reached him as round after round of RPGs slammed into the outpost, tearing jagged holes in the plywood walls. One of them exploded just as Bell left the quarters below. The force of it sent him sprawling onto the ground, the air knocked out of his lungs. Bell's first instinct was to get away from all of this. Escape. So he climbed to his feet, turned, and rushed back inside the hooch. But in seconds Bell realized this was no course of action for a soldier—his war had started.

*Either I sit here and die . . . or I'm going to run out and do my job.*

He steadied himself, counted to three, and barreled out the door, heading to the rear of the outpost, firing his 9mm over his shoulder in the direction of muzzle flashes up the hill. Gonzales was suddenly standing over him, up above in the ruins of the fighting position. Bell noticed how odd it was that the wooden canopy over the position was gone. Gonzales was yelling something down at him, but Bell couldn't understand it over all the noise and called out for him to repeat it. "Go to Post Two! Run to Post Two! Tell them the radio's down at Post Three and that the enemy's at the wire!"

Bell holstered his pistol and started racing down the steep slope. Post Two was about seventy-five yards ahead, and he felt a mix of relief for getting out of that kill zone and shame for feeling that way. Behind him on the wrecked outpost Delo was asking Gonzales to dig him out from under the collapsed canopy. Almost at the same moment a bullet struck Delo in the right shoulder and passed right through it. "Fuck! I got shot!"

Gonzales saw it happen. "I have to go," he said. "They're coming through the wire. I have to go."

And he was out of there, leaving Delo on the floor of the tower.

→  ←

With Post Three down and the twin compounds for Afghan security guards and Afghan Army soldiers captured, the entire eastern sector of the base was wide open to the attackers. The Afghan soldiers had left a mounted machine gun behind that enemy fighters quickly spun around and put into action against the American defenses ahead. Enemy fighters broke open captured cartons of bottled water and started passing them around.

The initial flush of victory left Hazrat Omar's assault momentarily unhinged. Fighters piled up around the captured fighting positions and barracks as their leaders urged them forward, one of them shouting into a hand mic that was wired into a bullhorn slung from a strap over his shoulder. A videographer panned the fighters and caught footage of Omar wearing an assault pack and desert-fatigue pants. He grinned into the camera before handing another fighter a grenade to throw down toward the paratroopers.

While a handful of more determined enemy fighters plunged forward toward the US positions, dozens of others crowded around the captured barracks. They searched rooms for spoils and found a cowering, befuddled security guard who got left behind during the defenders' hasty retreat. The man was ushered away. A seized crate full of RPGs—the missiles still in their factory plastic wrapping—was broken open and the rounds distributed to fighters who started launching them down toward the Americans. The cache included eight AK47 rifles, six radios, and dozens of ammo cans and magazines full of 7.62mm rifle rounds.

Down at the center of Ranch House Baldwin and White emerged from the barracks of Post One and saw Afghan security guards streaming past them and down the hill. Baldwin was struck by how peculiar it was that some of those running away were smiling. He and White could hear rifle and machine-gun fire and see RPG explosions. An uphill landscape of oak trees and tall grass disrupted their field of vision, and there was a sense that the security of Ranch House base was slipping away. They wanted to find someone in charge and start fighting.

A short distance to the east in the aid station Erich Phillips had just rolled over and sat up on his cot after automatic weapons fire woke him. It was 4:45 A.M. He'd set his alarm for 4:50 to start a shift in the TOC at 5:00. But all of a sudden there was machine gun fire outside. Phillips stood and listened, trying to decipher what and who was shooting. There was an M240 machine gun and Kalashnikov rifles like those the Afghan guards and Afghan soldiers carry. Some kind of drill? Then an RPG round exploded outside the aid station.

No drill.

The door to the aid station swung open, and a wild-eyed Baldwin was standing there. Kyle White was right behind him. Baldwin announced that the base was under attack, but the news didn't trigger the kind of reaction Jason expected. Phillips calmly geared up, pulled on his ammunition rack, and strapped on his helmet before finally reaching for his rifle. "Yeah, no fucking shit," Phillips said and stepped out the door, only to see fleeing Afghan security guards going right past him in full gallop. Dzwik had stepped out of the TOC to find himself in the same stream of fleeing humans. He literally grabbed ahold of one Afghan soldier and placed him in a defensive position near the aid station.

The security guard commander, Abdul Gafar, was right on the heels of his own men. Phillips was red-faced with anger: "What the fuck are you doing? Get back to your post!" he yelled.

Gafar kept repeating: "Taliban! Taliban!"

"No shit! Get back to your post!"

But now bullets were starting to kick up dirt where they were standing. Phillips sprinted to the nearby mortar pit and dove in.

→ ←

Far down the valley at Bella, Sergeant First Class Stockard roused Matt Myer with news that Ranch House was under attack. The captain was out from Blessing for a few days to visit Bella. He got on the radio with Begaye and could hear firing in the background.

Begaye was still trying to make sense of what was unfolding. Agitated young voices reporting by radio from different guard posts conveyed a sense of utter confusion. He had lost all communication with Post Three and could hear someone yelling over the radio, "Hey, they're in the wire!" When Myer came up on the link from Bella, Begaye tried to make plain to his company commander how serious the situation was becoming at Ranch House.

"All right, roger that," Myer said. "Keep calm."

That didn't sit well with Begaye.

*Fucking keep calm! What the fuck? YOU'RE not up here!*

Meanwhile Matt Ferrara had moved outside the headquarters to gather his own assessment, and as he neared the corner of the TOC, bullets started whizzing past.

*They're that close already?*

At Post Two Private First Class Sean Langevin saw what looked like a wild man running down the rocks toward him dressed in combat boots, long underwear, and body armor. It was Chuck Bell, and he didn't slow down until he reached the bunker. Bell swung around the MK19 grenade launcher on the roof and trained it on the area around Post Three up the hill, then started blasting away, hoping to keep the enemy from getting close enough to kill Gonzales and Delo. Firing the stream of grenades from the large, boxy automatic weapon gave the Missouri country boy at least a measure of relief from the guilt he was feeling for leaving his friends behind.

Post Two was a single-story bunker, with its grenade launcher and an M240 machine gun oriented toward the south and west in the direction of Aranas and down the valley. The living quarters for paratroopers manning the post was a separate, plywood hooch located about fifty-five yards southeast in the direction of the post headquarters. Langevin, who had a squad automatic weapon—or SAW, a light machine gun—had climbed up onto the roof of the Post Two bunker so he could start firing east in the direction of the enemy.

He and Bell suddenly saw Gonzales running toward them from Post Three. The sergeant had a gash on his foot after picking his way through boulders and prickly undergrowth without shoes. Worse than that, he had a shrapnel wound to his shoulder. Bell's grenade launcher jammed up after an enemy bullet lodged in the trigger mechanism, and he took Gonzales inside the bunker to treat his wounds. Bell was frantic about Delo and demanded answers from Gonzalez. "Where's Deloria? Where's Delo?" Gonzales said Deloria was still up in the guard post buried under its collapsed roof.

"I told him we would be back. We're coming back for him. Just stay quiet and no one will even know you are here," Gonzales said.

Bell called up to Langevin to continue pouring cover fire in the direction of Post Three to keep the enemy away from Delo: "Hey, you make sure they don't get up that ladder."

Langevin was hunkered over his light machine gun, playing out bursts of ammunition. He didn't need anybody telling him his job: "Don't' worry. I got this, Bell."

→ ←

Johnson and Remmel over at Post Four could see militants pouring into the Afghan National Army compound.

*There's nobody there fighting back at them. . . .*

Enemy fire on Post Four was only getting more intense. Remmel had crouched behind a sandbag wall in the tower to reload his machine gun. At six-feet-five and more than 250 pounds, he was one of the biggest men in the platoon. He got back up on his feet to resume firing and was cut down by a burst of automatic weapons fire from his left. Johnson pulled off his body armor and found three bullet holes in Remmel's side. Johnson strapped the protective vest back on the wounded soldier and called for Gregg Rauwolf to come help Remmel climb down and start dressing his wounds in the barracks.

Between the heavy machine gun fire from across the valley and rifle fire from the east and north, the post was literally under siege. Johnson picked up the radio mic and began reporting his first casualty to headquarters when a bullet shot the handset in half and communication was cut off.

→ ←

At the center of the base Ferrara was back inside the TOC and had taken over briefing Myer on the radio. For an odd moment the company commander felt like he was getting mixed signals because his young platoon leader at Ranch House sounded unusually calm, the tone of his voice almost conversational.

But the circumstances had actually grown more dire by the minute and remained confusing. All four guard posts had reported being under attack. Post Three communication was lost entirely. Post Two was reporting incoming gunfire to the rear of its location, clearly from inside the combat outpost. And Johnson over at Post Four had just informed headquarters about Remmel's gut wound.

When Ferrara took the radio from Begaye to get more detail, the line to Post Four went dead. It was still unclear whether there were friendly troops at the Afghan Army and security guard compounds up the mountain toward the east. Headquarters couldn't raise any of the Afghan commanders by radio. Even the Marine advisors for the bulk of the Afghan soldiers, who were bivouacked down by the landing zone and base entrance, were out of radio contact. Clearly, though, there was automatic weapons fire and RPGs coming from the east, particularly plunging fire, and it was only getting worse around the aid station and TOC. But without knowing for certain whether those compounds were in enemy hands, Ferrara couldn't order any mortar rounds fired in that direction.

*We have to find out what happened to our allies.*

Myer down at Bella was starting to absorb some of this from Ferrara when the radio connection with Ranch House suddenly dropped as the lieutenant was in midsentence. The captain radioed back, but there was nothing. By now there was little doubt that some enemy fighters had overrun a large portion of the base and were now within hand-grenade range of the base headquarters where Ferrara was on the radio. The more minutes that ticked by without reestablishing radio contact, the more alarming the prospects.

*Was the command post just now overrun?*

At Ranch House it took several minutes to restore order. An RPG had slammed into the headquarters' roof, blasting a hole in the ceiling and cutting communication to the outside world. Overhead lights in the operations center had come crashing down, and shrapnel went flying across the room. Fortunately no one was hurt. But it took time before Ferrara got his hands on a working, handheld radio with a whip antenna that he could use outside to reconnect with Myer.

Meanwhile Phillips had started organizing a defense of the headquarters area. He moved Sergeant Kyle Dirkintis, the medic, up to the TOC and ordered Schilling to take a position on the northwest corner of the aid station where he could fire at insurgents higher up the mountain at the Afghan National Army compound.

Chavez, who was up in Post One just to the west, was trying to track on his radio how events were unfolding across the base, and he heard that Post Three had been overrun with all but one of the Americans evacuated.

"What do you mean one man's unaccounted for?" Phillips yelled.

"Nobody knows where he is—it's Deloria."

→ ←

At Post Three the enemy was still shooting into the tumbled-down guard tower. Delo, who was alone now, already had a bullet wound through his left shoulder. A portion of the collapsed roof was pinned against his body armor, keeping him from moving, so he shimmied out of the vest. But while he did, a second bullet ricocheted into his right thigh and then a third drilled though the meaty part of his right backside. "Come on, you got me!" Delo yelled out. "Time out! Stop!"

Now free to crawl around a bit, Delo found his M4 jammed under the wreckage, but he couldn't pull it loose. Explosions had wrecked both the machine gun and grenade launcher. He saw detonators for the Claymore mines—clackers, they call them—hanging down off the front sandbags. He reached over and tried to set off the mines, but it didn't work. Someone must have cut the wires.

It was just a matter of waiting for the enemy to come kill him. The radio was nearby, but Delo couldn't get it to work. It had sensitive frequencies on it that should never be allowed to fall into enemy hands, so he twisted the knob to render the device useless.

Then he waited. He could hear insurgent voices down below, men shouting directions or orders at one another. It sounded very much like they were moving past him and continuing down the hill.

He was now behind the advancing enemy lines.

→ ←

At the mortar pit Phillips called over for Baldwin, who was in a sand-bagged position near Post One, to come help him fire the 60mm mortar. From that location looking east there was virtually a wall of oak trees and waist-high grass and bushes. It was good concealment for the paratroopers in the mortar pit, a portion of which was an ammunition supply bunker. But it also made it tough for Americans to see the advancing enemy. Phillips had preplanned targeting coordinates for the mortar that would allow them to pummel the ground around Post Three. He had assembled the data as a contingency in the event of an attack like this.

But the gunfire raining down from higher elevations to the east made it impossible for him to reach and operate the mortar. Bullets were actually pinging off the launch tube.

Schilling, meanwhile, spotted an insurgent slipping up behind a plywood latrine just several yards east of the aid station. He started yelling, "He's behind the shitter!" And everybody opened up on the shack, splintering the plywood with M4 rounds.

From where the troopers had taken positions in and around the mortar pit and the aid station, they could see muzzle flashes from the vegetation and trees on the rising slope to the east. Rocket-propelled grenade rounds whooshed out of the underbrush to explode nearby. But it was hard to see individual enemy fighters who were little more than shadows passing quickly from one tree to another. The soldier only had a split-second to react and Phillips felt certain he dropped a few of the enemy. He kept calling out, "Oh, I see one." Then he would fire. "Got 'em!" And then he'd do it again. It was driving Baldwin bananas because the spectral figures with their AK47 rifles were just moving too quickly for him to get a bead on.

The volleys of RPGs escalated, and Phillips called out for his soldiers to ratchet up their return fire. Phillips wanted fire superiority—force the enemy behind cover.

Let 'em have it.

And it seemed to have some effect. Up at the Afghan National Army post, on images captured by the enemy cameraman, a row of attacking fighters were forced to take cover, crouching behind a sand-bag wall.

The fighting there raged for several minutes. One enemy fighter un-leashed an RPG round that struck the far end of the aid station, sending small pieces of shrapnel into Schilling's face, and he had dust and blood in his eyes. The paratrooper instinctively started to pull back, but Phil-lips hollered at him to stay put.

"I need you to hold that center or we might not go home!"

Schilling, who was for the moment more intimidated by Phillips than the enemy, stayed put.

Dzwik came down from the headquarters, and Phillips shouted for him to relieve Schilling, who fell back to the mortar pit. Phillips sur-veyed his wounds and decided they were superficial, but he could tell Schilling was stunned from the blast, so he had him stay low behind the ammo bunker and fill magazines for the rifles. "Roger that, Sergeant."

Half of the mortar pit doubled as an ammunition storage area, a bunker four feet high and covered with plywood overlaid with sandbags, and some of the RPG rounds coming in at an angle literally skipped off the sandbags like pebbles on a lake and flew off into the trees. Schilling was mesmerized watching two deflected RPGs spin end over end high up into the sky in a kind of aerial ballet. Each time an RPG roared in, Phillips and the others yelled "RPG!" and ducked down into the bunker as the missile caromed off to explode someplace else, then they would pop right back up with their M4s firing or throwing hand grenades. There was a strange rhythm to it all. Phillips was amazed how they were spared over and over again from being blown to pieces.

*You want to talk about some lucky bastards.*

# 5

> > > PHILLIPS FIGHTS BACK

*Luck was scarce* for several other Chosen Few defenders. At Post Two, where a wounded Carlos Gonzales was being treated, Sergeant John Relph and Private First Class Adam Spotanski tried to fight their way back up the steep, rocky terrain to reach Post Three and Deloria. But enemy fire was too intense, and they were forced to fall back.

The enemy advancing toward Post Two from the opposite direction had an easier time of it. They were scurrying downhill, a series of limestone outcroppings acting like stone walls that provided perfect fighting positions as the insurgents moved closer to the bunker.

An AK47 bullet literally drilled its way through the breach of Langevin's SAW, but the firing mechanism somehow still worked. Spotanski climbed up on the roof to help Langevin lay down fire, but rounds were coming so fast and furious that eventually he headed back down inside the bunker. "Fuck this. I'm outta here." Shrapnel from an RPG blast wounded Langevin in his thigh, but he didn't cry out or even mention it to anyone and kept fighting. Chuck Bell, down below in the bunker, was on the radio when a round passed through his right triceps—a neat hole in and a neat hole out. Gonzales was sitting nearby getting bandaged and saw the whole thing. "Yep. You were shot."

But Bell shook it off. He didn't see much blood, and the pain wasn't any worse than when he got vaccinated before deployment. He remained more troubled by the thought of his friend Delo, still possibly alive up at Post Three. Bell never had much patience for organized religion and had his doubts about a higher deity, but this one time he prayed to God.

*I hope you keep Delo safe.*

Far to the south at Post Four the fighting strength of the paratrooper team there had been cut in half. With Gregg Rauwolf treating Remmel in the barracks, only Johnson and Shaw were outside defending the bunker. Shaw was fighting from the secondary position, walls of sandbags stacked up on the ground near the outpost. He dropped down to reload his rifle, and when he reemerged to start firing, an enemy round passed cleanly through his right bicep and burrowed into his left bicep—one bullet, two limbs shot. Shaw was initially stunned by the wound, uncertain of what happened or why he was having trouble moving his arms or holding his rifle. By this time Johnson had been forced out of the tower by increasingly heavy gunfire and reached Shaw, saw that he was bleeding, and sent him back into the barracks. Now the sergeant was left outside to defend Post Four by himself.

→ ←

Lieutenant Colonel Bill Ostlund was down at Blessing in the Pech Valley, where the battalion had two 155mm artillery guns capable of wreaking some havoc on the enemy. He wanted to know why Myer wasn't employing them in the battle at Ranch House. Myer explained that the enemy was inside the perimeter. "We can't shoot artillery. They're too close to us," he told his boss.

The captain did call in fire from 120mm mortars located at Bella to hit ridgelines two to three hundred yards away from the base just in case there were enemy reinforcements positioned up there. Forty-five minutes into the battle enemy fighters had captured roughly half of Ranch House, with the area around Post Three and the Afghan Army and security guard compounds now under their control. The front line for the fight ran north to south through the center of the base.

There was further confusion because many of the attackers were wearing camouflaged military clothing, leaving some of the paratroopers uncertain whether they were seeing Afghan soldiers or security guards moving behind the dense vegetation. As the militants worked their way west, they began closing in on the base headquarters, the mortar pit, and aid station. They were within ten to twenty yards in some places. To the far right of the enemy advance was the Post Two guard station, where paratroopers were forced to turn their weapons toward the interior of the base to defend themselves. Between that fighting position and the aid station were the empty barracks for the paratroopers assigned to Post Two, and behind that building was a storage shed.

The enemy was pushing toward those structures. If they captured them, they would split what was left of the American defenses, isolating Post Two. The enemy would also have succeeded in outflanking the center of Ranch House—the headquarters.

→  ←

At the mortar pit Kain Schilling could hear over a radio that Gonzales had lost blood from his wound and was slipping in and out of consciousness at Post Two. It was the first time the men at the mortar pit had heard of someone seriously wounded, and Erich Phillips decided he needed to get up there with Sergeant Kyle Dirkintis, the medic.

*Nobody's going to fucking die on my watch.*

He grabbed Kyle White and low ran over to the TOC, where he found Ferrara standing in the doorway, one hand carrying the heavy portable radio, the other holding a mic to his ear. Phillips left White there to augment the headquarters defense, took Dirkintis, and returned over to the mortar pit. By this time enemy fire was so intense that rounds were tearing holes in the sandbags over the ammo bunker. Phillips was working on how he and Dirkintis were going to get across open ground uphill to Post Two—the first stop would be the Post Two barracks.

He wanted Baldwin to throw grenades into the oak trees where there were enemy gunmen and indicated where he wanted them to go and where he wanted Baldwin's covering fire after that. Then they each pulled pins and lobbed grenades. Schilling watched in amazement as even before the bombs detonated Phillips and Dirkintis took off up the slope toward the barracks thirty yards away, crossing an area swept by enemy bullets. To the east of the barracks was a storage shed and a line of trees and trails that led east toward the captured Afghan Army compound. Figures were moving from the ANA post down through that foliage heading west toward the barracks. Phillips and Dirkintis picked their way through waist-high grass to reach the far west end of the barracks building. From there it was still another fifty yards across largely open and uphill terrain to Post Two. Enemy fighters were filtering in among the trees on the opposite, east end of the barracks building, which was about twenty feet long. They saw the two paratroopers move out in front of them, effectively blocking their infiltration. Phillips, in his bid to get a medic to Post Two, had disrupted an enemy maneuver to cut through the American line. The militants unleashed AK47 fire down along both sides of the barracks toward the west end of the structure where Phillips and Dirkintis had taken refuge. Other enemy fighters fired down from the direction of Post Three.

Phillips ordered Dirkintis to get inside the barracks out of the line of fire: "Lay flat on your belly. Don't get up until you hear me call your name, dude. Like don't fucking move. I can't lose you."

→  ←

At the edge of the Afghan Army Compound Hazrat Omar was back in the lens of the video camera, this time with a cluster of his men and an AK47 in his hands. He started to lead them down a trail that sloped toward the center of Ranch House.

Jason Baldwin, at the mortar pit, could hear insurgents shouting "Allahu Akbar" as the gunfire grew even more intense, and it felt like they were on the verge of finally being overrun. He called over to Hector Chavez for help and then in the other direction toward Phillips. But both yelled back that they too were pinned down. Baldwin was left to struggle with the prospect of his own annihilation. He laid out three grenades near a support beam for the ammo bunker. Baldwin reasoned that if the worst happened, he would use one to destroy the mortar tube, another to roll into the ammo supply bunker, and a third on himself.

The twenty-one-year-old soldier could feel panic welling up inside. Then something in his head clicked. He realized there was nothing he could do to change fate.

*Okay, I'm gonna die. So what.*

After that, he could think straight. He remembered how Phillips once showed him how the elevation on the 60mm mortar could be raised up so that a shell would go straight up and come straight down and blow up the weapon. Baldwin figured if he just dropped that setting a smidgeon, 20 degrees, he might slam rounds just fifty yards away where the enemy fighters were clustered around the Afghan National Army compound. That could really mess things up for them.

Baldwin yelled over at Ferrara who was near the TOC with the radio. "Hey, can I blow up the ANA compound?" Matt Ferrara pondered for a moment the irony of bringing artillery down on a portion of his own combat outpost.

"Fuck it," the lieutenant yelled back, giving the green light.

Baldwin adjusted the tube so that it was almost straight up and down. Then he dropped a round in. Schilling was nearby as Baldwin watched the shell fly upward and then appear to actually arc back over their heads in the wrong direction.

"Schilling, oh fuck, I think I've killed us."

But the shell rose higher and finally pitched forward, dropping into the ANA compound.

Now Baldwin started launching more 60mm rounds. In his excitement he forgot to pull the arming pin on about four of them, so they landed harmlessly among the enemy. David Dzwik, over by the TOC, could hear Baldwin shouting obscenities at himself for the blunders. But the mortar man finally started to lay waste to the Afghan Army compound.

After several minutes the Afghan security guard compound was burning.

This was good news for Ferrara over near the headquarters, but it wasn't good enough. He and Matt Myer knew the situation demanded air support. The closest available aircraft were two Air Force A10 ground attack jets that were prowling up and down the Pakistan border.

"We need to do something to get them off of us," Myer told Ferrara about the insurgents closing in. "We need to figure out how we're going to use the A10s to do that."

The A10 is one of the ugliest aircraft in the American arsenal, even its most ardent supporters concede. Its nickname, after all, is Warthog. But the infantry love it—they know it can rain death in tight spaces. The aircraft doesn't have the sleek, aerodynamic lines of an F16; it has big, boxy wings and vertical stabilizers—a muscle-bound, armored fuselage—that is actually wider than it is long. If airplanes were athletes, pilots like to think of A10s as weightlifters, powerful in small turns, if not fast—a homely child of the skies that only a pilot-parent could love.

The aircraft can carry a payload of bombs, rockets, and missiles, and from its inception in the 1970s it was designed to support troops on the ground by destroying tanks. So the entire airframe is built around one of the most distinctive weapons on the battlefield: a seven-barrel cannon called the Avenger that works like a supersized Gatling gun. It shoots 30mm cannon rounds—each the length of a forearm—at a rate of seventy shells per second and at a muzzle velocity three times the speed of sound.

The noise made by the cannon when it's fired is a sustained, sky-rippling BRRRRT that can be heard for miles and that every soldier knows by heart. Whatever is targeted erupts in a riot of explosions and smoke. The cockpit actually vibrates when the gun is loosed, and even the Heads-Up Display on the cockpit window momentarily blurs out.

The two jets aloft this Wednesday morning were just waiting for a mission. The lead pilot was Dan Cruz, the son of an electrician and dental hygienist who grew up near Luke Air Force Base in Glendale, Arizona. He first fell in love with the F16 fighter aircraft, a machine he thought looked like a sports car in the sky. After graduating from the US Air Force Academy, Cruz got his second choice, the A10, and simply transferred his affections from one airplane to another.

His wingman flying the second A10 was Andrew Wood, another Academy graduate who grew up outside Memphis, Tennessee, and followed into the Air Force his father, Bill, who had flown F4 Phantom jets and was now a pilot for Federal Express.

Cruz and Wood had become minor sensations within their combat flying circle. On the occasions when they were assigned to fly together, ground attacks almost always seemed to materialize. Some pilots deploying to Afghanistan almost never use their weapons. But not Clyde and Freaq, the respective call signs for Cruz and Wood. Each of them had fired thousands of rounds since arriving in theater in April for no other reason than they just happened to be the pilots aloft when trouble or targets arose.

In the wee hours that morning Cruz and Wood had taken off from the sprawling US airbase at Bagram twenty-five miles north of Kabul. Before takeoff, with their night-vision goggles, they spotted huge camel spiders the width of a human hand skittering across the runway. The stars shimmered with an otherworldly glow through the eye devices that amplified ambient light, and the nearly full moon seemed to fill the entire night sky. As the twin-engine jet climbed to cruising altitude, electrostatic charges sent rippling spider webs of light playing across the front of the cockpit.

The two airmen were in plane-to-plane radio contact chatting about almost anything to pass the time as they cruised to the border to begin surveillance for any enemy fighters crossing into Afghanistan. The topic for tonight: the physical endowments of a certain female officer. The first few hours of the early morning passed without incident as they orbited up and down the Pakistan border. The pilots were ready to provide ground support if any coalition troops got into trouble. And that was precisely the emergency call that came in just as the sun rose.

It took them about twenty minutes to get over Ranch House.

→ ←

Down below on the slopes of the mountain Phillips was virtually alone in his fight from the west end of the Post Two barracks. He'd been shifting from one corner of the building to the other, moving across a concrete pad in front of the door to the barracks, always firing east into the oak trees where insurgents had taken up positions. If he was lucky, they might think there were multiple defenders in their way. He peered around one of the corners, cracking off a couple of shots with his M4, and could see enemy fighters running down the trail from the east, right in his direction. He was certain that one of those times when he changed position and moved around a corner to open fire there would be an enemy gunman waiting for him.

Phillips was at the south corner of the building when an RPG came whooshing right toward him.

*This one's got my name on it.*

It passed just over his shoulder and exploded a few yards behind, the concussion knocking him forward, flat on his stomach. Dirkintis heard the blast and decided he couldn't sit inside the barracks out of the fight any longer. Phillips was already back up and shooting and when the medic emerged, he yelled at Dirkintis to take the north corner.

Just as Dirkintis started to return fire, a bullet struck him right in the collar bone, burrowed through his chest, and exited out his back, collapsing the soldier to the ground. Phillips reached him and started firing around the corner, dragging Dirkintis by his foot behind the building.

Langevin, still lying prone on the roof of Post Two with his SAW light machine gun, was pouring fire into the far end of the barracks and yelling, "You got two guys on the back of your building, Sergeant Phillips!"

Phillips started lobbing grenades over the roof to the other side, but he knew he was in trouble. Enemy fighters were just a few feet away, he had a wounded man in need of medical aid, and getting him anywhere from there was going to be dicey.

First thing was to see if Dirkintis could move on his own. Phillips, while continuing to fire at the enemy, started yelling at the medic, urging him however he could to get on his feet: "I need you to get the fuck off your ass."

Dirkintis tried mightily to comply. Over and over he pushed up onto one hand, and then both feet, only to fall back down. Blood was oozing from under his body armor, and he was spitting it out of his mouth and moaning. Phillips figured the medic probably had a collapsed lung from a sucking chest wound. He started stripping ammo off Dirkintis to replenish his own and got ready to make a move. Phillips wanted a grenade blast for cover. But he was out of frags. He yelled over to Post Two for a little help. There was a parachute draped over the entryway into the bunker, and the fabric was suddenly pulled aside as John Relph emerged with a grenade in his hand, pulled the pin, and drew his arm back to lob it when he was struck in the right leg with a bullet and went down. Phillips could see the whole thing. The sergeant fell back into the bunker, and someone grabbed the live grenade and threw it outside, where it exploded.

Langevin, still on the roof with his SAW, could see it too and decided to act. As Phillips watched, the private first class popped open the feed tray on his weapon, laid in an ammo belt from a new drum, slapped the cover closed, pulled back the charging bolt, and opened up. He worked the barrel left to right, laying down a wall of fire across the far east end of the barracks. Phillips took the cue. He spun Dirkintis's sprawled figure around, grabbed the medic by a handle on the back of his body armor, and, with his other hand firing his M4, started dragging him back down toward the aid station. Phillips found a deep-slotted depression in the ground about midway there and called for assistance from Chavez, who had moved down from Post One to join Baldwin at the mortar pit. Chavez came running.

Back up at Post Two, four of the six soldiers were wounded, and there was no sign of a medic coming any time soon. Langevin kept firing from the roof. The enemy had gotten closer, and Langevin trained his machine gun wherever he saw a head poke out from behind a rock. Paratroopers from down below started passing him grenades, and he lobbed them as far as he could, watching in frustration as some rolled back down the hill toward Post Two. But a few found their mark, and soldiers could hear insurgents screaming out in pain.

The fight had been raging for more than an hour, and the men in the bunker were exhausted. A battle-weary kind of giddiness settled in, and Relph blurted out, "Okay, guys, if I die, I want you guys to go ahead and delete all the porn off my computer so my wife doesn't see it." He actually looked serious about his request, but everybody else started laughing, a moment of comic respite in the middle of a disaster.

The same urge to step back a bit from the suffocating sensory overdrive of combat played out earlier when Phillips and Baldwin were side by side in the mortar pit, throwing grenades, and Baldwin, apropos of nothing, blurted out, "Hey, Sergeant Phillips, what day is it?"

It was actually a Wednesday, but that didn't seem to be the point. Phillips turned and grinned at Baldwin and did his best bad-ass imitation, "I don't know, motherfucker, but it's a good day to die." Baldwin picked up the cue and responded with a faux whine: "No, man, I just turned twenty-one. I haven't even been able to drink legally in the States yet."

A single fragmentation grenade was looped onto the ammo rack Baldwin was wearing, and he was thinking that now, in the midst of this terrible fight, he was like a kid excited about the chance to lob his first frag at an enemy, just like in every war movie he ever saw. Except Phillips turned and demanded the explosive so he could throw it, and Baldwin reluctantly gave it up. There would be time for dozens of grenades to be thrown. But just now, as Phillips called for another, Baldwin, without missing a beat, reached into his tactical vest and pulled out a plastic bag full of ready-to-fill, water-bomb grenades and stuck them in the NCO's outstretched hand. "What the fuck is this, ass-clown?" Phillips said and threw the bag into Baldwin's face. Baldwin grinned and handed him a real one.

The two men were alternating between firing their M4 rifles and throwing the grenades when Phillips all of a sudden asked for cover fire. He dropped down and opened a can of Copenhagen Long Cut smokeless tobacco, grabbed a pinch, and stuffed it between his cheek and gums.

"What the fuck are you doing?" said Baldwin, realizing he was providing cover for a tobacco break.

"Hey, I need a dip, man."

At Post Four Sergeant Mike Johnson's solitary defense finally got some relief. One of the Marine trainers made his way down to Johnson's position with four Afghan Army soldiers and left them there to help the sergeant hold the beleaguered outpost. Still, the situation was dire. Remmel was suffering inside the barracks from the wounds to his stomach. He was bleeding internally, and his skin was turning pale. They needed to get him on a medevac helicopter.

→ ←

As the A10 jets arrived over Ranch House there was a bank of purplish haze covering the mountains in the distance and tufts of cotton candy clouds rolling through the valleys down below, enough to make a pilot queasy about low-level strafing runs through the narrow caverns. Equally disconcerting was how the ground below was in shadow at this early hour, complicating the task of spotting targets. But the sky directly overhead was a clear blue, and as the aircraft passed low over the surrounding ridgelines, the feminine-sounding altitude warning alert—the pilots called her Bitching Betty—sounded out, "Altitude, altitude."

The pilots bore in for a "show of force" display over the broad spur on which the battle was unfolding. They saw a column of white smoke billowing out of a burning structure to the east.

Down below at Ranch House headquarters the paratroopers could tell the show of force was doing nothing to deter the jihadist gunmen. In fact, Dzwik, from his position near the TOC, could hear the enemy forces from two different directions yelling at one another, as if they were coordinating a final assault.

"Hey, they're massing," Dzwik yelled over to Ferrara. "They're getting ready to do something."

Dzwik had been alternating positions between the TOC and the aid station. That kind of close-quarters combat was more difficult and desperate than anything the squad leader expected. Killing a man wasn't as simple as pointing a weapon and firing. Everything just moved so fast, and there was so much confusion. Dzwik felt like all he could do was shoot where he thought the enemy was. By the time he actually spotted a shadowy figure shifting behind the trees and bushes, the insurgent was already halfway to his next defilade position, and Dzwik had been too slow to react. He got off a round that went nowhere.

It's not like the movies.

→ ←

Back at Bella, Chosen Company commander Matt Myer raised A10 pilot Dan Cruz on the radio and told him there were as many as forty enemy fighters closing in on the Ranch House base headquarters. Ferrara had been filling Myer in.

"We're going to do a gun run here shortly that's going to be danger-close," Myer told the pilot.

Thirty-millimeter shells slamming into a hillside at high velocity could create a lethal splash pattern of debris and shrapnel flying up to seventy yards in any direction. If there were US troops within that zone, that was considered a "danger-close" attack and required explicit approval from ground commanders. There must be a clear understanding—and agreement—of the risks to nearby friendly forces.

Just then, though, both pilots tuned their radios to the frequency Matt Ferrara was using on the ground, and they could hear him calmly relaying a casualty report for medical helicopters that were on their way in. He already had seven wounded.

"Shit, dude, this is a fuckin' medevac [report]," Cruz said to his wingman.

The enormity of what the pilots faced was becoming clear. During so many of their missions over these eastern provinces the attacks were often against enemy fighters hunkered down hundreds of yards away from US forces, and the goal was simply to kill the insurgents. This was different: there was a desperation in the facts being relayed, even if the men relaying them didn't sound desperate.

Even more startling was something the facts they were hearing only hinted at: the attack mission would be carried on inside a US military base, something never done before in the war in Afghanistan.

For now, however, Cruz made radio contact with Ferrara and told him what he needed: coordinates for the gun run, where the nearest "friendlies" were in relation to the targets, and whether Ferrara had training in air combat support: Was he a joint terminal attack controller (JTAC)?

"No, I'm not a qualified JTAC," Ferrara said. Cruz could hear gunfire in the background and was struck by how calm and unmoved the young lieutenant sounded. What he heard was quintessential Ferrara. When Kyle White, who was firing at the enemy from a position near the TOC, would call over for more ammunition, Ferrara, without missing a beat in his radio communications with Bella and incoming aircraft, would grab a magazine and toss it to his soldier.

Ferrara had ordered men at his outposts to lay signal panels near their fighting position to mark them for the incoming fighter planes, and he told Cruz this. The pilot didn't react. The reality was that these VS17 panels, although they might be helpful to alert slower-moving aircraft like attack helicopters, were useless for jets streaming at tree-top levels at four hundred miles per hour, particularly over a densely vegetated hillside like this one.

Ferrara told Cruz he had a major worry. "I have one post, highest post on my installation . . . highest up on the spur all by itself. I have one person in that installation. Do not hit that installation. It's the only special instruction I have."

He was talking about Deloria trapped in the ruins of Post Three.

With the Afghan National Army compound now in enemy hands, Ferrara wanted it destroyed, and he passed along its latitude and longitude coordinates to Cruz. Myer came up on the radio to elaborate using the pilot's call-sign, Hawg 1-7.

"Hey, roger, the friendly situation on the ground is they have their position, which is the TOC, marked by VS17 panels," Myer said. "To the south of that location there's a bondeh [cottage], which used to be friendly local national forces. Break. That location has been compromised, and they need a gun run."

Myer provided his initials—M.M.—to certify as commander that a danger-close strafing run was authorized. He told Cruz the nearest US forces to the target were fifty-five yards away.

Cruz could see people down in the area where smoke was rising above a building. Was that the target?

"Roger," Ferrara said. "That compound is on fire."

To make absolutely certain what he would be bombing, Cruz told Ferrara he would fire a rocket filled with white phosphorous that would burn and mark the intended ground zero. With US troops so close, the pilot wanted there to be no question he would be killing only the enemy.

Cruz rolled his big plane to the left and then right and nosed it down, his right hand on the hand-grip of the weapons control stick between his legs and his left hand on the throttles for maneuvering his aircraft. The instrument panel before him was a panoply of levers, dials, knobs, and switches for radios, flares, speed breaks, weapon settings, and a host of other functions. Bitching Betty started sounding off about altitude.

"This is hard, dude," Cruz said to Wood while he maneuvered for the best approach. "I don't want to frag the friendlies with the rocket."

"Yeah, you might want to get in close and spike that shit," Wood said. "I see some muzzle flash down there."

Cruz fired the rocket and pulled up hard to get out of the valley. The rocket left an orange streak as it straight-lined into the mountain, hitting close to the burning compound. Ferrara quickly confirmed for Cruz over the radio that he had marked the right target.

Dzwik was nearby and growing anxious that the A10s were taking too long.

"They need to engage now," the staff sergeant called out.

The lieutenant said the pilots were worried about hitting Americans.

"It doesn't matter," Dzwik said as he fired his rifle from the corner of the operations center. "We're dead anyway. Might as well take some of them with us."

Ferrara raised the radio and mic and gave the go-ahead as clearly as he could: "I want you to hit that [Afghan security guard] building and any personnel maneuvering south below that building or along the side of that building."

As an afterthought Ferrara asked about what kind of munitions the planes would be firing.

"Thirty-millimeter high-explosive incendiary rounds," Cruz radioed back, "and be advised this is going to be danger-close, so fifty meters. We're going to be pushed in there pretty close to you guys."

"Roger."

Ferrara began calling those posts that he could still reach to warn paratroopers about taking cover, then he called out timeframes for the men hunkered down around him.

Thirty seconds. Fifteen. Ten.

The jets came in low. Cruz flew his A10 only about one hundred feet off the ground, and Wood was thirty seconds behind him, the hulking silhouettes of their aircraft casting fast-moving shadows across the battlefield. Cruz flew straight toward the target with its white plume of smoke and fired for three full seconds, unleashing about three hundred cannon rounds in the time it takes to exhale. The Heads-Up Display momentarily vibrated into a blur in front of him, and just as Cruz lifted his finger off the trigger, another automated voice in the cockpit blared a warning about plowing into the ground: "Pull up! Pull up!"

But the Air Force captain had already throttled for altitude and was in a sharp ascent, banking right. In a few seconds he was looking at nothing but blue sky.

Wood was right behind, laying down more shells.

→ ←

On the ground it felt like one continuous explosion rocking the entire planet. Baldwin had replaced Chavez in treating Dirkintis, who had been sucking on a fentanyl lollipop pain killer and had also gotten a morphine injection. Dirkintis was feeling good and, in his woozy state, kept asking Baldwin to go get his wallet so he'd have it when the medevac helicopter arrived. Baldwin had his head down, trying to listen to the medic's labored breathing when suddenly everything ten yards off to their left seemed to explode.

Erich Phillips was back in the mortar pit and turned his head to the side like he was facing away from storm winds when the hillside erupted and rocks and debris pelted his helmet. He was thinking about the enemy.

*They're probably thinking, "What the fuck are we facing? These guys are willing to shoot their own base."*

Dzwik remembered peeking up a few seconds later and seeing a wall of exploding dirt in front of him and all along the area where the enemy had been advancing. He was ecstatic. "That's it! Right there! Do it again. Do it again. Just like that. That's perfect," he yelled over to the platoon commander.

Dzwik called out, asking if everybody was okay, and got a scattered chorus in response, "Yeah, I'm good. . . . No injuries, nothing, we're good. . . . Hell, yeah."

Ferrara, for the first time with a hint of excitement in his voice, lifted the mic to his mouth, "Hawg, Hawg, that was a direct hit."

They needed one more strafing run on the enemy, and Ferrara wanted them to shift the attack about fifty-five yards south of that last strafe. He also warned the pilots to be careful. "You can't get any closer," he said. "That hit was perfect. It was hitting where the fire from the enemy was coming from. But it was also very close to us."

Both pilots bore in for a second run.

Ferrara started his countdown again. Thirty seconds. Fifteen. Ten.

Cruz changed his angle of approach ever so slightly, and some of the 30mm rounds went just too far. Begaye was down on one knee in the TOC bracing for the attack, and he felt the earth shaking from the explosions and the building rocking back and forth. He felt trapped in the headquarters during the fighting without his battle gear and even fashioned a shank out of antenna in case the enemy came barreling through the door. But just then something struck him in the back of the head, and he fell forward, unconscious for a few seconds. When he regained his senses he felt light-headed and reached back with his hand to discover he was bleeding.

*Holy shit, how did this happen?*

Dzwik was in the middle of telling everyone to get down again when suddenly the hillside seemed to explode, and he was on his back in a sea of brown. When he sat up it was eerily quiet until he heard Begaye from inside the TOC.

"Hey, I'm hit! I'm hit! I'm wounded!"

Dzwik headed inside to find Begaye on his feet, holding the back of his head.

Ferrara got on the radio to the pilots in just a few seconds. "Hey, that was too close, that was too close.... Cease fire, cease fire!"

It's a pilot's worst nightmare. What was too close? Did they kill someone? Fratricide? What happened? Cruz kept asking for details to understand whether there was a miscommunication. "Too close to what?"

Ferrara, his hands full trying to sort out the aftermath, put him off. "Stand by. Let me get a report from my post. Like I said, that was too close, and I need to make sure any kind of missions after it are safe."

A few agonizing minutes later the pilots got the word that no Americans had been killed. They were not told about Begaye's wound. But the shooting had died down across the eastern side of the base. The A10 attack put an end to the assault. The insurgents began peeling away, sweeping the battlefield clean of enemy casualties.

They left just one. Up the trail leading to the smoldering Afghan Army compound paratroopers found the body of Hazrat Omar. His remains were evidently too far forward for his fighters to recover and remove. It was unclear exactly what killed him. Phillips thought he might have shot the militia leader when he was firing at shadows in that direction. Baldwin thought it was one of the countless grenades he threw. Some speculated he died in the A10 attack. On his body they found attack plans, pictures of insurgents, and even payroll documents for his fighters. They also discovered a video camera with footage of the meeting where he discussed battle plans for Ranch House. The number of other enemy dead and wounded were difficult to assess. Some intercepted radio chatter suggested that four or five insurgents were killed and two wounded. Military valor citations later cited a killed-in-action total for the enemy of ten, and an intelligence analysis concluded there were a dozen attackers killed.

Helicopters arrived to evacuate the US and Afghan wounded and to deliver reinforcements. There was word that some of the wounded enemy fighters might have been carried down and treated in the school house the Americans built in Aranas. Ferrara discussed with Phillips the idea of forming an assault team to go down there, but the staff sergeant told him that they were all too shot up or exhausted and that the risks were too high.

After the strafing was over and the mountain finally fell quiet, Phillips turned to see Ferrara walk up to him, blackened from head to foot from dirt thrown up by the storm of 30mm shells. The lieutenant looked Phillips in the eyes. "Hey, I need you to go to Post Three." Someone needed to get Deloria. Phillips said he'd go. "Trust me, I've got it. I'll get him."

Phillips gathered up Baldwin and a Marine advisor for the Afghan soldiers, Specialist John Paul Atchley, and headed first to Post Two. There Spotanski and Langevin joined the group before they started the careful climb up to the ruined guard post high up the mountain. Langevin, his leg wound now bandaged, carried his light machine gun along to provide cover fire.

→ ←

From where he lay in the wreckage of Post Three, Delo could hear the familiar sky-ripping sound of the Gatling gun unleashing as the Warthogs made their runs.

Oh shit, that's us.

He had been there for a long time now. An hour or more before, when the fighting was still heavy, Delo had tried to ease his way over to the edge of the building to get down. But there were so many rounds hitting nearby that he, struggling to move his left leg and blind out of his right eye, pulled back and stayed inside what was left of his guard post.

What he didn't know was that Langevin at Post Two, while providing cover to Phillips pinned down at the barracks, now and again turned his SAW in the direction of Post Three and opened fire to discourage enemy fighters from trying to climb up on top of it. Langevin was still hoping Delo was alive up there.

But then the A10 Warthogs showed up like cavalry, and nearly all the shooting died away.

Delo just lay there, his mind racing. Were his buddies coming for him? He started dwelling darkly on how damaged his body was. He knew his right eye was in a really bad way. Would he someday get a bionic replacement? Could he emerge from all this even better than he started? His thoughts were foggy, and he was tired and losing track of time.

Then he saw figures down the mountain slowly making their way toward him. He recognized Phillips and Baldwin. Then Langevin. Then Spotanski. They were moving carefully. Phillips and Baldwin were pointing their rifles right at him until they approached close enough to recognize their wounded comrade.

"What's wrong?" Baldwin called up to Delo, a teasing edge to his voice.

"What do you mean?"

"You're not smiling."

"I got hit by a fucking rocket," Deloria said, his face finally relaxing into that familiar Delo grin.

"Oh, he'll be fine."

→  ←

In the days immediately following the attack on Ranch House on August 22, 2007, intercepted enemy communications led Lieutenant Colonel Ostlund and intelligence officers to estimate that 120 to 150 insurgents mounted the assault. Once the Afghan security guards and many of the Afghan Army melted away in the opening phases of the assault, the remaining defenders were outnumbered by as much as six or seven to one.

The small US force suffered a 50 percent casualty rate, unusually high for the wars in Iraq and Afghanistan. Four of those Americans wounded required evacuation from the war zone back to the United States: Private First Class Jeddah Deloria, Sergeant Kyle Dirkintis, Sergeant John Relph, and Specialist Robert Remmel. The others eventually returned to duty. One of the last to be injured was Spotanski, who fell off of the ruined Post Three after they recovered Delo, impaling himself on a stake. One Afghan National Army soldier and one Afghan security guard were killed, and a second Afghan soldier was wounded and was evacuated by helicopter.

No US combat outpost in the Iraq or Afghanistan wars came that close to being overrun. Historians say not since the Vietnam War was a bombing mission necessary inside the perimeter of an American base to stop an enemy assault. An intelligence analysis later concluded that the attacking force was filled with men from the Waigal Valley villages as well as members of Hezb-e-Islami Gulbuddin, or HIG, and the Islamic Movement of Uzbekistan. Some fighters came from as far away as the Punjab Province of Pakistan. Every indication was that enemy commanders viewed the battle as a success against the Americans.

For many of the Chosen Few who fought in the battle it was their first true taste of combat. Even among those who had been in firefights before, the struggle on the mountain that morning was more ferocious than anything they had experienced. In the hours after the fighting, as soldiers explored the ruins of Post Three and repaired the damage to the headquarters, they marveled at how close disaster had come and took pride in fending it off.

"Didn't take down the Chosen Few, now did they?" Dzwik said as he climbed up after the battle onto the shattered landing where Delo had held out on Post Three. "Try to kill my boy—what were they thinking?"

The paratroopers felt they had stubbornly stood their ground, absorbed everything the enemy could throw at them, and carried the day.

Several gathered around the Post Two barracks for smokes and stories. Langevin was there. So was Baldwin.

Phillips saw them jawing with each other and made his way over. He had learned a few lessons about himself that day. It was the toughest fight Erich had ever been in, and at age twenty-three, he had learned to trust his instincts. He didn't have to get bollixed up second-guessing every move but could rely on intuition. Something that flowed unfettered through his cerebral cortex when everything around him was in chaos took him where he needed to go when he needed to go there.

He also realized how proud he was of the men he fought with—of Matt Ferrara, calmly directing the battle on the open ground outside the TOC, or Baldwin taking the initiative to lob mortar shells into the enemy, or Langevin blasting away from the roof of Post Two.

Phillips wanted to say something about how he felt, but didn't want to make a big deal out of it. He strolled up to the paratroopers gathered at the barracks.

"Hey men," and their faces turned toward him. "I want you boys to know you fought your asses off. And I'm proud as hell of you."

Then he just turned and walked away.

→ ←

For his actions at Ranch House Staff Sergeant Erich Phillips received the Distinguished Service Cross, an award second only to the Medal of Honor. A Silver Star was awarded to Specialist Jason Baldwin and another to First Lieutenant Matthew Ferrara. A Bronze Star for valor went to each of seven soldiers: Sergeant Kyle Dirkintis, Private First Class Jeddah Deloria, Staff Sergeant David Dzwik, Private First Class Sean Langevin, Sergeant Mike Johnson, Sergeant John Relph, and Specialist Kain Schilling. A Distinguished Flying Cross for valor, equivalent to the Army's Bronze Star, was awarded to Air Force Captain Dan Cruz.

# 6

## > > > GIVING GROUND

*First there were the initial sprinklings* of jet fuel from water bottles, and then it was just a matter of putting a match to it. On a shirt-sleeve fall evening in September Chosen Company torched Ranch House, the white smoke billowing northeast in the direction from where the assault had come weeks before.

The paratroopers loved it, watching the hooches burn, flames eating up the inside of each bunker and barracks until breaking through the outside walls in long, yellow tongues that rippled thirty feet into the sky. They set fire to the structures one by one. The popping, the cracking, the wood-burning smell. Outer shells of stacked sandbags had been left in place around the buildings so that when the plywood walls and ceilings burned away, it looked like some giant snake had shed its skin and slithered off across the mountain.

By nightfall it was a glorious bonfire, dozens of upturned soldier faces cast in the glow. "Fuckin' weird," said Erich Phillips, a big wad of dip bulging out of his lower lip as he squatted on his haunches nearby and shook his head, watching the flames swallow up the aid station that had been home for nearly five months.

"I burned it," he played to David Dzwik's camera in a moonshiner's drawl, "to the ground."

Chosen Company was pulling back in the Waigal Valley, and it had been a long time coming. For months Bill Ostlund had kept up a steady drumbeat with his immediate commanders and any senior leader who made a trip into the Rock Battalion's area of operation. *Shut it down,* Ostlund would say, arguing that the Waigal Valley could be dealt with more effectively from the southern end of the valley, closer to Blessing.

*I need to get these guys out of there. I know there's a lot of bad guys, and I know I can't get there in a hurry if something goes wrong. It makes no sense to me as a commander to have people I can't reinforce.*

His bosses were ready to approve the withdrawal, but the August 22 attack actually had the effect of further delaying matters. The brigade commander for the 173rd, Colonel Charles "Chip" Preysler, didn't want to hand the enemy an immediate propaganda victory. How would it look to leave the base so soon after it was nearly overrun?

*Don't want to make it look like the enemy's gaining ground.*

So it meant delaying the closure for another month or two and pushing back a timetable of plans already under discussion for closing down Bella and putting a new base near the district center in a small village called Wanat.

In the weeks immediately after the battle Captain Matt Myer flew additional troops to Ranch House, shifting two squads from 2nd Platoon to bolster the mountain base defenses while decisions about its future were made. Those soldiers would also provide the manpower and muscle necessary to tear it down. Even before the August attack Myer had planned to have 2nd Platoon replace 1st Platoon in staffing Ranch House and Bella late into 2007 and give Ferrara's men a chance to live with hot meals and showers at Blessing and take over patrolling the western reaches of the Pech Valley down below. The switch-over was still in the works, but it would involve trading places only between Blessing and Bella now that Ranch House was being closed down.

The Afghan security guards at Ranch House had been fired for their cowardice or complicity, whichever was the case, and 2nd Platoon troopers took over security at their positions, reinforcing the burned-out buildings there with sandbag defenses. Paratroopers lived in and around the charred ruins and learned the hard way that the area that had been staffed by the local Afghans was infested with fleas.

The final move to put a match to the hard-luck mountain base came in late September. After that, 2nd Platoon pulled back to Blessing for a few months and 1st Platoon consolidated at Bella. With Ranch House now history, Myer felt he had a certain measure of freedom in the Waigal Valley. He could staff Bella with a full platoon, and that would allow him enough people to defend that base and also send out squads more frequently to extend Chosen Company's presence.

When an Army military historian, Major Dave Hanson, showed up at Blessing in late summer to talk about the Ranch House battle, Myer spoke encouragingly about his revamped operations: "[It] allows us to be somewhere where the enemy might not know we are instead of being at the Ranch House where they do know where we are."

Ferrara dutifully began leading patrols to villages in the Waigal Valley, including a November 2 trip to Muladish, a village southeast of Bella. The patrol was on its way back from there, approaching the ridgeline above Bella, when they came under mortar attack. The column altered direction, and the rounds just kept following them. It was clear they were being watched, and enemy spotters were adjusting the mortar fire. Staff Sergeant Kyle Silvernale ordered his soldiers to take cover near any tree they could find, and they started scanning to find the insurgents' version of forward observers. Private First Class Joe Lancour was the first to spot them on the opposite side of the Waigal Valley, two men perhaps twelve hundred yards away, a distance that pushed the effective range of his SAW. Lying prone near a tree, Lancour opened up. Silvernale stood over him with a small pair of binoculars, giving direction, "walking" tracer fire closer to the two insurgents in the distance.

"Yeah, right there. Fucking light 'em up."

Lancour started pouring out rounds. He loved his M249 squad automatic weapon and had nicknamed it Reese Witherspoon. Silvernale could see one of the insurgents down on one knee and then he saw the man collapse. The second fighter just seemed to disappear. The mortar fire ended, and the patrol returned to Bella.

In many respects Bella was even less defensible than Ranch House. Stockard, for one, hated it from the beginning. It was really only a small crossroads hamlet with an inn, a bazaar, and a medical clinic. A small valley shot off to the northwest from the location, and farther up the Waigal River there was the canyon that ran northeast to Aranas. Chris Cavoli and his 10th Mountain troops had built the base next to the Bella hamlet and used its central location in southern Nuristan Province as a nexus for gathering information.

Still, it was a tough sell as a place to build a fort. Mountains on both sides of the river rose several hundred feet, creating a geographical setting they likened to being in the bottom of a Dixie Cup. There was a narrow mountain road heading south down the Waigal Valley that was navigable only by small pickup trucks at least as far as Wanat, about five miles down the river, where the road broadened enough for military vehicles. So supplies were delivered primarily by helicopters that had to thread between the mountains, making them vulnerable to anyone with an RPG launcher standing on a ridge. The river itself frothing past the Bella operating base on its way south toward the Pech Valley offered perpetual white noise that gave the area a touch of the wilderness.

The key to defending the bottom of the Dixie Cup was an aerie brimming with guns that sat on a ridge two hundred feet above the Bella base and had a sweeping view of valleys and ridgetops to the north, east, and south. It was simply designated OP1 (Observation Post One).

Throughout much of Chosen Company's time in the Waigal Valley Army Specialist Gabriel Green—the soldier who had fallen in love at first sight on a city bus back in Vicenza—was the denizen of OP1. The place was perfectly suited for his skills as a forward observer trained to call in artillery and air support. Other squads would rotate in and out.

But twenty-six-year-old Green always stayed, climbing down to Bella once a week to call his new bride, Addy. The soldiers started calling him the Mountain Man. He was at OP1 when Ranch House was nearly overrun in August. From OP1 he could see for miles across the Hindu Kush and down the Waigal Valley as it wound its way south. Green would snap pictures of the graceful, intersecting lines of ridges stretching off into the distance with those cotton candy clouds nestled in the valleys or capture the image of a Chinook helicopter flying in for a landing at Bella hundreds of feet below. He would send a video stream of these images back home to Addy, interspersed with photos of himself staring pensively into the lens while standing in his barracks holding up a piece of paper with a message: "*Cuando vamos a tener una nena?*" (When are we having a baby?) "*Te amo, bebe.*" (I love you, baby).

He learned every crevasse, every corner of the outpost constructed high above Bella. It was half fortification, half man cave. Like other forts for the Americans, it followed the pattern of plywood hut barracks—"cribs" GIs called them—with a shell layer of sandbags buttressed with HESCO bastions. HESCOs were ubiquitous fortifications for US military outposts across Afghanistan and Iraq of simple design—a steel wire-mesh basket several feet high lined with fabric and filled with rock, dirt, or sand. The kitchen was a U-shaped pile of flagstones with a grill set over burning logs. An outdoor "living room" was an Army cot set out on a platform rimmed with sandbags under a canopy of camouflage netting where troopers could sit on ammo cans and play spades or poker. A light machine gun on a swivel stand was close by in case they needed to go to work. One level down was the "love shack," where a soldier could indulge carnal thoughts with the right magazines or videos and not be bothered.

One level up was an ammo bunker with a sandbag wall through which Green had proudly inserted a defunct grenade-launching tube that soldiers could use to piss through so they didn't have to go far in the middle of a fight.

One more level up was the "penthouse," the highest observation post, a square-shaped hut made out of wood and sandbags that afforded a broad view of the surrounding country. It sprouted heavy weapons, including the outpost's .50-caliber machine gun. A fortified sniper's nest nearby overlooked the Waigal Valley and held the automatic grenade launcher. Directly adjacent was the "tanning salon," an open-air platform surrounded by sandbags where a soldier could sun himself sans clothing without worrying about getting shot.

*We're ready for war.*

In the winter the climb up to OP1 was so steep and icy that soldiers ordered crampons to wear on their boots. In the warmer months Afghan children would climb up to visit the Americans and sell them quartz or other precious stones as souvenirs. For a few dollars Green purchased a black and tan puppy he would call Peanut. The dog was adorable, and Green used the excuse that he would be a security investment, barking at any unfamiliar human smells wafting in from the dark. They kept Peanut in an ammo can during firefights so the noise wouldn't make him run away. An old man visited each morning with his goat, and Green let him graze the animal around the concertina wire to keep the grass low. The old man spoke perfect English and would bring Chai tea and sugar bread to share with the Mountain Man each morning. Green paid him five rupees for the pleasure.

Down below at Bella the living conditions were not quite as austere as at Ranch House, but it was only a difference of a few degrees. Trays of food were brought and heated, and that was a notch above the packaged MREs. A delivery of fresh produce occasionally arrived by helicopter. There was a shower that worked intermittently. Otherwise soldiers bathed in the frigid eddies of the Waigal River, shivering even in the summer. Paratroopers would wade in two or three at a time where boulders diverted some of the white water, while buddies stood guard.

The recombining of all four squads of 1st Platoon at Bella made for something akin to a big family reunion. Soldiers got a chance to reconnect. Long hours of guard duty provided an opportunity for some serious reflection on a twentysomething's military life—where it was headed and where it might go. Gabriel Green would muse to Joe Lancour about his dream of having a baby with Addy. It always all made perfect sense to Joe, and that was all Gabe really needed to hear. James Takes and Sean Langevin, who ran naked together through the streets of Vicenza before their deployment, now spent hours discussing what would really matter when they put the guns and uniforms away. Langevin was exuberant about soon becoming a father—Zoe was due in a couple of months. Takes listened quietly, a little envious about how his subordinate seemed to have life all figured out.

*Man, this guy's got his shit together. He knows what he wants. He has a wife and a child on the way. He's an old soul. . . .*

Meanwhile there would be a change of command for 2nd Platoon, with Lieutenant Devon George moving up to become Chosen Company executive officer, replaced by a young lieutenant who had been pushing paper at Battalion headquarters at Blessing, Jonathan Brostrom.

Brostrom had just turned twenty-four and was a graduate of the University of Hawaii, earning his commission through the ROTC program there. He was a true Army brat, raised in a dozen different places as the eldest son of an Army officer, David Brostrom, who had moved his family twenty-two times in thirty years.

The elder Brostrom had joined the Army as an infantryman, earning his Ranger tab. But he eventually switched to flying helicopters and rose in the ranks to command a combat aviation brigade, finishing his career at Fort Drum in upstate New York. Jonathan was born in an Army hospital in Germany. The toughest move growing up was the last one when the Brostroms shifted from Fort Drum to Hawaii, and Jonathan was enrolled in a Catholic school in Honolulu. One of a minority of white children, he got into a few dozen scrapes his first year and was a frequent guest in the dean's office.

In his senior year of high school Jonathan began thinking about the Army and won an ROTC scholarship to the University of Hawaii. He wanted infantry, and when his father suggested the aviation track he had followed, the son rejected it out of hand. "I don't want to be a wimp," he said. When Jonathan saw cadets attending a Navy scuba-diving school in the pool where he was a lifeguard, he got his father to pull strings to get him into the course to earn the badge. He went through airborne training and then, after graduation, enrolled in Ranger school, where he finally earned his black and yellow tab after retaking portions of the course two times. Jonathan had his heart set on joining the 173rd Airborne Brigade in Italy, even though he had orders for the 1st Cavalry Division at Fort Hood. Once again he turned to his career-officer dad to make it happen. It turned out the brigade commander for the 173rd, Colonel Chip Preysler, once worked under Dave Brostrom. So the retired colonel gave Preysler a call, and Jonathan was soon on his way to Vicenza.

Dave Brostrom had been worried about his son's safety from the moment Jonathan chose infantry. But by the time he reached out to Preysler, the 173rd was committed to Afghanistan, and Dave felt that had to be safer than war-torn Iraq, with the infamous surge underway.

Jonathan headed off to Afghanistan, leaving behind a five-year-old son, Jase, whose mother was Jonathan's high school sweetheart. The couple's relationship had been stormy.

Brostrom liked the physicality of soldiering. He lifted weights with his troopers in a makeshift gym at Bella, and they admired how he looked like he was in perfect physical condition. Brostrom could be serious when circumstances warranted, and his tactical decisions seemed smart. But he had a playful side and was utterly unpretentious, a big kid with a grin that seemed to fill up half his face.

When 2nd Platoon was assigned to Bella, Sgt. Ryan Pitts brought his sewing machine, a little table-top model that came in handy for sewing on patches. He used it one day to sew shut Brostrom's T-shirt sleeves, then sat in the early-morning darkness watching him fight with his underwear. "Did you fuckin' do this, Sergeant Pitts?!" That was Brostrom, a Joe who was also an officer. His soldiers loved that about him.

→ ←

Downtime at Bella or Blessing or any of the tiny outposts and guard shacks that ringed those bases was a contest between imagination and boredom. Humor was a high art practiced in strange and glorious ways.

Jacob Walker did a send-up of the popular MTV *Cribs* program where celebrities give tours of their resplendent homes, except Walker's tour was of battle-damaged Ranch House in the weeks after the fight there. It would produce one of the oddest videos of the entire deployment. Walker was already a man built for comedy, gangly with a paunch that he would push out on occasion to make himself look even less like the member of an elite airborne unit. In the video Walker strikes a kind of karate pose outside the former Afghan security compound at Ranch House renamed Post 5. He's wearing only tight black underpants, combat boots, a skull cap, a face bandana, sunglasses, and an Army T-shirt; for some reason there's a gas mask container strapped to his left leg.

"This is Post Five! This is where it goes down! Okay? Good and bad." Walker says at the start of the footage. He's looking offstage and not at the camera. "My identity, my name, has been withheld for reasons of homeland security. You'll find out later why, okay? We're going to give you a little tour of the place, and you'll find that Post Five is the SHIT." Then he starts doing a jig.

There were countless days of exhaustion from all-night patrols or day-long mountain hikes. But these were young men in the finest condition of their lives, and every idle moment was a gauntlet thrown down before the gods of mirth and mischief.

They'd spray paint "Chosen Few" on a wall of Post Three at Ranch House, stencil "Welcome to Thunderdome" on a wooden crossbeam at OP1 high above Bella, and scrawl "Deposit in Osama's Ass" or "Have a Nice Day" across fragmentation grenades.

They'd trap scorpions and giant camel spiders in MRE boxes before mashing them up and marveling at the result, ride a village burro in full battle gear until falling with a clatter to the ground, or use helmeted heads to butt a farmer's billy goat, the animal responding by rearing up on its hind legs and meeting Kevlar with a set of curled horns.

You might find the powerfully built Pruitt Rainey pinning the skinniest and youngest member of 2nd Platoon, Gunnar Zwilling, to the floor of the Camp Blessing barracks, twisting him into a painful pretzel to force the phrase "I'm a bitch" out of the twenty-year-old paratrooper. Zwilling never did say it.

Zwilling was born in California but raised in Nashville and St. Louis. He had a gift for mimicry, loved playing the guitar, and was a huge Metallica fan. When he was a teenager and his parents divorced, Zwilling turned rebellious and dropped out of high school. He joined the Army after earning a high school diploma equivalency certificate and was one of the Chosen Few's youngest, entering the Army at eighteen in early 2006. When he came home from Italy to see his family, Zwilling could hardly wait to get back to his buddies in Chosen Company. His mother died halfway through the deployment from a medication overdose, and he was allowed to go home for her funeral. An older brother, Alex, was in the Air Force serving in the United Arab Emirates as a flight mechanic while Gunnar was in Afghanistan, and they kept in steady contact by e-mail, signing off missives with nicknames from a favorite movie, Top Gun. Alex was Dude and Gunnar was Maverick.

Spare time in the combat zone was how James Takes wound up posing nude up at OP1 with nothing but bandoliers wrapped around his body for a photo portrait. Or why Staff Sergeant David Dzwik videotaped a large marijuana patch near a schoolhouse built with American dollars in Aranas, all the while joking about drug-free school zones. Or why Staff Sergeant Kyle Silvernale captured footage of Specialist Shane Burton on shit-burning duty at Bella, stirring a big steel receptacle filled with smoldering feces. Everybody had to take their turn. "It looks like the cafeteria's sloppy joe," Burton says to the camera.

Bathroom humor was always big. It inspired Conrad Begaye to sneak up on the latrine at Ranch House and peer with his camera under the door to film a straight-up shot of Erich Phillips taking care of business while reading a magazine. Phillips spots the intruder and breaks into a broad grin that says, "What the fuck."

When a platoon rotated back to Camp Blessing for vehicle patrols through the Pech Valley, they'd throw scotch candies out the windows of Humvees to giddy Afghan boys skittering along the roadway, muttering "You little bastards . . . don't be a Taliban when you grow up!"

At Bella there were jackals who came out of the woods at night to rummage through garbage for any scraps they could find. Their cries in the dark—which sounded like human babies wailing—were just another element of alien weirdness that was Afghanistan. The men hated it.

Contests were part of the fabric of barracks life—shot-gunning near-beer through a funnel to see who could guzzle the fastest or who could stuff the greatest number of lighted cigarettes or the biggest dip of Copenhagen into his mouth. It was like endless fraternity rituals, only with assault weapons sitting around. Often it wasn't over until people started throwing up. They might capture a scorpion and put it in a box with a camel spider and watch the creatures battle to the death.

There were hours spent in the conventional pastimes made possible with laptops brought to the war. The men of 2nd Platoon for some reason were fascinated with the MTV reality show The Hills, which tracked the personal and professional lives of Lauren, Heidi, Audrina, and Whitney, young women in Los Angeles. The show had launched the year before the Chosen Few deployed. During downtime it wasn't unusual to see a cluster of young warriors with shaved heads huddled around a laptop, fixated on the tangled personal relationships of blond twentysomethings half a world away.

Platoon sergeant Matt Kahler would hike to OP1 to spend a day or so with his men up there, barbecuing cheeseburgers on the grill or cooking up some risotto. Kahler would warm up this cheese ramen dish his family sent him that his soldiers thought was really stinky.

"Sergeant Kahler, that smells like straight ass," Pitts told him.

But Kahler would ignore him and spoon it up while watching the HBO series Rome, with Pitts in the tiny barracks up at the outlook post.

Like most Americans, the paratroopers—when they could establish an Internet connection to the outside world—relied for their virtual interaction on what was then the leading social networking site on the planet, MySpace.

Poker was huge, Texas Hold 'Em mostly. And there was real money at stake, hundreds of dollars in some games. The undisputed champion, hands down, was 2nd Platoon's Pruitt Rainey.

They called him "The Big Polar Bear." Rainey was muscular and physically intimidating. He was a champion wrestler in high school and during a short stint in college, and he would sometimes prowl the barracks looking for someone to take down or put in a headlock. But it was never malicious, and beneath his tough exterior was a vein of compassion. He had earned a reputation as a good soldier, technically proficient, knowledgeable.

Rainey was yet another example of one of the lost boys of Chosen Company. His mother got pregnant dating a college boy from South Georgia. They never married, and Pruitt was raised by his grandmother in Haw River, North Carolina. He joined the Army in 2005 when he was nineteen and went to Chosen Company early the next year. Before heading off to war Rainey called his father, Frankie Gay, and tried to reconnect with the man he had seen only a few weeks a year, at most, during his childhood. Gay was a competitive gambler, a talent his son inherited. During Chosen Company's deployment the sergeants refused to let Rainey in their games because he took all their money.

He told them they were gay.

Access to software for splicing and synching digital video was an opportunity for the more creative—or obsessive—soldiers to practice amateur filmmaking. Begaye assembled a sort of stream-of-consciousness footage, a mindless blend of inane skits, stunts, and life scenes at Ranch House. He labeled his creative efforts "Meow Meow Productions and Manic Hispanic Pictures." They made very little sense. He'd do miniplots where he'd shoot a close-up of his round face earnestly

consulting a medical-treatment guide before pretending to stick his index finger into Kain Schilling's eye. A second version has him emerging
from the book proclaiming, "Anus! I got it!" and then lubing a long,
plastic prod apparently bound for some GI's naked backside appearing
in the left side of the image frame.

There was footage of sweaty hikes up the mountain, shirtless rave
dances with glow sticks in the barracks, and a long sequence of soldiers
trying unsuccessfully to build a potato gun using a length of PVC pipe
and a hunk of high explosive. Fortunately it never went off. Throughout a twenty-minute video Begaye would keep showing the same three
seconds of Erich Phillips spinning around, dropping his pants, and
mooning the camera.

But when it came to filmmaking, Chosen Company's uncontested
virtuoso was 2nd Platoon's Jason Bogar, a Seattle native who arrived as a
replacement late in the year and displayed a true passion for capturing
what life was like there. Everybody else collected the requisite footage
of mountains and rivers or bullet holes and blood trails, but Bogar was
fascinated by people. He'd take his camera up to OP1 during guard duty
and start filming the soldiers working with him, waiting for something
interesting to happen.

He was enchanted by Afghan children and loved to zoom in on a
cluster of tiny faces with huge eyes staring up into his lens. He did still-
life portraits of belted machine gun rounds glistening in the sun. He
had an artful skill for setting videos of weapon fire at Bella to music.
Even as a kid his art was how he coped. The son of a Baptist minister,
Jason was seven when his parents divorced; his mother left the church
and took her children with her. He expressed himself through drawing,
videos, and photography and dreamed of being a photojournalist but
wound up in the National Guard.

Bogar was an exception in Chosen Company in a way that really annoyed him when he first arrived. He wasn't a paratrooper. He had not
yet been through airborne school when he was suddenly shipped off to

Afghanistan as a replacement. It didn't matter that he'd seen more combat than many of the Chosen Few, having served in Iraq and Afghanistan as a member of the Washington National Guard. The fact that he
was sent overseas without the chance to earn his wings was the subject
of endless razzing when he arrived at Blessing.

Unlike many other soldiers who grew indifferent or resentful or
worse toward Iraqi or Afghan people, Bogar went to war a true believer
who honestly felt he was a part of something that was helping people
improve their lives while safeguarding America. "Mom, I really believe
that I'm supposed to go to Afghanistan and help the women and children," he told his mother, Carlene Cross.

But he had also learned some of the hard lessons of war and
passed them on to other replacements, like Chris McKaig, for whom
it was all new. He schooled McKaig about one crucial truth: anytime
violence was unleashed there were no guarantees—the training, the
equipment, being in the right place at the right time—none of it mattered. The bedlam could still find you and kill you. There was no staying safe.

Nevertheless Bogar loved being 2nd Platoon's designated videographer. He even took to wearing a helmet cam, stubbornly focusing on his
brothers until they did something strange or hilarious or flashed the
universal symbol for fuck off. Mostly they gave him what he wanted—
Michael Denton and Jason Hovater would launch into their well-
rehearsed version of a classic *Saturday Night Live* sketch, the one where
Will Ferrell and Cheri Otari play Craig and Ariana, the Spartan High
School cheerleading duo. Hovater was Ariana, his fists on his hips
screeching in falsetto, "Who's that Spartan in my teepee?" Denton behind him would crouch down on all fours and pop his head out from
under Hovater's crotch squealing, "It's me! It's me!" The bit ended when
Hovater launched himself into Denton's arms in a frozen, toe-pointed
cheerleader pose.

In the barracks Denton and Gunnar Zwilling would start busting
dance moves with a kind of crazed synchronicity while Bogar, filming

from the top of a bunkbed, egged them on like a thrilled Hollywood director, "You're scuba diving. . . . You're mowing the lawn. . . . You're in the turret, you're gunning. . . .You're cleaning out earwax and throwing away the Q-tip. . . . You're having dirty, dirty anal sex. . . ."

A star attraction for Bogar videos and for many other soldiers with cameras in 2nd Platoon was Jason Hovater. The paratroopers adored the Tennessee native with his blue eyes, all-American good looks, and wickedly funny comic timing. Hovater was a complicated young man who lived in two very different worlds—the profane, harsh reality of the combat grunt and the deeply spiritual, highly consecrated life of a born-again Christian.

He wasn't one to proselytize. But if the listener was curious and open to a discussion, Hovater could inspire. He had a profound influence on Mike Denton after a conversation they once had about religion. Denton was impressed with his friend's strong set of beliefs and knowledge of the Bible. They began to pray together regularly, and the relationship strengthened Denton's faith.

Jason Hovater was raised in the tiny town of Dylis just west of Oak Ridge on twenty-five acres of land, where he helped his father build a house and a barn and where Jason, an older sister, Jessica, and younger brothers, Joe and Jesse, were homeschooled. They led lives dedicated to Christ, with morning devotions of prayer, singing, Bible reading, a Bible lesson, and then time alone for communing with God. They attended Pentecostal churches and performed like a religious Von Trapp family, all lined up before a congregation singing contemporary Christian music. The children would sometimes be filled with the Holy Spirit and speak in tongues. Jason rededicated himself to Christ with his two younger brothers at a church when he was fifteen.

Jason was also a huge Arnold Schwarzenegger fan and became immersed in body building, sending off pictures of himself to Flex magazine when he was thirteen.

A strong influence was his grandfather, Francis Michael "Hank" Sullivan, who served as a ball turret gunner on a B17 that was shot down over Germany during World War II and spent a harrowing ten months as a prisoner of war. Jason, inspired by his grandfather's war stories, shocked his family when he enlisted a few years after high school. By that time Jason had fallen in love with a young woman he met at church and married her six months before he deployed.

Hovater's impressions of people were a hoot during the months Chosen Company was at war, particularly his drop-dead imitation of the squared-away battalion commander, Bill Ostlund. Troopers would pester him to do his Ostlund, and all eyes—and often Bogar's camera—would turn toward Hovater, who would sit for a moment as if waiting for a muse to inspire, then transform himself before their eyes—the muscled bearing, the grin so wide it put dimples in his cheeks, the gung-ho Army idioms.

Hooah!

He'd stiffen the corners of his Army cap so it sat on his head like a small box and push his ears out to mimic Ostlund's jug handles, and the other soldiers would pull out their iPhones and cameras to capture a few seconds of comedy footage for families back home.

Even Ostlund had to hand it to him—it was spot on.

As Bogar's camera recorded rituals like the birthday takedowns—a cloud of shaved heads moving through the barracks, muscling the birthday boy to the floor and delivering the requisite number of open-handed whacks to his exposed belly—it sometimes offered a glimpse of what it meant to be one of them.

Matthew Phillips—the soldier who had spent his bachelor party before the deployment pub-crawling through Vicenza dressed in a wedding gown—turned twenty-seven the spring of 2008 and got mobbed. At the end of all the torture Phillips climbed back to his feet, his belly covered in welts, as the men herded past him out the door, many of them wrapping him in a congratulatory birthday bear hug. Bogar's camera captured the look on Phillips's face with each one—pure, unabashed joy.

They love me.

To be sure, there were still resentments and rivalries among some of the men, but ill will was often leavened by the reality that every one of them depended on the other to stay alive. Jeff Mersman came to terms with an old adversary in this way. He and James Takes had always clashed: two sergeants—one battle hardened, the other a veteran of the flashy honor guard in the nation's capital.

This was Mersman's fourth deployment since 2003. The twenty-three-year-old team leader, tall and fair complexioned with a heavy build, had gone to Iraq the first three times with the 82nd Airborne Division and, on his last time to war, had been shot by a sniper, although his armored vest stopped the round.

Mersman was born and raised in the flatlands of Kansas south of Kansas City amid fields of corn, soybeans, and oats. He also came from a broken home and was raised by his mother in Parker, Kansas. As a little boy he idolized his grandfather, Marvin Mersman, who had served in the Marine Corps, and they spent hours fishing for bass and bluegill on the elder Mersman's ranch where there was a lake. Jeff Mersman enlisted right out of high school.

He married while serving with the 82nd Airborne, and his wife, Lynn, already had four children. The ready-made family moved to Italy when Mersman transferred to the 173rd Airborne in August of 2006.

What frustrated Mersman was watching James Takes, who had no combat experience, move ahead of him on the promotion ladder. Takes was approved during the deployment to become a staff sergeant. Takes sensed major resentment from Mersman, but in fact, the combat veteran was smarter than to let things fester. As soon as Takes returned from his promotional board at Blessing and dropped his bags in his barracks, Mersman pulled him aside.

"You're a sergeant promotable now, and you're going to be a staff sergeant," Mersman told him. "You're going to be a squad leader, and I want to be your team leader. I'm going to be the best I can do for you. I don't like it, but I'm going to do it."

They shook hands on it. Takes respected him for putting aside their past differences.

In these austere settings on the far rim of Afghanistan's war—where young men who were really only boys with a few years tacked on lived with guns and Claymores and concertina wire—lives became so folded into each other that it was sometimes hard to see where one left off and another began. There was, to begin with, zero privacy. All modesty and introversion was sandpapered away, the hard edges of personal space erased. Each became an expert on the other's personality quirks, speech patterns, even body smells. Soldiers would likely live out their entire lives never knowing or being quite so utterly relaxed around anyone else, not even a wife or a girlfriend.

Any one of them could die in the next attack. Nobody had a leg up on good fortune. There was no logic in this place. Afghanistan was the great leveler. When they arrived at Ranch House or Bella or, later, at a place called Wanat, they were reborn as equals.

They were absorbing the great lessons of war every generation had to relearn—no matter what the training or the equipment, no matter what army they belonged to or what high-minded aspirations lay behind the mission. Once the violence started, there was something new and terrifying to be discovered. As Shane Stockard so often liked to say, "It would not end well."

So they only had each other. They actually grew toward each other, becoming this multiheaded organism prone to farting and belching and the orgiastic release of gunfire and grenades, and that was perfectly okay. The timeworn metaphor was that they had morphed into a family, one they had chosen.

One day at Bella 1st Platoon squad leader Kyle Silvernale hauled out his camera to shoot some goofy footage of some of his men bouncing up and down, toboggan style, on a fuel blivet, trying to drain every drop out of it.

"What are you fucking ferret faggots doing?" Silvernale says teasingly.

As the blivet flattens, the row of five soldiers—Shane Burton, Scott Derry, James Takes, Justin Kalenits, and Andrew Hagerty—dissolve into a tangled mass of legs and arms, like a pool of young boys reveling in a pile of leaves on a fall afternoon. Specialist Gabriel Green shows up to drop himself on top. One other soldier, Stephen Johnson, hesitates.

"What's wrong, Johnson? You want none of that?" Silvernale says.

Johnson pauses and then opens his arms wide, grins, and falls face-forward into the jumble of brothers.

→ ←

By early November the Rock Battalion was nearly halfway through its fifteen-month deployment and losing soldiers at the rate of about one every other week, a pace just about as bloody as the 10th Mountain Battalion it had replaced. The peak fighting season of warm months was coming to a close, and winter was approaching, a period when enemy operations historically slowed down until spring.

Nine Rock paratroopers and a Navy corpsman assigned to the battalion had been killed since the unit arrived in late May. The very first to die was nineteen-year-old Private First Class Timothy Vimoto, who was killed in the Korengal Valley just a few weeks after the Afghanistan deployment began. It was his first firefight, and he died instantly from a gunshot to the head. The loss was stunning in so many ways. Not only was Vimoto the youngest member of the Rock Battalion, he was also the oldest son of the senior enlisted man for the entire 173rd Airborne Brigade, Command Sergeant Major Isaia Vimoto.

Although half the Chosen Company soldiers at the Ranch House battle were wounded, all had survived. A month after Vimoto died, Able Company, while patrolling the Pech Valley, lost two soldiers. A Destined Company first lieutenant was killed a little more than three weeks after that.

But the hardest hit up to that point was Battle Company. All of the others killed in action through early November were part of that beleaguered fighting unit in the Korengal Valley. All had died or been mortally wounded in a series of intense firefights or long-distance shooting exchanges that seemed to occur almost every day for weeks on end. The catchphrase for Battle Company paratroopers was a simple "Damn the Valley." They scratched it on the walls of firebases, wrote it on their helmets, and shouted it during firefights—or a variation like "Damn the motherfucking Valley!" They even tattooed it on their bodies, sometimes signified with just three letters: DTV. Many of the Battle Company dead had close personal ties throughout the Rock Battalion, including among the Chosen Few.

One evening in September up at Ranch House a hail storm had struck the base, and Chosen soldiers were outside waging a snowball fight when news about a casualty in the Korengal Valley arrived. Sergeant Brian Hissong saw Sergeant Ryan Pitts approach him with a dark expression on his face. The casualty was one of their best friends in Battle Company, Sergeant First Class Matthew Blaskowski, and he was dead. The three had a long history together. They'd all attended Pathfinder school in Europe before the deployment, a three-week course in setting up landing zones and directing aircraft. Pitts walked away, and Hissong found a quiet place to himself and wept. He would write a eulogy for Blaskowski's memorial service.

Blaskowski had earned a Silver Star during the battalion's previous deployment to Afghanistan in 2005 when he led a weapons squad that killed seventeen of the enemy, and he pulled a wounded paratrooper to safety even after being shot in the leg. He had since risen to the rank of platoon sergeant and was killed on September 23, shot through the neck by a sniper.

A month later, during a massive six-day operation that Lieutenant Colonel Ostlund launched in the Korengal Valley aimed at driving a stake through enemy resistance there, almost the entire Rock Battalion was put into action. The mission was called Rock Avalanche, and it essentially used almost all of his force to clear the east and west ridge-lines of the north-south-running Korengal, flush out all enemy fighters from their havens, and then kill them from the air and ground. There were periods of vicious fighting. Battle Company lost three paratroopers in four days. Ostlund would later estimate that they succeeded in killing anywhere from three hundred to five hundred enemy fighters during those six days, and he scored it as an overwhelming American battlefield victory.

With their backs against the wall in some sectors, the militants displayed flashes of increasingly sophisticated tactics. They overran a fighting position manned by a battalion scout and two Battle Company paratroopers on October 23, killing one American and wounding the other two before escaping with two assault rifles, two sets of night-vision goggles, and an M240 machine gun.

Two days later eighteen Battle Company paratroopers were coming down a narrow mountain trail from Honcho Hill in the Korengal Valley after manning a lookout position all night when they walked into a textbook L-shaped ambush. There were enemy fighters armed with automatic rifles and arrayed in hidden positions across the paratroopers' path, and there were more along the left flank with machine guns and RPG launchers.

In his book *Living with Honor*, Battle Company Staff Sergeant Salvatore Giunta, who was among those caught in the ambush, described the tactics as laden with "shocking efficiency and precision. To this day, I still have trouble believing it happened." Giunta, who was twenty-three at the time, displayed uncommon valor that day by charging forward through enemy fire to find the mortally wounded point man on the US patrol, Sergeant Josh Brennan, tied hand and foot and being carried away by two Islamist fighters. Giunta shot and killed one of the insurgents and wounded the other, who managed to escape down a cliff. Giunta dragged Brennan back; he later died in surgery. Also killed that day was Specialist Hugo Mendoza, a twenty-nine-year-old medic who was shot and bled to death before he could be evacuated.

For his extraordinary heroism in his effort to save Brennan, Giunta would later become the first living recipient of the Medal of Honor for battlefield actions since the Vietnam War. A day later, shaken by the death of the friend he tried desperately to rescue, Giunta bitterly expressed to *New York Times* reporter Elizabeth Rubin, "The richest, most-trained army got beat by dudes in man-jammies and AKs."

Word of the improved enemy tactics quickly spread through Rock Battalion. Chosen Company soldiers would talk among themselves about how a fighting position manned by their Battle Company brothers had been overrun. They would put considerable thought into how that ambush of Giunta's unit had been carried out, particularly the part that made it clear that the enemy was intent on dragging away an American soldier alive or dead.

That reality would influence decisions to come. But for the meantime Ostlund believed he had dealt a stunning blow to militant operations south of the Pech Valley with his Avalanche campaign. In fact, almost all of Rock Battalion unknowingly passed a milestone in their 2007–2008 deployment when Mendoza and Brennan were killed during that October fight. Although there would still be soldiers from the 2/503 who would fall wounded on the battlefield in the remaining months before everybody went home, nearly every company in the battalion would be spared the death of another paratrooper.

The only exception would be Chosen Company.

# 7

## >>> AMBUSH—MY FRIENDS ARE MY ENEMIES

*The song was everywhere that day.*

> On the 8th of November the angels were crying
> As they carried his brother away
> With the fire raining down and the hell all around
> There were few men left standing that day.

The summer before Chosen Company went to Afghanistan country western stars Big and Rich—Kenny Alphin, aka Big Kenny, and John Rich—released a documentary on the Great American Country Television network that told the story behind their recent hit single, "8th of November."

The ballad was a bit of a departure for the singer-songwriters, enshrining in lyrics the sacrifices made in Vietnam by soldiers of the 173rd Airborne Infantry on November 8, 1965, in a battle waged north of Saigon. Big and Rich wrote "8th of November" after meeting a veteran who told them the story of the battle in which he and other members of two companies from the 1/503 Battalion—the sister of the Rock Battalion—were locked in sometimes hand-to-hand combat with a Vietcong regiment of twelve hundred for hours in the jungle, losing forty-eight soldiers and leaving more than four hundred of the enemy dead. One of the paratrooper medics, Lawrence Joel, would become the first black man since the Spanish-American War to receive the Medal of Honor. He moved throughout the battlefield caring for wounded even after being twice shot himself. The worst casualties were hoisted out of the jungle by helicopters.

As the eighth of November 2007 approached in Afghanistan, the song weighed heavily on the Chosen Few at Bella. The men who were heading out on a mission that very day played it over and over on their iPods or laptops and through speakers in their barracks. They let the mournful lyrics wash over them as they gave their weapons a last thorough cleaning, listening to the words of a young soldier saying "goodbye to his momma as he left South Dakota to fight for the red, white, and blue . . . just doing what he had to do."

A lot of them called home. Sean Langevin reached his mother, Roxane, and his wife, Jessica, back in Walnut Creek, California, who was seven months pregnant with their daughter, Zoe, and asked for prayers. Jon Albert phoned his mother, Chele, though he didn't elaborate or tell her he was nervous. He just wanted to hear her voice.

*You don't want to go on this operation and not say good-bye.*

Their fears of surviving the next twenty-four hours stood in sharp contrast with life back at brigade headquarters on the sprawling US military base in Jalalabad, where troops were planning a twenty-four-hour relay run around the airfield to commemorate the November 8 battle. The disparity illustrated how this war's hardest fighting was in the distant margins in places like the Waigal Valley.

The mission for Ferrara's men was a hike back to Aranas. An Afghan messenger had arrived a few days earlier bearing an invitation for Matt Ferrara to come and visit with village elders at a *shura*, or meeting, in Aranas. Matt had participated in several shuras before when he was based out of Ranch House. But although the village was only about three miles away from Bella, it would be slow going over rugged terrain and would take hours each way. It would mean staying overnight. The route was either narrow goat trails cut into the sheer sides of a small canyon or a partially finished dirt road winding through uneven ground. Getting to Aranas meant following the Waigal Valley north before turning east and entering a narrower canyon that led to the village.

Ferrara really wanted to go. He wanted answers. He still felt the village leaders had somehow deceived him because of what happened at Ranch House six weeks earlier. He wanted to know how such a coordinated attack could have been carried out without any warning from the Aranas elders he had worked with for months. And Ferrara's boss agreed. Matt Myer had told the Army historian, Major Dave Hanson, that they wanted explanations from the village elders at Aranas.

"They were definitely people who did a one-eighty on us, who were playing both sides. We felt betrayed by a village that we had a pretty good relationship with," Myer said to Hanson.

But for his senior enlisted officers like Shane Stockard, David Dzwik, and soon-to-be-promoted James Takes, it was the elders' deceit that led them to urge Ferrara to call off his November 8 plans to take a patrol up to Aranas. Moreover, no one had recognized the runner who delivered the invitation purportedly from Aranas elders, yet another unsettling twist. Couldn't this just as easily be a trap? Have them come down here to Bella, they argued.

Going back to Aranas, that vertical village that cascaded down a mountainside just below where the fated Ranch House had been located, was like returning to the scene of the crime. In the TOC at Bella, Ferrara discussed the mission with Stockard and Begaye. Takes sat on the floor near the open doorway and added his two cents, even though he was only a sergeant-promotable. He had just returned from Blessing, where he sat before a promotion board, and it would be a few more months before he got his stripes as a staff sergeant. But he was already assuming leadership of a squad, and this would be his first mission as their leader.

"Sir, this is a fucking terrible idea. Why are we going up there?" Takes asked his lieutenant as the late-afternoon sun cast a column of light across the TOC's wooden floor.

"They invited us up there," Ferrara said.

"Why? So they can ambush us?"

Takes knew he was being a little too cocky for a new squad leader. But he could sense Stockard shared his concerns about the mission, and Takes knew he would be left with the unsavory task of convincing his soldiers that the Aranas trip was an order and they needed to buck up and carry it out. Ferrara outlined the precautions to be taken. They'd travel up there under cover of darkness—and it was really dark at night right then, with periods of moonless nights and zero illumination. They'd be shadowed by a scout team of six paratroopers led by Staff Sergeant Christopher Choay, a tough, highly respected squad leader who had received a Silver Star for heroism during Chosen's previous deployment to Afghanistan. Choay would lead his small group high along a southern ridgeline to overwatch the patrol after it arrived in Aranas. There might be some air cover for at least part of the mission, although that sought-after resource was usually reserved for missions where enemy contact was anticipated. Ferrara would lead a reinforced squad of thirteen paratroopers and link up with fourteen Afghan soldiers and their Marine advisor, Sergeant Phil Bocks, once they arrived at Aranas. Ferrara and his men would travel at night on November 8, sleep at the empty schoolhouse the Americans had built for the village, finish up early with the shura, and be back on Friday before dark.

A few hours before the mission started, Dzwik pulled Ferrara aside and tried one last time to change his boss's mind. "You really should not be doing this. There's one way in and one way out, and they know you're coming," he told him. Ferrara argued that the elders would be violating their own cultural covenants if anything happened. If they extended an invitation, Ferrara argued, you're assured safety going in and coming out.

"It doesn't matter," Dzwik said. "I'm telling you it doesn't matter."

Ferrara was losing patience. "I don't understand why guys don't want to do their job."

The mission was on.

Langevin told his team leader, Sergeant Mike Johnson, that he really had a bad feeling about this patrol. He said he'd feel a lot better if Johnson went along. Langevin was one of the most likeable soldiers in 1st Platoon. He was like Jason Hovater in 2nd Platoon, someone who could just naturally put a buddy at ease and make him feel like he had a real friend. A lot of them respected and cared about the guy, not the least of which was Johnson. They both had fought at Ranch House and received Bronze Stars for valor. Johnson said he would be absolutely willing to volunteer for the mission if it made Langevin feel better. But he also assured him that the patrol would prove boring and uneventful.

The plan was for Bocks and his Afghans to head out during the day on November 8. The Afghan troops didn't have night-vision equipment and needed to travel during daylight. Bocks would accompany them, and they all would link up with Ferrara and his men at Aranas.

Bocks was a twenty-eight-year-old native of the Detroit suburbs. He held the distinction of being a mountain warfare specialist for the world's greatest amphibious fighting force, the US Marines. He joined up when he was twenty-one, was eventually promoted to sergeant, and became a trainer at the Marine Corps Mountain Warfare Training Center in Bridgeport, California. Deploying to the mountains of Afghanistan was a chance to practice what he had been teaching.

Bocks was assigned as a mentor for the Afghan Army soldiers as an Embedded Training Team (ETT) member. He, too, was from a broken home. His parents had divorced when he was eight. He grew up with his mother, Peggy, before moving to California to spend part of his high school years with his father, Kent, in Truckee. He had married the year he joined the Marines, but he divorced the year before he went to Afghanistan. Phil was a tall Marine, over six feet tall, well built, with a distinctive, dimpled chin resembling the actor Kirk Douglas.

After darkness fell, the patrol assembled at the front gate. The only one missing was Staff Sergeant Conrad Begaye, who was the mission's senior enlisted officer. Stockard went looking for him. He found him back in his barracks in full battle gear, sitting on his bunk. Begaye was in prayer. He truly believed in the ways of the Navajo. He had his arrowhead and his medicine pouch out. Alone in his room with a few minutes to prepare himself for the mission to Aranas, Begaye had been chanting a Navajo prayer for warriors on the eve of battle.

After a time Stockard opened the door. "Hey, what are you doing?"

"Waiting." Begaye didn't want to explain himself

"Well, everyone's waiting for you. They're all in line out here."

The troopers gathered at the gate were a mix of men who had fought at Ranch House or had been assigned to Bella since the deployment began. Ferrara, of course, was going. His radio man would be Kyle White. Kain Schilling would be along as forward observer for calling in artillery, and Lester Roque was their medic. Takes had his squad in tow—his team leader Jeff Mersman, Justin Kalenits, Scott Derry, Jon Albert, and Joe Lancour with his beloved SAW. Albert had been at Ranch House until he got transferred to Bella right before the August 22 attack. So he had missed the firefights that members of 1st Platoon at Bella had fought that summer, and then he missed the Ranch House battle. He was one of the few in 1st Platoon who had yet to fire his weapon in combat, and the others razzed him about it.

Last-minute safety checks were underway. CamelBak water containers were topped off. Takes walked up and down the line tugging at gear and rapping on helmets to make sure all heads were in the game. He was getting a lot of let's-get-this-over-with feedback. And then Stockard, whose outsized leadership style had shaped and nurtured many of the young men heading out, did something wholly uncharacteristic. He began to go from man to man, shaking hands, wishing a safe trip or similar words of encouragement. Some, like White and Schilling, who had spent most of their time at Ranch House and had not worked as consistently with Stockard in Afghanistan, didn't really think much of the farewell gestures.

But the send-off left others blinking in disbelief, a display of senti-ment born of genuine concern seemed out of character for the tough-as-nails platoon sergeant. It was a side of Stockard they hadn't seen.

*Just how fucking dangerous is this mission?*

Although the terrain largely dictated the general route to Aranas, Ferrara wanted to guard against predictability as much as possible. So he planned to cross the Waigal River at Bella and climb the oppo-site ridge before taking a partially finished dirt road north and then east, edging along the southern rim of the small canyon running to Aranas. They would be shadowed by Choay's scouts, who would then take up a position across the valley from Aranas to keep a watchful eye through the duration of the shura before paralleling Ferrara's troops on their return Friday. On that trip back to Bella the lieutenant planned to take his men along a goat trail on the opposite, northern slope of the canyon so they wouldn't be repeating their steps from the previous night.

Traveling up there on the night of November 8 put a lot of the men at ease about a potential ambush because their movements were under cover of darkness. Vision through their night-observation devices, or NODs, always gave them a distinct advantage in this war, particularly under these kinds of moonless conditions. The enemy was all but blind on a night like this, but the paratroopers could see where they were going. Still, that didn't make the hike easy. The green-tinted vision the NODs afforded was a two-dimensional world—there was no depth per-ception. This made stepping across uneven ground tricky. Although the soldiers were generally following a dirt road up there, there were times when they went off into the bushes and traversed gullies to avoid am-bush choke points. They had to keep high-stepping to make sure they didn't stumble over clumps of dirt or rocks that looked lower to the ground through their NODs. It was exhausting. Men were sweating, and they sounded like a herd of elephants despite efforts to maintain noise discipline.

At one point where the road had partially collapsed, Jeff Mersman fell hard and badly hurt his wrist. Begaye thought he might have shattered a bone. The pain was intense, but the sergeant didn't complain. A couple of soldiers came down to help him back up on the trail. Roque later bandaged him up.

It was all so characteristic of this place. Mersman's grimaced face could have been the poster image for what Afghanistan inflicted on people, beyond even the existential threat of an enemy out to kill them. The very earth they walked on, the gnarled trees and roots they grabbed for support, those mysterious critters slithering from under rocks and bushes all seemed to conspire to cause pain and injury. Some Chosen Few feared the terrain almost as much as they feared the enemy. The rocks and crevasses and caverns and valleys oozed hostility and threat, ready at any time to grab and twist ankles, shave off skin, or send some unfortunate paratrooper humping seventy pounds of gear tumbling down onto boulders. Everything animate and inanimate seemed in league. Even the Afghan soldiers, many who came from less daunting regions of the country than these Hindu Kush Mountains, complained about it. If they uttered any English at all, it was two words they knew would elicit an approving grunt from any American within earshot: "Fucking Nuristan."

Ferrara and his men finally reached the schoolhouse just short of Aranas and started setting up security and working out watch rotations so soldiers could get some sleep. By morning they were up and ready to head into the village for the shura.

Except the village wasn't ready for them. The soldiers waited all morning. Ferrara kept strolling up and inquiring, but there was always some delay, always someone who hadn't shown up yet.

The soldiers bided their time pulling security. It was one of those slack periods that come with soldiering, endless hours waiting for no apparent reason, without any explanation. You were a cog in a military wheel that for the moment had ground to a halt. So you stood or you sat. You bitched or you munched whatever MRE snacks were in your assault bag. One pleasant surprise was the US jets orbiting overhead, which lowered tensions a bit.

By early afternoon the shura finally got underway. Ferrara took his translator, an Afghan named Alex Drany, and his radio operator, Kyle White, and met with about twenty people in what amounted to a kind of town square but was really little more than a courtyard.

White tried to follow the exchanges between Ferrara and the elders as Alex translated. But if he stared out over and beyond the village and the surrounding countryside, the mountain-scape looked very much like home.

White grew up in the spectacular setting of Bonney Lake, Washington, south of Seattle, in the shadow of 14,400-foot Mount Rainier. He was the only child of parents who worked for Boeing, the biggest employer in the area. He watched television images of the towers falling in New York while sitting in a middle school English class. His father, Kurt, had been in the Army, and Kyle listened to his stories. Being a paratrooper seemed a good fit. He was already an adrenalin junkie addicted to downhill mountain biking in the Cascades. Plus, there was something compelling about the idea of serving his country in uniform. When Kyle failed to get accepted into Central Washington University, he felt the Army was his next move. But his parents resisted, and he agreed to give community college a shot. That didn't work out, and by January 2006 White had enlisted and was off to basic training.

On this crisp November day in the village of Aranas White wanted to hear something hopeful come out of this shura. So much had changed. The first three months of his deployment up at Ranch House had felt very nearly like the paratroopers were just camping out, as if the war in Afghanistan was someplace else. The people of the Waigal Valley didn't seem to be looking for a fight.

But everything shifted violently on August 22 when they were fighting for their lives at Ranch House. It was clear there were enemy in the valley intent on killing the Chosen Few. Ranch House had been attacked at the weakest point in its defenses. The base had been nearly overrun. The video taken off Hazrat Omar's body was a chilling indicator of how cunning the enemy could be.

*These people are organized. They know what they're doing.*

White hoped the village elders might at least show some remorse for what the Islamist fighters had done at Ranch House. Maybe there was a relationship with the village that could be salvaged. But as White listened after the meeting finally got underway at 1 P.M., the discussion didn't seem to be going in any purposeful direction.

Ferrara and White leaned on a courtyard wall and faced a collection of older village leaders, while several young men of fighting age watched and listened nearby. Begaye, who was the senior enlisted man on the patrol, cycled back and forth between the shura and his soldiers. Sergeant Mike Johnson and Marine Corps Sergeant Bocks, who was mentoring the Afghan troops, did the same.

Ferrara brought up the Ranch House attack, but it seemed to get glossed over. There were complaints that local children had been killed by explosives they found up near Ranch House after it was abandoned. Ferrara assured the elders that the kind of devices they were describing were not from the US Army. The villagers seemed hostile during much of a discussion that just dragged on.

Bocks approached Ferrara at one point looking worried. The Afghan soldiers had been monitoring radio bands and overheard a lot of chatter, some of it in languages they couldn't understand. Something seemed to be going on out there, and it didn't sound good. "We gotta go," Bocks told Ferrara.

Ferrara agreed and wrapped up the largely disappointing shura. All he really had to show for it was a wish list of winter supplies the elders had asked for. He wrote it all down and stuffed it in his pocket.

When the US aircraft flying overhead finally departed, Begaye and Johnson approached him about staying in the village until nightfall, when the Americans would again have the advantage of night-vision goggles, and then heading back under the cover of darkness. It was highly unlikely anyone would attack them while they were in the village, the two men argued. Ferrara listened to his noncommissioned officers and seriously considered their idea. Just like at Ranch House, the more anxious a situation became, the cooler and more relaxed the lieutenant seemed to get. He decided they should go ahead and head home. As long as they made steady progress, they could probably stay ahead of any attack.

As the Chosen Few and their Afghan allies left Aranas, Begaye radioed Takes and said they needed to keep moving down cliff trails along the narrow valley connecting Aranas to the Waigal Valley. Just on the other side of the canyon was where a patrol of 10th Mountain soldiers had been attacked the year before, with three killed.

"It's a bad area. Let's move through here quickly," Begaye warned.

For this route back to the Waigal Valley there were two parallel trails along the north side of the east-west canyon. One trail was high and one was low. The patrol would take the lower of the two. They could see and hear the mountain stream running down the center of the valley below. The weather was a perfect fall day—crisp, cool, and clear.

But there was a troubling flurry of activity as they left the village. Some young men came racing up from behind and squeezed past them on the trail. Kain Schilling saw a few of them take the higher trail. Some of them actually looked like they were laughing as they raced ahead of the column. Over their radios Begaye and Takes took note of the commotion as the young men finally went out of sight.

The goat trail that followed the canyon westward to the Waigal River Valley narrowed in places to little more than a catwalk cut into the steep slope of the canyon's northern wall. Large spurs defined that side of the canyon, and the trail hugged them like a waistband so that troops walking the route single file could round a bend and be out of sight of those who were behind them.

The trail had been there forever and was surfaced with broken shale that made for unsteady footing, particularly on an incline. So the paratroopers tended to be focusing on their next step rather than looking out for threats. On this narrow trail the mountain slope rose steeply to the right, and a sheer cliff dropped perilously to the left. Worse yet, it was almost totally devoid of places to take cover. There was the occasional tree that somehow took root among the boulders. But otherwise the troopers might just as well have been walking a plank suspended over the valley.

They ended up coming to a frustrating halt at least a couple of times, primarily to let the Afghan soldiers who were lagging behind catch up. Each time someone would radio in their precise grid location to Bella. During one of the pauses Ferrara pulled out his camera and snapped a couple of pictures. One of them shows Kyle White right behind him, leaning up against the mountain on the narrow trail and staring across the valley almost as if he were enjoying the view. The other looks forward and captures Private First Class Scott Derry, Private First Class Joe Lancour, and Sergeant Jeff Mersman taking the opportunity to sit down and relax before pushing ahead. Mersman, with his helmet off momentarily, and Derry stare at the camera. Lancour looks like he's deep in thought.

From across the canyon—where, in fact, enemy fighters with automatic rifles, machine guns, and RPG launchers lay in wait—the coalition column of Americans followed by Afghan soldiers looked like ducks in a shooting gallery moving from right to left.

Choay's overwatch team, which had kept a lookout over Aranas during the shura, headed back to Bella when Ferrara's troops left Aranas at about 2:30 P.M. Choay and his scouts largely retraced their outbound route, and this took them farther south to where a ridgeline blocked their view of Ferrara and his column of men moving west through the small canyon toward the Waigal. Choay wanted to get back to where he could overwatch that last leg down the Waigal Valley toward Bella.

With intelligence reports suggesting for weeks that enemy fighters were gathering around Bella, Ferrara's last stretch leading to the base seemed the most obvious place for an ambush. But in fact the Islamist fighters were setting a trap in a different location. Local fighters and, potentially, elements of the Lashkar-e-Tayyiba terror group were taking positions at a point along the trail roughly five hundred yards from the valley crossroads located a little less than a mile north of Bella. At that point the paratroopers could be targeted from three different ridgelines: one directly south across the canyon, another due west across the Waigal River Valley, and the third, the ridge towering directly over their heads. Up above them someplace was a fortified position that was supposed to be manned by hired Afghan security guards. They called that outpost Lone Ranger.

Ferrara and his men had been delayed in Aranas long enough that by the time they reached the ambush site, the sun was in their eyes to the west, all but blinding them to targets shooting at them from that direction.

There were enemy preparations even beyond the ambush site, with militants taking up fighting positions above Bella and across the valley from the US observation post known as OP1. Others were shadowing Choay and his overwatch team. These forces would be ready to attack to prevent reinforcements from reaching Ferrara and his men.

Just like Ranch House, the Islamist fighters were intent on videotaping the battle for propaganda. Different cameramen from different angles were prepared to capture the ambush on film and recorded some images of the American column before the shooting started. One videographer across the canyon to the south panned along the goat trail where the Chosen Few could be seen walking single file in regimented fifteen-yard spacing, steadily trying to make their way home.

In the final video product the film editor did a freeze-frame at this point in the footage and inserted red arrows pointing at each paratrooper in view. There's a subtitle in Persian. It reads, "The Americans and their slaves are doomed."

→  ←

At the very beginning most of them heard a single gunshot and suspected it was an accidental discharge by the Afghan soldiers.

Oh, these idiots.

And then the hillsides erupted. It was like being caught out in the open during a sudden cloudburst, only the rain was made of fire and steel. The surrounding amphitheater of rock walls not only amplified and reverberated the sounds of gunfire so that it grew into a sustained roar but also made it very difficult to discern exactly where shots were coming from. In fact, there were teams of gunmen firing from about five different locations in a semicircle around the column, positioned as if shooting into a giant fishbowl from the rim. It was 3:30 in the afternoon, and there was almost an hour and a half of daylight left.

The paratroopers reacted instinctively. The only way to check a fusillade of incoming enemy fire was to throw out a competing wall of lead all your own. After that it was a matter of maneuvering for advantage and calling in artillery or air support. The soldiers had this drilled into them endlessly in the training fields of Germany. In a place like the exposed goat trail along this narrow valley of northeastern Afghanistan, where there was no room to maneuver, their training would call upon them to stand and fight.

Each of them did just that.

Takes was leading the column, something he always insisted on doing because he liked the responsibility and felt he could handle it. As the shooting started and Takes brought his rifle to bear, his choices were to go forward, backward, or off a cliff. The trail ahead rounded a bend that would separate him from the rest of the paratroopers. So he retraced his steps back toward Jon Albert, who was armed with a SAW, or light machine gun, and in the first gunfight of his life.

Albert spotted Takes and sprinted toward his squad leader.

The pair found what they could tell right away was a pitiful place for cover: a rock along the trail maybe two feet high and about as long. Both paratroopers tried to make themselves small behind it, crouching

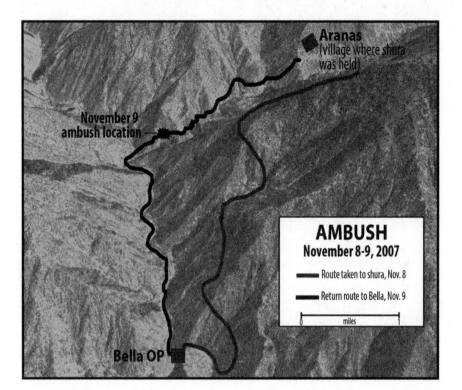

shoulder to shoulder and bitching back and forth as bullets slammed into the rocks all around them.

"Slide over!" Takes yelled. "I'm getting shot over here!"

"Fuck you! I'm getting shot over here! You slide over!"

Just behind them in the column Private First Class Justin Kalenits ran back to take a knee next to Staff Sergeant Begaye, who was already returning fire. The pair was caught in a cloud of dust thrown up by the RPGs that were exploding everywhere. Kalenits was a grenadier, so Begaye, who was working to clear his jammed M4, started picking out enemy positions for his soldier to target with the brass-headed grenades that Kalenits fired from a launcher slung under the barrel of his carbine.

Beyond them around a bend in the trail were Private First Class Sean Langevin; Sergeant Mike Johnson; and the medic, Specialist Lester

Roque, who all simultaneously started returning fire. Like everyone else, they were caught in the open. Langevin dropped to a knee to bring his light machine gun into action, aiming at muzzle flashes across the valley. Johnson went flat on the ground and opened up with his M4.

Roque yelled that he could hear someone behind them on the trail crying out for a medic. Mersman, Joe Lancour, and Scott Derry were next in line in the column and back beyond another bend in the trail. Johnson told Roque to stay put until they could maneuver in that direction as a group.

Meanwhile enemy gunmen were zeroing in. Johnson felt an impact to his right thigh. It actually shoved his leg backward. But there was no pain and very little blood, so the sergeant figured it was just a rock kicked up by an explosion.

As he looked to his right, Johnson could see Langevin rolled over on his side, as if he'd been shot. But then the SAW gunner reassuringly popped right back up again. The three started retracing their steps, but RPGs exploding in that direction forced them to stop.

Langevin called out that he was reloading, and Johnson took the cue to start firing at the ridgeline across the valley to provide cover. Now Johnson could hear someone calling for a medic back on the trail, and the next time he looked to his left, Roque was gone, obviously bent on reaching whomever was in need.

Even farther back on the trail was Matt Ferrara. As the ambush began, the lieutenant had reached the end of a spur where the trail cut back into the mountain. All of his paratroopers were ahead of him with the exception of his artillery forward observer, Kain Schilling, and his radioman, Kyle White. Behind those two soldiers was Marine Sergeant Bocks and then the Afghan troops he oversaw, arrayed out along the winding cliff trail for several dozen yards. Ferrara found himself caught in the open at the end of the spur and decided to lay flat on the ground and immediately put his rifle into action. Behind him Schilling, whose twenty-first birthday would be in three days, and White also opened fire with their M4 rifles, although none of them could tell precisely where the enemy fusillade was coming from. Bullets zipped and cracked through the air. The paratroopers simply aimed at the opposite ridgeline to the south and blasted away. White pivoted on the loose shale, slipped, and fell right down on his butt. Firing one round with each trigger squeeze, he emptied a thirty-round clip in seconds. He dropped that mag and started to slip in another one when an RPG exploded right behind him, knocking White to the ground unconscious, face flat on a rock. Schilling caught a piece of the shrapnel in his left hand before bounding over to climb behind a rock outcropping just above the trail.

White began to stir, and just as he lifted his head off the rock, an enemy round exploded against it, inches away from his face. Shattered bits of metal peppered his nose and around his mouth. He felt with his fingers and pulled his hand back—blood.

This is bad.

Climbing to his feet, White followed Schilling behind the outcropping. Both hoped this would cover them from the torrent of gunfire and RPGs coming from the opposite ridgeline. What they didn't realize was that insurgents were dug in high up on the north ridge above their heads and could target them.

The Afghan Army soldiers scattered along the trail were by now in a near panic, scrambling back and forth, searching desperately for cover. Some dropped to the ground and lay still in hopes the enemy would believe they were already dead. In the midst of the confusion Phil Bocks, their Marine advisor, was a study in contrast. The Marine followed his training, picked a firing position near some low-lying rocks and bushes, and sent rounds across the valley with his M4. Bullets whizzed past him until Bocks realized he was caught in a crossfire. An enemy round hit him in the upper right thigh. Bocks didn't flinch. Instead, he swung his rifle from where he was firing across the valley and took aim at a group of insurgents high up on the ridge above him.

One of the enemy cameramen was filming. In the footage that was later posted as propaganda on the Internet, it looks as though Bocks is pointing his weapon directly into the camera lens. Just as he starts to shoot, an enemy bullet hits him near the upper part of his right shoulder. His body goes slack and his head slumps forward. He rocks first to his left, absorbing the shock of the impact, then rolls to his right as his legs go limp. His feet slip on the loose gravel, and he tumbles down the trail, gripping his weapon all the while with his right arm and hand.

The man with the video camera chants the same phrase over and over in a Nuristani dialect as the lens follows the falling, wounded Marine.

"God is great! God is great!"

→  ←

More than a mile south down the Waigal Valley in their fortified post high up on the ridge above Bella, six paratroopers manning OP1 could hear the sustained roar of gunfire in the far distance. It was clear that something had gone terribly wrong with Ferrara's patrol. One of them manning the radio, Specialist Stephen Johnson, tried to contact the patrol. He could hear someone key the intercom, and the same cacophony of gunfire was in the background, only amplified over the radio.

One of the first people Johnson finally reached was Takes, and he asked the sergeant whether Bella could start firing at the high ground around the patrol with 120mm mortar rounds.

"Oh yeah, fucking let it rip!" Takes yelled into his mic.

The sergeant was still crouched with Albert behind a rock that seemed to grow smaller with each passing second as enemy gunmen zeroed in on them. Takes searched hard for targets on the opposite side of the canyon and saw muzzle flashes, so he started aiming and shooting at them. Each time he cut loose on one, another flashed nearby.

It's like playing whack-a-mole.

Albert, for his part, couldn't see any targets, so he just kept firing his light machine gun all along the opposite ridgeline. There were sudden explosions to their left and right. Takes figured they were mortar rounds closing in. "They're bracketing!" he yelled at Albert. Then Takes realized the explosions were RPGs. Either way, they clearly couldn't stay where they were.

Begaye was in exactly the same predicament just several yards back on the trail. He'd been directing Kalenits, who was down on a knee right next to him, where to launch his 40mm grenades, the hollow-sounding THOOMP going off as Kalenits fired away. But the incoming rifle fire was getting more accurate and intense. Enemy bullets were hitting the ground or zipping by them very close, and then an RPG slammed into the hillside just over their heads, raining down rocks and debris. Begaye's sunglasses were blown off his face. A bullet passed through the meaty part of his upper right arm. Clearly it was coming from behind them, up on the mountain. They were caught in a crossfire. He tried to radio OP1, but the amphitheater of noise was so overwhelming that Begaye couldn't make any sense of what was being said. He realized he had to make a decision and fast.

"Follow me!" Begaye yelled.

He took a few steps and threw himself off the edge of the cliff, choosing a spot where the drop appeared less sheer and there was a tree offering at least some concealment. But as he slid down between the rocks, Begaye got tangled up in the tree trunk, and suddenly there was a traffic jam of soldiers as Albert and Kalenits barreled down behind him.

Takes saw the exodus off the trail and started laying down cover fire at the far ridgeline across the canyon, boiling through magazines of ammo. He stood up and started to follow the paratroopers when he felt a dull pain—a bullet had sliced through his left shoulder. He was surprised it didn't hurt more. Takes kept firing his rifle as he moved to the precipice and looked down to see the pileup of paratroopers.

*It is an honest-to-God clusterfuck.*

Then he followed, picking a slightly different course around the opposite side of one of the boulders, as enemy gunmen began to focus more attention on this scrum of Chosen Few.

Mike Johnson and Sean Langevin were headed right in the same direction. Johnson figured Roque had managed to backtrack around the bend in the trail behind them because he couldn't hear anyone calling out for medical aid. Roque must have reached whomever was wounded. Johnson ordered Langevin to move forward down the trail, and he followed. As the pair progressed one behind the other, it looked like Langevin was in distress. He stopped at one point and took a knee, got back up, moved some more, then slumped to the ground. Johnson felt certain his friend was wounded and moved toward him to assist, only to watch Langevin climb back up on his feet, take a few more steps, then dive off the edge of the cliff, following the troops who had followed Begaye. Johnson was right on his heels. He couldn't know that Langevin already had gunshot wounds in an arm and a thigh.

Somewhere farther back on the trail Scott Derry found himself in a kink that almost had him in a corner. He couldn't see Ferrara, who was directly behind him, though he could hear the lieutenant firing his carbine. He couldn't see Joe Lancour, who was right up ahead, but he could hear him blasting away with his prized squad automatic, the one he'd nicknamed Reese Witherspoon. Lancour had dropped off the trail into some kind of cover area where he could bring his weapon to bear.

Derry was a grenadier like Kalenits, so he was launching brass-covered grenades at muzzle flashes across the canyon and watching them explode on the opposite ridge. Dropping round after round across the canyon, Derry felt an enemy bullet graze his right shoulder. He knew he had to move.

*And do it now.*

Derry took several steps and almost immediately an RPG exploded right where he had been standing. Derry ran as fast as he could. His world, certainly his vision, was like a tunnel he wanted to pass through as quickly as his legs would allow. There was a second explosion close behind him. He rounded a short bend, caught his foot on something, and went flying onto the trail. It was a dead American—Roque. Derry had tripped over Roque's boot. Derry got up and kept moving. Enemy fighters were trying to track and kill him as he headed down the trail. The air was full of flying lead. A bullet had sliced through the barrel of his grenade launcher, cutting it in half; another ricocheted off the helmet mount for his night-vision goggles.

The whole desperate flight through the gauntlet of fire had strangely played out as if in slow motion for Derry, his adrenalin pumping so hard that the world around him was in crystal-sharp focus. The endless drills the Army had put him through instilled muscle memory so that there was no second thought to running, finding cover, firing across the valley, and then doing it all over again as he made his way along the goat trail. Somehow he was staying alive.

He finally reached a part of the trail where the drop-off was less sheer and there were a few trees for cover. He dived off.

→　←

For Matt Ferrara, far back in the kill zone that Derry had fled, it was death by a single bullet. An enemy round struck the lieutenant near his left collarbone and passed through his body and out his back as he lay in a prone fighting position, killing him, the wish list for winter supplies from Aranas elders still tucked in his front pocket.

None of his men saw him die.

Several yards back on the trail a wounded Phil Bocks had rolled down the slope to a point where the ground began to flatten out, and he started half scooting, half crab-walking his way down the mountain path. Three Afghan soldiers who were laying on the ground nearby still pretending to be dead suddenly sprung to life and were on their feet, scrambling down the hillside, all but running over the stricken Marine as they frantically sought a place to take cover.

They left Bocks, their American mentor, behind, awkwardly sitting up in the dirt in the open, bleeding heavily from his wounds, with more blood oozing out of his mouth. He knew he had some real damage internally, and it was terrifying.

Not far away an enemy sniper found Kain Schilling. A bullet slammed into his collarbone and then shattered the bone in the upper part of his right arm. It sliced some nerves in the process, and for Schilling it felt like his right arm was gone. It was twisted awkwardly around behind him, so at first he didn't even see it.

*Oh shit, my arm just got blown off.*

Gunfire was coming from above him. The rock outcropping Schilling had found wasn't enough cover. He realized, thankfully, his arm was still with him. Climbing to his feet, the soldier headed farther down the trail to a place where a tree sprouted from below the edge of the cliff, and he took refuge under the canopy of leaves.

White heard Schilling cry out and saw him run down the trail, his right arm dangling at his side. He saw his friend reach the canopy of leaves and followed him. White began returning fire at muzzle flashes on the opposite ridge to the south, shooting through leaves above his head when he suddenly found himself struggling to breathe. There was a strange metallic taste in his mouth, and his lungs were burning. Schilling, nearby, felt some of the same symptoms.

Then Schilling noticed smoke coming from the large radio pack on White's back.

"Your bag! It's on fire!" he yelled.

Bullets had ripped through the lithium battery, spewing toxic smoke. White pulled off the backpack and hurled it aside. Out of the corner of his eye he spotted Bocks sitting out in the open, bleeding badly. The sergeant looked disoriented, and there was a good ten yards of open ground separating them, all of it swept by enemy gunfire.

→ ←

The column of American and Afghan soldiers that had started out from Aranas and extended along the goat trail for a couple of hundred yards had disintegrated. Utter chaos unfolded. Where Begaye had led his soldiers off the trail, paratroopers remained bunched together around two large boulders where the only possible cover was a gnarled tree. It barely shielded more than a few of them and provided no protection at all from incoming rounds. And still more men fleeing killing zones along the goat trail were arriving. Sean Langevin had slid down nearby with Sergeant Mike Johnson right behind. Scott Derry would be there soon. Directly below, where the paratroopers were clustered, there was a thirty-foot drop-off to the canyon floor. The bottom of the canyon was wide and treeless except for foliage and rocks at the base of the cliff. Enemy gunmen were firing from several directions and, within a span of just a few minutes, the Chosen Few were trapped and getting shot to pieces.

Langevin called out: "Sergeant Begaye, I'm shot." The staff sergeant was just about to answer back that Langevin wasn't the only one wounded, but just then an enemy sniper round struck Langevin in the head. Johnson saw it happen—Sean's head snapping backward from the impact. The father-to-be went limp and tipped over, spilling down the slope, his body brushing past Begaye. Albert caught a glimpse of a lifeless figure somersaulting all the way down before coming to rest in a sprawl near a stream at the bottom of the valley.

Just as Scott Derry reached the group, an RPG exploded against the mountain along the upper edge of where the soldiers were clustered. Pieces of shrapnel stitched across Derry's left side, almost from head to toe.

James Takes, farther down, was facing uphill in the direction of the blasts, taking aim at muzzle flashes on the ridgeline above their heads. The RPG explosion threw a cloud of steel particles into his face and all the way down the front of his body to his genitals. The force of the blast literally spun him around so that the sergeant found himself sitting against the mountain, stunned and groggy, and staring down at the bottom of the canyon.

Johnson was closest to the explosion, and the force of it caused him to lose footing and slide diagonally down the mountain until he became wedged between two large rocks. The ground was steep, and he tried to brace himself on the rocks to keep from falling any farther. He was feeling faint. Hunks of shrapnel had passed through both legs, where he already had bullet wounds. But what caught his attention was how an enemy round had drilled cleanly through the center of his green Suunto tactical military watch.

*What are the odds?*

He knew he needed to stop his hemorrhaging soon. Derry suddenly showed up behind him, astonished by how much the twenty-six-year-old sergeant was bleeding. Derry could see the cargo pockets on Johnson's trousers literally bulging with blood. The two men worked together for the next several minutes placing tourniquets on both of Johnson's legs and his left arm.

Back where other soldiers were grouped near Staff Sergeant Begaye, Kalenits suddenly cried out. A bullet had smashed into the upper part of his left buttock—a Forrest Gump wound, Takes would call it. The round splintered bone as it passed through Kalenits's pelvis and then exited out the inside of his left thigh. Meat from the inside of his upper leg hung from the exit hole, and blood gushed so thick that Kalenits thought both his legs had been shot.

Begaye felt a growing sense of helplessness and anger. He'd led his men off the cliff to try to protect them. Now they were dying right before his eyes. He was determined to save at least one in this mayhem. He and Kalenits were just below a kidney-shaped boulder where there was a crevasse in the crook of the rock. It was almost a small cave. Begaye grabbed Kalenits and shoved him into the hole as far as he could, then covered him with his own body. He pulled a HemCon bandage out of his aid kit—an Army field dressing actually made with a shellfish substance that works as a strong clotting agent—and started stuffing the dressing into the gaping wound in Kalenits's backside.

Nearby Takes started to clear his head from the RPG explosion, and his eyes focused on the body of a US soldier lying near the creek below.

"Who is it?" he yelled over to Begaye.

"He's dead," the staff sergeant shouted back. "Don't worry about it."

Then they heard Specialist Jon Albert scream out in pain. The twenty-two-year-old SAW gunner had run through nearly one hundred rounds of ammunition firing his light machine gun. He was struggling to unload a bag of fresh ammo from his assault pack when it felt like his right knee exploded. He saw his pants ripped apart from where the enemy bullet grazed his kneecap. The pain was excruciating. Sitting against the mountain, Albert had his legs planted to keep himself from slipping down. But the right one, now damaged, gave out, and the soldier started to slide down the slope.

Takes snagged him at the last second, gripping Albert by the handle on the back of his body armor with one hand and clinging with the other to some vegetation sprouting from between the rocks. Albert could see the strain in his sergeant's face as he struggled to hang on. Between the relentless enemy fire, Albert's agonizing wound, this godforsaken mountainside, and the laws of gravity itself, it was as if everything was conspiring against them.

"Just let go," Albert called out.

"Shut the fuck up," Takes said.

The chorus of gunfire and explosions reverberating across the valley was by now unbroken thunder. Albert had been supporting his weight with his left leg, but the limb finally gave out. Takes couldn't keep a grip. The Army specialist tumbled down the rocks, cracking his face on the edge of a stone before coming to rest on the creek bed about forty feet from Langevin's body. Albert's SAW gun had gone flying off in one direction and his helmet in another.

Takes watched and then started working his way over toward Begaye and Kalenits. He suddenly felt like he couldn't breathe and his chest was constricting. A bullet had drilled through a spare radio battery in Takes's assault pack, and just like White on the trail above him, the sergeant was choking on the toxic fumes. He peeled off the backpack.

The enemy rounds rocketing in at two thousand feet per second, had turned this corner of the battle into a horrifying game of Russian roulette. The rounds that hadn't torn through flesh had stitched the dirt and rocks all around the crouching paratroopers, perforating folds of their uniforms. One bored a hole through the CamelBak water carrier on Begaye's back so that warm liquid ran down his backside. Too busy to investigate it, Begaye figured it was probably blood and, as he was no worse off, ignored it. Bullets deflected off helmets and flattened up against body armor plates. Each time the impact was displaced across the entire ceramic shield it felt like a blow from a baseball bat. The bullet-proof shield smacked up against the body in a microsecond so any air caught between plating and skin blew out the sides like a tiny burst of wind.

Derry's wallet, stuffed with $300 in cash he had just won playing poker with the guys up at OP1 the night before they left, stopped one bullet, but it penetrated some of the $10 bills. Another round hit a frag-mentation grenade that Derry carried in a pouch on the front of his assault pack. The bullet broke loose the safety pin that held in place the spoon or lever that, when freed, would ignite a fuse and explode the grenade. Somehow, though, the bullet had damaged the spoon so it miraculously stayed in place. (After the battle Derry duct taped the spoon to the grenade to make sure it stayed put and carried the bomb on patrols for months afterward, like some kind of good-luck charm.)

After Takes abandoned the assault pack with the burning battery, he turned his attention to Albert, who was lying down in the creek bed, and yelled to him, "Hey man, quit fucking moving around! Just lay there for a bit. I know it hurts. But they're going to think you're dead."

Albert lay in this shooting gallery, completely exposed. Taking a bul-let to the head was what scared him the most. Rounds were hitting the stream bed all around him, and he figured it was only a matter of time before one of them drilled into his skull and it was all over. A flat rock stuck out of the ground a few feet away, and Albert, on his stomach, crawled over to it, lifted it up with his left arm, stuck his head under, and just let it rest on top of him. But the weight was too much, and in short order he pulled it off.

Takes could see the enemy had not stopped shooting at Langevin's lifeless body.

*Playing dead doesn't work. I'm not going to leave Albert out there.*

He spotted an overhang at the bottom of the cliff and told Begaye he might be able to drag Albert over there to get him out of the line of fire.

"Hey, if you want to make it down there, make it down there," Begaye told him. "I have Kalenits right here."

Takes, rifle in hand, slid the last thirty feet to the canyon floor and made his way over to Albert. The soldier was lying parallel to the creek with his head facing downstream. Enemy gunmen started to pay attention, and incoming fire picked up. Takes realized the only alternative for the moment was the Army doctrine of return fire: put those shooters back on their heels. He took a knee, straddled Albert where he lay flat on the ground, and started firing at targets high up on the ridge.

Back up on the slope of the mountain Begaye was transfixed by the scene playing out in the open down below—one American soldier covering his wounded comrade with his body and fighting back at the same time.

*Wow, that is badass.*

## 8

> > > **A RADIO MAN TAKES CHARGE**

*Those who have experienced intense combat,* where fear verges on sheer panic, often speak later of a moment of clarity that comes once they've accepted death. Only when they reconcile with the fact that life is over—that they are, in a sense, already dead—does the paralyzing terror subside. Then they are able to do what they need to do.

Kyle White, who turned twenty the previous spring, reached this point as he stared out at the direly wounded Sergeant Phillip Bocks who, although just several yards from him, might as well have been a mile away for all the enemy gunfire raking the dirt between them. From where he lay in the open, with wounds to his upper body and his right thigh, Bocks called for White to come get him.

"Hey, you got to use all your strength," White yelled back. "Get to me."

Bocks shifted himself and tried to crawl. But it was no use. He didn't have the strength to move. White knew he had to go out there. Bocks had a good fifty pounds and four or more inches on him, not to mention the body armor. Pulling him back to the relative safety of the tree would almost certainly kill them both.

*I'm not going to make it through this.*

With that thought, White got to his feet and sprinted toward the wounded Marine. It was exactly what the militant snipers were waiting for. Enemy fire pelted the ground White covered. Schilling, who was also badly wounded and depending on White to get him through this nightmare, watched from beneath the canopy of tree leaves. He saw sparks where bullets were hitting rocks. Even the air seemed to turn hot and hostile. White could feel rounds snagging at his clothes. He grabbed the handle attached to the back of Bocks's body armor and began dragging the big man. But the gunfire escalated, and White was convinced the next shot would hit one of them or the other. He let go and ran back toward Schilling, hoping to draw fire away from Bocks. Schilling watched in amazement from under the tree cover as White moved through this open ground without a scratch.

Don't die.

White waited for a lull, then sprinted out a second time, grabbing and pulling the Marine that much closer. He repeated this once or twice more, until he finally had Bocks under the tree.

The first order of business was applying a combat tourniquet to Bocks's right thigh. Each of the paratroopers was equipped with a specially designed tourniquet with Velcro and a plastic windless that could be applied with one hand. White's own tourniquet had been used on Schilling's arm. Now he took a tourniquet from Bocks's med kit, applied it to the Marine's leg, and stopped the bleeding there. He could see Bocks had a second wound—a small entry hole—on his upper left shoulder. He bandaged that. But White knew there had to be more. All the paratroopers were trained in a high level of combat emergency medicine. He pulled off Bocks's body armor and ammo harness and ripped open his shirt. Sure enough, there it was—a gaping exit wound on his right side near his rib cage. The Marine was losing a lot of blood, and White guessed there was probably serious internal damage. He said nothing of this to Bocks, who stared back at him with a glassy look.

"I don't think I'm going to make it through this one," Bocks said.

→ ←

Down below in the streambed Takes was still multitasking as he straddled Albert on the valley floor, using one hand to apply a tourniquet
to Albert's right leg just above his bloody knee and firing his M4 with
the other. By this time Albert was bleeding from wounds all over his
body. In addition to the searing pain coming from his right kneecap,
which the Army specialist hadn't yet brought himself to look at, he
had a through-and-through wound to his left thigh. That leg had gone
numb and was unresponsive. There was also shrapnel to his right leg,
and a bullet or piece of shrapnel had passed through the triceps of his
right arm.

Amidst the dust and debris clouding the air, Takes's M4 rifle jammed,
and he worked to clear it. There's a protocol for this, and just like everything in the Army, it's rendered into an acronym, S.P.O.R.T.S.: Slap the
magazine to make sure it's seated, Pull the charging handle all the way
back, Observe ejection of shell or round, Release the charging handle to
feed in a new bullet, Tap the forward assist, Shoot.

As Takes began to work the procedure, Albert looked up at him from
the ground and started yelling. "Sports! Sports!" The admonishment
was maybe the last thing Takes needed to hear. He shot Albert a look
just as an enemy bullet caught his upper right arm through the bicep,
burning as it tore through. Albert watched his squad leader as if in slow
motion, like a car wreck, as his expression turned from pissed off to
stunned.

"Gosh, they still see us," Takes said, shot now through both arms.

The sun was starting to drop below the mountains, and a merciful
dusk and eventual darkness was minutes away. Takes looked around
and knew what he needed to do: get them both over to a small tree at
the edge of the cliff that might offer some cover.

He dragged Albert with his left arm and kept firing his M4 with his
right. Albert tried to help by pushing himself along with his right leg.
Gradually they moved up an embankment to the tree.

Takes connected with Begaye, who was several yards higher on the
rock face. "I'm good. But Albert, I just put a tourniquet on him because

he got another gunshot on the other leg. We could use some fucking air support, dude."

→  ←

Back at Bella they were beginning to grasp the gravity of what was going on at the ambush. Staff Sergeant David Dzwik pulled an all-nighter Thursday monitoring radio traffic, while Ferrara and his team headed out to Aranas; Dzwik stayed on duty Friday too, and by early afternoon he looked exhausted. Once they got word that the patrol was heading home, the platoon sergeant, Shane Stockard, told him to get some sleep. Dzwik headed for his bunk, relieved that the worst was over. Before he even closed his eyes someone burst in with word of the ambush. He raced back to the tactical operations center and resumed his vigil at the radio. Stockard was in overall command of the base with Ferrara gone, and he ordered that the 120mm mortar start firing onto the high ground above the ambush site.

Chris Choay had moved his scouts from their hide over Aranas to a point where they could track Ferrara and his men heading down the Waigal Valley. They could hear the ambush gunfire erupt just north of them and beyond a ridge from their new position. He set off with his men on the fastest route into the Waigal to join the fight.

At Blessing the Chosen Company commander, Captain Matt Myer, was in his office when word of the attack came. He rushed to the TOC. Lieutenant Colonel Bill Ostlund had just entered battalion headquarters when he heard and started monitoring the radio traffic.

But for the moment, because of the geography of mountains and valleys, it was the soldiers far up in the OP1 outpost on a ledge overlooking Bella who were best positioned to communicate by radio with the men under fire. The senior enlisted officer there was Staff Sergeant Joshua Salazar. They had already heard briefly from Kyle White when he initially reported the ambush. Takes now was in contact. OP1 was in near-continuous, if sometimes broken communication with Begaye.

Reports of heavy casualties were coming in fast, and the men at OP1, huddled around the radio, reacted with shock, anger, and expletives.

What followed was a cumbersome bucket-brigade of electronic communication: Dzwik, at the command center in Bella, feeding Salazar up at OP1 questions and commands to relay to Begaye and White at the ambush site. Responses from the field followed the same arduous path in reverse back to Dzwik, who was both briefing and, in turn, taking orders from Myer and Ostlund by radio or telephone from Blessing. In the communication center at OP1 was a receiver dedicated to intercepting enemy radio conversations. There were almost constant verbal exchanges in a foreign language coming from the receiver. It added a disturbing element to the drama playing out at OP1: hearing the voices of the men trying to kill their friends even as the paratroopers at the outpost were trying to save them.

Mortar rounds out of Bella started to hit the high ground around the ambush, but it was basically blind firing because they couldn't tell precisely where the enemy was yet. Artillery rounds from a pair of 155mm cannons at Blessing were soon employed. Under Dzwik's direction, Salazar, at OP1, pushed Begaye for his GPS location, or grid, so command would at least know where the paratroopers were located and could adjust their fire.

"Hey, are you guys good on the 120s? You still need 120s? I need a grid where you're at so we don't blow you up, over," Salazar radioed.

Begaye delivered the coordinates, certain that the enemy was firing down on them from the Afghan security guard outpost high up on the ridge above, the place they called Lone Ranger.

"They're moving right above us," he told OP1. He wanted artillery fire concentrated there.

Salazar asked Begaye if he could spot where the 120mm mortar rounds were landing and let him know how to adjust that fire so the enemy could be more effectively targeted.

"I can't," Begaye said. "They got us pinned down. I got hit in the arm."

The frustration at the mountain outpost was palpable as the soldiers heard the 120mm mortar firing from down below in Bella, sending rounds someplace they prayed was near the jihadist gunmen.

"I hope you fucking die, bastards," one soldier muttered under his breath.

In all of the chaos of the moment there was one piece of information commanders wanted to know more than any other: What had they lost? How many dead and how many wounded? The Rock Battalion had seen a total of ten men killed in combat up to that point. On two occasions—in the Korengal Valley when Sal Giunta's heroism was on display October 25 and in the Watapor Valley to the east on July 5—the battalion had lost two soldiers in one event. That was the most at any single time.

So how bad is this?

Dzwik relayed the request through OP1. He knew the men out there were in the middle of a gunfight, but he wanted a casualty report now.

"It doesn't have to be in so many sad details. Just quick."

Begaye was the first to respond, sounding impatient and out of breath, still trying to fire his weapon and brace the wounded Kalenits up in the little cave.

"There's a fucking KIA," he said, meaning Langevin. "I don't know about the rest of us. We got knocked down. We're at the bottom of the fucking river."

From where he sat with Kalenits, Begaye put out a call for anyone else on the patrol to respond, specifically Mersman or Roque.

"Anybody copy, over?"

Kyle White answered. The fact that he was on the air at all was a small miracle. His own radio had been shot up, and it turned out Kain Schilling's was too. White had found Bocks's radio and was just about ready to key the handset when a bullet came through the canopy on the hand mic, knocking it out of his hand.

Really? Come on.

Somehow in all the chaos White caught sight of some of Matt Ferrara's gear just down the trail at the end of the spur. He could see his platoon leader's helmet and his assault pack. Once again White ventured out from under the thin canopy of leaves where he and Schilling and now Bocks had some concealment, and he low-crawled about fifteen feet to find the lieutenant face down in a pool of blood, his rifle still cradled in his arms.

He checked Matt's pulse. Nothing. He headed back. Schilling had always been paranoid about a neck wound and was lying there with his helmet pushed back to cover the back of his neck when an enemy round came through the canopy of leaves and tore through the back of his leg, shattering the large femur bone and exiting out of his knee. He cried out in pain.

"I'm shot again!"

"I know, I saw it," White yelled back and made his way over. He had seen Schilling's pants rip and flare open when the bullet hit. Out of tourniquets, he pulled out his belt and wrapped it around Schilling's leg above the wound as blood poured out.

"Hey, this is going to hurt."

"Whatever, just do it."

White tightened it down hard, which seemed to stem the bleeding. He turned back to Bocks's radio and finally managed to get it to work without the hand mic, and when Begaye called out for anyone to respond, White gave his casualty report.

"We got one KIA. Three wounded."

Begaye told him to take charge at his location. "What you need to do is assess casualties, roger?"

"Roger."

Dzwik, on the radio from Bella, wanted to know if the dead and wounded were all American. He was told that they were, and radio communications fell silent for a few seconds.

"Who is controlling the fight, over?" Dzwik asked.

Salazar up at OP1 said that was not entirely clear. He was in contact with Begaye and White but was not at all certain where they were in relation to each other. And there was no word at all yet from Sergeant Jeff Mersman.

It had become starkly evident to commanders just how out of control the situation was. In a half hour the sun would set, and they did not know where all their people were, who was missing, and who was alive.

"They need to find out what the situation is. You need to keep trying to get coms with 1-1 Bravo," Dzwik told OP1, referring to Mersman's call sign.

Begaye said he had no communication with Mersman, adding that the sergeant had been nearest to White in the column when the fighting broke out.

Up on the goat trail, under the canopy of leaves, Marine Sergeant Bocks lost consciousness. Within minutes his breathing stopped. Schilling, through the pain of his own two wounds, watched Bocks slip away, the first time he had seen someone die.

→ ←

Ten minutes after sunset Navy F18 fighters from an aircraft carrier out in the Indian Ocean showed up, and Dzwik, at the Bella headquarters, was working with the soldiers up at OP1, trying to provide the jets some targets. Begaye was in contact, doing his best to assist while also complaining that he couldn't stop the bleeding from Kalenits's wound.

"I'm trying to apply pressure on it!"

White came up on the radio, saying he couldn't see where Mersman was, couldn't really move anywhere, and his GPS has been destroyed in the fighting.

There was still chaos even as the sun was setting. The enemy suddenly broadened its attack. Teams of gunmen were high on the eastern ridgeline opposite Bella. Anticipating the Americans would try to rush reinforcements to the ambush, other jihadist fighters had pinned down Staff Sergeant Choay and his scout team as they tried to make their way into the Waigal Valley. More were shooting down across the valley at OP1.

"Hey, they're up there on that fuckin' mountain over there!" Juan Diaz, one of the paratroopers at the outpost, yelled out. The mountain-top observation post was bristling with weaponry, and in seconds soldiers were firing every major weapon at any enemy fighters they could see. Stephen Johnson, an Army specialist, blasted away with the MK19 automatic grenade launcher. Private First Class Ken Turner weighed in with a light machine gun. Specialists Juan Diaz and Tom Hanna took the M240. And Gabriel Green manned the .50 caliber. The outpost erupted in a cacophony of weapons fire. Over in a corner Peanut the puppy cowered and squealed in a high-pitched yowl.

Gabe Green had taken over communications with the ambushed patrol and Bella.

"We're trying to get the Mark-19 rocking, over," he radioed Dzwik.

Dzwik gave Green his orders: keep engaging the enemy to kill or force them away. But above all, Dzwik said, maintain contact with the wounded at the ambush site.

"You are the lifeline for that patrol out there."

Word reached Begaye that OP1 was under attack. He could hear machine guns and the grenade launcher firing in the background over the radio transmission. His first thought was that the ambushers would use the opportunity to reload, reorganize, and then sweep back through the battlefield to kill or capture anyone they found.

"We need that fucking air support," Begaye told his comrade over the radio.

Up at OP1 Specialist Stephen Johnson spotted enemy fighters behind the outpost, and Green opened up for seven seconds with the .50 caliber.

"There ain't nobody there no more," he hollered out with a note of triumph, then cut loose for another nine seconds for good measure.

For eighteen minutes this collateral battle raged around Bella. The paratroopers at OP1 focused on targets along the ridge across the Waigal Valley—at an enemy fighter spotted carrying RPGs or at muzzle flashes in the trees—and tore loose with machine guns or the MK19, its rhythmic BOOM-BOOM-BOOM followed by an echo of explosions as the grenades detonated on distant impact. Shouted commands punctuated the combat: "Light that place up where they were shooting before! . . . Ammo! Ammo! Ammo! . . . Shoot that motherfucker!"

Salazar, Green, and OP1 could see that soldiers manning their guard posts down at Bella were firing toward Afghan National Army soldiers making their way along another trail on the opposite ridge.

"Bella, cease fire! . . . All battle stations, cease fire!" Green shouted over the radio.

With the fight around Bella finally winding down, headquarters was asking again who was alive and accounted for out at the ambush site.

"I need a good status on casualties, over. I need a really good status on casualties, over. I need a really good sit-rep," Dzwik told OP1.

Begaye gave what numbers he had. But his biggest concern, as he sat in the dark at the ambush site, was the fact that they couldn't get up and move. Too many of the wounded were hit in the legs. He worried the enemy would walk up on them and kill any Americans they could find. Jets could not maneuver in this narrow canyon, and Begaye couldn't help wondering why they hadn't sent in attack helicopters yet—the Apaches.

In the meantime he started sending through possible target locations for GPS-guided bombing missions for a B1 orbiting above. All of the bombs had to be dropped several hundred yards away to make sure the wounded paratroopers weren't hit. OP1 relayed the targets, and the jets responded in seconds. The night sky erupted in explosions of white light from the bombs, and the Chosen Few at the outpost sent up a cheer.

→ ←

Fifty miles south at a large US airbase in Jalalabad, Afghanistan, the crew of a pair of Blackhawk medevac helicopters had just finished a brisk game of whiffle ball on the tarmac when an alert came in for a rescue mission in the Waigal Valley.

The crews from the 82nd Combat Aviation Brigade were veteran combat flyers, medics, and crew chiefs who had spent nearly a year in Afghanistan plucking wounded American and coalition troops off battlefields and delivering them to field hospitals. They flew the Skull and Crossbones over their headquarters at Jalalabad. Their most experienced pilot, Chris Ryan, a thoughtful, easygoing chief warrant officer there, was marking his thirty-fifth birthday. He was a true child of military flight: his father was a retired airman, and Chris was born in a military hospital on the grounds of Andrews Air Force Base outside Washington, DC.

They were led by twenty-seven-year-old Army Captain Clayton Horney (pronounced Hore-NAY), who grew up in Tucson, Arizona, fell in love with helicopters and the adrenalin rush of air rescue when he was a high school senior, and got an internship as a tag-along with a state police helicopter crew. While his classmates were earthbound, Horney was flying several times a week on observation and rescue missions.

The senior flight medic was Staff Sergeant Peter Rohrs, who, at thirty-one, was older by a decade than many of the men he worked to keep alive during his third combat deployment. Like others in the Army who grew up knowing they wanted one day to be a soldier or a pilot, Rohrs always wanted to be a medic. Whereas others drew inspiration from cinematic portrayals of fighting men, Rohrs liked the tough, ever-caring "Doc," consumed with ensuring the wounded came home—if not entirely in one piece, at least alive.

He had treated hundreds of casualties airlifted off the battlefields of Afghanistan. Not only had he been deposited on battlefields under dangerous conditions to treat wounded soldiers and prepare them to be hoisted and evacuated, he also took considerable pains to teach other medics what he had learned.

But nothing that he or Horney or Ryan or any of the others on their team had done before—or would do again—would match the harrowing experience they faced that night over the Waigal Valley.

When Clayton Horney arrived for his tour of duty he pulled data on medevac missions across Afghanistan, using as a metric the frequency of hoist missions. These are often the most hazardous assignments because they are, by definition, the rescue means of last resort when the wounded are so inaccessible in the mountains that the only way of collecting them is to pull them up by cable.

He found that medevac missions flown into mountainous Kunar and Nuristan provinces out of the Jalalabad Air Base had the largest number of hoist missions, and Horney requested his platoon be assigned there. No sooner did they arrive in January to replace crews attached to the 10th Mountain Division than they learned just how treacherous the missions could be. During the transition between the crews, when Horney and his men flew some missions with the 10th Mountain medevac crews, they saw how pilots would dodge and jink their way through narrow valleys to be hard targets for enemy gunmen.

Horney pushed for his teams to conduct hoist-training missions in the valleys near Jalalabad during their down time. Over and over they would practice lowering and raising the hoist cable next to cliffs or in narrow valleys in the day or night, using night-vision goggles, all so they could grow increasingly confident in steadying their seven-ton aircraft and using the hoist even when rotary blades were only several feet from a rock face.

But the mission on this night was shaping up to be even tougher than what they had practiced. During the preflight briefing Horney and Ryan recognized the location. Ryan, working with Rohrs, had pulled casualties out of Ranch House after the battle in August, and he knew well those knife-edged ridges and narrow canyons.

Even worse, it would be a moonless night. Their NODs were a real asset, but the goggles operated by amplifying ambient light. Without even a sliver of moon in the sky and with high mountains obscuring many of the stars, the view through their NODs would be scintillated like a snowy image on a television screen. By the time they were wheels-up in Jalalabad heading out on the mission, the sun had already set.

→  ←

As darkness approached at the ambush site, enemy fire had finally started to dwindle off, and the cluster of casualties around Staff Sergeant Begaye was huddling more tightly together. Derry and Johnson worked their way down the steep slope, startling Takes, who was pulling security in that direction and almost shot them. Johnson was growing weaker, and they got to a place where Derry could administer saline solution through a needle into Johnson's arm. Derry had been assigned to carry a medical bag with additional supplies, except that after all the gunfire and shrapnel, the bag was riddled. All but one of the IV bags was drained empty. As the liquid dripped into the sergeant's right arm, he almost immediately began to feel a little better. He eventually wound up near the creek at the bottom of the valley next to Albert. It was getting cold, and both of them were covered up with ponchos. Albert thought it was the coldest night of his life.

The wounded men were growing thirsty. Takes had given Albert his single IV bag, and the soldier drank it down. As night fell, Begaye pulled Kalenits out of the small cave and passed him down to Takes. The two men sat awkwardly on a steep section, their backs against a large rock. Kalenits had his right hand braced on Takes's wounded left shoulder for support and was pleading for water.

"I'm so thirsty."

From where Takes was braced against the mountain, he couldn't stretch the spout of his CamelBak far enough to reach Kalenits. So he improvised. He sucked in a mouthful of water and then, through pursed lips, launched a stream of it in a small arc through the air toward

Kalenits's open, waiting mouth. Kalenits lapped it up. Some of it spilled onto his face.

Takes, his mind always drifting toward dry humor, couldn't decide whether the whole thing looked like a mother bird feeding her hatchling or a gay porn scene.

Derry, nearby, cracked up. Kalenits was loving it.

"Oh, thank you. This is the best water ever. I appreciate it, bud."

They were a wrecked bunch. Derry had a bullet graze to his right shoulder and shrapnel up and down his left side, with a chunk of steel embedded in his left triceps—and he was the least damaged. Begaye was shot in his right arm, Takes in both arms. The three of them were the only ones still capable of fighting. Both of Johnson's legs had been hit by bullets and shrapnel. Albert had four wounds in three limbs and couldn't walk. And Kalenits had the gaping gunshot hole to his backside along with a shattered pelvis and considerable loss of blood.

They were all getting cold, but Kalenits was freezing and kept telling Takes, "I'm going to die. I'm going to die." Each time Takes told him to shut up. He pulled a poncho out of his assault bag and wrapped Kalenits up in it.

"You're not going to die. You're fine."

Some six hundred feet above them, up on the goat trail, where Kyle White and Kain Schilling were hunkered down, a night of interminable waiting had only begun. Schilling's greatest fear was losing consciousness and then losing his life, as he had just seen happen to Bocks. His plan to stay awake and stay alive was unorthodox—he kept bumming cigarettes from White.

→  ←

As the medevac helicopters lifted off from the US airbase in Jalalabad, each aircraft had four men aboard. Chris Ryan's copilot was Chief Warrant Officer 2 Christopher Carson. They were the "two Chrises." Carson was born and raised in Frederick, Maryland, and liked to fly with a

99-cent Ricky Bobby Novelty Slogan Car Air Freshener from the movie *Talladega Nights* hanging inside the cockpit. Ryan had Peter Rohrs in the back as his medic, and the crew chief was Specialist Timothy "Matt" Johns, a native of South Dakota. Horney was flying with First Lieutenant Eric Doe, a New Yorker who was the novice pilot on the mission and deployed shortly after the birth of his son, Gavin. In the back of their aircraft was the medic, Sergeant Shon Crowley, and the crew chief, Sergeant Isaac Johnson.

From Jalalabad the most direct route for Horney and his medevac helicopters was straight north. But that would require flying over soaring mountains and through the deadly Korengal Valley, so they headed northeast up the Kunar Valley along the Pakistan border and then west through the Pech to Blessing at the base of the Waigal. It was a forty-five-minute trip.

Both helicopters touched down temporarily at Blessing, keeping their engines running, as a pair of Apache helicopters flew ahead to attack any enemy fighters they spotted in the dark with their night vision and to prepare the ambush site for medevac helicopters. Just shy of two hours after the ambush began, the rotary attack aircraft that Begaye had been begging for finally arrived.

"As soon as we can clear the enemy off that high ground we can get the medevacs in. They're just waiting for that," Dzwik told OP1.

In minutes the Apaches, each with a two-member crew, were firing at suspected enemy positions high on the southern ridgeline across from the ambush site. The weapons operator used a heavy "chain" gun slung on a swiveling mount under the cockpit that could be aimed merely by the gunner turning his head in the direction of the target. The chain is a broad belt that feeds 30mm cannon rounds into the gun. The rounds don't hit as hard as those fired by Air Force A10 jets, but they can still churn the landscape into a cauldron of atomized rock and earth.

It was 6:05 P.M., and the moonless sky was in full, oily blackness. The wounded paratroopers had been waiting a long time for deliverance.

"We need those medevacs over here," a weary Begaye radioed Specialist Ken Turner up at OP1. "I got guys bleeding to death."

They told him it would be five more minutes, and he passed that along to White by radio. The young Army specialist wanted some direction. As the shooting died down, Afghan Army soldiers from farther back on the trail had been making their way into his position. By now he had ten of them gathered there, half of them were wounded. Close by was an eleventh Afghan soldier who'd been killed. At Begaye's urging, White had formed the Afghans into a defensive perimeter around their location. When the helicopters arrived, he asked Begaye who should get on.

There would be limited space on the Blackhawk. The staff sergeant told White to get his wounded and himself on the copter and make sure the bodies of the dead Americans went too.

"We're not leaving anybody behind, roger?"

Down in the creek bed Begaye and Takes had set up their own defense. There wasn't much to work with, so the plan was simple: Takes would keep watch toward the west, Derry toward the south across the valley, and Begaye to the east.

→ ←

At Blessing the medevac crews took on two more medical personnel from Rock Battalion—a physician's assistant and a medic, one for each helicopter. They would need the extra hands in what was shaping up to be a complex mission.

Two and a quarter hours after the fighting started, the medevac helicopters finally arrived over the wounded Chosen Few. The biggest problem was finding people. And fuel. The Blackhawks hold about two and half hours of fuel. Pilots usually give themselves a thirty-minute buffer, so they try to ensure a pit stop after two hours. It took forty-five minutes to an hour just to reach the casualties on this night. From there the nearest refueling base was about twenty minutes away. That would give them maybe forty-five minutes over the rescue zone before they would have to leave.

They zeroed in on Begaye and his casualties thanks to the staff sergeant providing Bella his exact coordinates. But White's GPS device was broken, so his location could only be guessed at.

As Ryan flew his Blackhawk down toward Begaye, his crew spotted the casualties. The rescue effort got an unexpected break in the darkness: a burning bush near the goat trail, evidently set fire in the attack, could be used as a landmark and also provide some ambient light for Ryan's night-vision goggles. Rohrs was quickly lowered down to a spot on the creek bed near Albert, who watched him materialize out of the blackness and touch down nearby, like some angel of mercy.

*Thank God this guy is here.*

Horney, in the other helicopter, orbited for about twenty minutes. The airspace was getting crowded in and over the narrow canyon, with Ryan's medevac helicopter hovering low over the first group of casualties and two Apache helicopters on the prowl for any enemy fighters. When Horney finally began his search for White and Schilling, he used some rough coordinates Chosen Company had provided. But he and his crew couldn't see them. They continued their search, moving up the canyon, but eventually they realized they had gone too far. They simply couldn't find the second group of wounded.

Rohrs finally solved the mystery from the ground. Working with Begaye, he got a better understanding of where White and the second group of casualties were located up on the goat trail and passed along more explicit directions using the burning bush, which was slightly west, as a reference. Chief Warrant Officer Chris Ryan, in the helicopter above, relayed to Horney, "Hey, if you find the burning bush, look up and to the right about two hundred meters or so, and that's where the next casualties are supposed to be."

Horney and his crew finally spotted White, Schilling, and the bodies of Marine Sergeant Bocks and Lieutenant Ferrara along with the Afghan soldiers huddled there. They noted the precise coordinates. But both aircraft were already running low on fuel, and before they could take on all of the casualities—a slow, methodical process that eats up a lot of time—they would need to refill their tanks. The nearest place for that was a US base in Asadabad at the far east end of the Pech Valley, about twenty minutes away.

Word of another delay was relayed to the paratroopers, who were stunned.

*The medevacs have only just arrived, and they're already leaving—and without the casualties?*

On the goat trail above, Schilling was listless from the cold and the loss of blood. It was getting harder for him to focus his eyes, and he was starting to fade in and out of consciousness. The first hour or so after he was wounded he had assured himself that help would arrive soon. They were so badly shot up that he was confident commanders would waste no time getting them out of there. The thought helped keep him calm at first after the shooting died off. But as time wore on without rescue and he grew weaker, the delay made less and less sense.

Down below, where Rohrs was already on the ground, there was time to take one patient, and the decision was made to hoist out Kalenits. The medic prepared the soldier to be lifted out using a rescue strop, a kind of upside-down horse collar that extended under Kalenits's arms. Rohrs had given him a shot of pain killer, fentanyl, and by the time the paratrooper was on his way up he was in a genial mood.

"I love you guys! I'll be back!" Kalenits called to the other wounded soldiers as he dangled from the horse collar and a crew chief reeled him up. "I'll be back! I promise! I love you!"

The bonhomie didn't last. When the hoist reached the open door of the Blackhawk, Kalenits had to be pulled inside, and with his shattered pelvis, the effort to grab ahold and drag him into the aircraft was excruciating. Even over the roar of the engine and through his flight helmet, Chris Ryan, in the cockpit, could hear Kalenits screaming.

The medevac helicopters peeled away and flew out of the valley. Rohrs stayed on the ground with the wounded. As the sounds of the engines grew distant, the canyon was plunged into an eerie silence. The flight medic had been dropped into battle zones before, but he had not experienced anything like this. He pulled off his helmet after getting on the ground and, using his night goggles, worked his way from one casualty to the next, checking tourniquets, examining wounds, assessing and trying to understand what he was dealing with. His presence was reassuring to the wounded men.

"You're doing good, man," Rohrs said to Albert as he inspected his wounds and tightened his tourniquets, gently adding, "I'm going to go up and check these other guys."

→  ←

The gnawing realization back at headquarters that some of Ferrara's men were still unaccounted for sent tremors through the command. This was already shaping up to be the deadliest combat the battalion had waged, worse than any of the gun fights, skirmishes, or battles fought by any other company; worse than any single event in the Korengal Valley ten miles to the south—and the outside world was beginning to believe that was the most dangerous place in Afghanistan.

Ostlund and Myer both knew that a missing American soldier would bring an entirely new level of gravity to the situation. Back at Blessing, Ostlund began entertaining dark thoughts of his soldiers now in the hands of the enemy. He could see their faces, knew their names, and understood they must be scared to death. If he had dead and wounded on the battlefield, as horrible as that was, he could do something about it. He could send in reinforcements and call in air support. But a paratrooper in enemy hands was utterly out of his control. A captured American soldier would be unprecedented. Although several American service members had been abducted and released or killed in Iraq, nothing like that had so far happened in the Afghanistan war.

Dzwik, over the radio, kept pushing for the walking wounded to do something about this—go out and search for Jeff Mersman or anyone else they hadn't yet seen. Begaye and Takes, down at the creek bed, and White, up on the goat trail, were getting pissed. Headquarters just didn't seem to get it: every last one of them was wounded. They had dead comrades nearby. They were out of ammunition—black on ammo, as soldiers called it—and they were separated by six hundred feet of vertical cliff. Organizing some kind of search party was ludicrous.

Dzwik then asked if they'd thought about policing up spare ammo from the dead. The guys at OP1 relaying the messages felt caught in the middle. Green passed back the response to Dzwik—they were in no condition to go search for anyone.

Dzwik said he understood, but he tried once more, this time with White, asking the radioman if he could have the Afghan National soldiers who were with him help carry Schilling down to join up with Begaye and Takes. But White had already tried that on his own. Earlier he attempted to hoist Schilling onto his shoulders to see if he could carry his wounded buddy down the slope to the creek bed. But Schilling had cried out in pain, so White gave up on the idea. Later he moved out on his own just to see if he might find any missing Americans. But again, Schilling called out for him in the dark and he dutifully returned.

Schilling "is doing badly. He needs to get out of here now," White told OP1. Moreover, half the Afghan soldiers were wounded too.

Dzwik, now sufficiently chastised, finally dropped it.

"Just thought I'd ask. Just trying to paint a picture of it . . ."

With most of the Afghan troops accounted for at White's position, the thought occurred to Bella: What about their US Marine mentor, Sergeant Phil Bocks? What happened to him? Dzwik decided to ask directly, using Bocks's call sign, Joker 2-2.

"He's KIA," White said.

This news took a few minutes for everyone at Bella and back at Blessing to absorb—the very first confirmed name linked to a dead US service member. With the uncomfortable topic finally broached, the command decided to find out all the names of those Americans known to be killed.

"Go ahead and send the names of our KIAs," Dzwik said.

Takes was first to respond.

"Specialist Langevin."

The paratroopers at OP1 were stunned and reacted privately with each other, off the radio.

The night before the patrol left, most of the men fighting for their lives had been up at OP1 playing poker—Langevin, Lancour, Mersman, and Derry. Now Langevin was gone.

"He has a daughter on the way," one of them said.

"Why the fuck did they have to do this stupid-ass, fucking mission, man?" Juan Diaz said in disgust.

"Hey, what the fuck, dude. A fuckin' shura could have been held down here, dog. There's no fuckin' reason why we had to go up there," said Green.

White reported the dead Americans at his location using the call sign for his platoon commander and the acronym for Embedded Training Team, Bocks's assignment as a mentor to the Afghan Troops.

"Chosen 1-6, Lieutenant Ferrara. Second one is the ETT, Joker 2-2. Not sure of his name," White said.

Back at Blessing the news confirmed what Matt Myer suspected from the start: if Ferrara had been alive, it would have been his voice coming in over the radio all these long hours.

A flurry of communications from headquarters followed to nail down who was alive and who was missing. The call signs for those un-accounted for came in absent any names, but it was clear that among the missing were Sergeant Jeff Mersman, Private First Class Joe Lancour, and a medic. The commanders might have known which medic was as-signed to this patrol, but the guys up at OP1—relaying and listening to the radio traffic—weren't sure and started guessing. Which medic went out on this screwed-up mission? Was it Roque?

The fact that there were missing soldiers complicated air support. The Apache helicopters and an Air Force AC130 gunship that would soon follow were equipped with heat sensors that could detect human

The Waigal River Valley

Image taken from a terrain map of Waigal Valley, showing the river valley running north and south, with many deep east-west valleys branching off.

*All of the photographs in this section have been graciously supplied by the paratroopers and families of the Chosen Few.*

The steep terrain that challenged the Chosen Few.

RIGHT:
Combat Outpost Bella, at the "bottom of a Dixie Cup"

Camp Blessing, Rock Battalion and Chosen Company headquarters

Observation Post 1, or OP1, high above Bella

Lieutenant Colonel William Ostlund

First Lieutenant Matthew Ferrara

Sergeant Ryan Pitts (left)
and Sergeant Israel Garcia

The Ranch House building,
which gave its name to the
mountainside outpost.

The uphill trek to Post 3
at Ranch House

The "vertical village" of Aranas

RIGHT:
Sergeant First Class Matthew Kahler

Staff Sergeant Conrad Begaye (left) and Staff Sergeant David Dzwik
in a candid moment at Ranch House. Begaye would earn a Silver
Star at the ambush. Dzwik would later become platoon sergeant
for 2nd Platoon at Wanat.

First Lieutenant Matthew Ferrara (left) and Sergeant Jared Gilmore stand before a burning structure during the abandonment of Ranch House.

Staff Sergeant Conrad Begaye's squad on the front steps of the "Ponderosa-like" Ranch House. *Back row, from left:* Sergeant Jose Canales Jr., Specialist Samuel Huxford, Sergeant Kyle Dirkintis (medic), and Sergeant Mike Johnson. *Front row, from left:* Private First Class Adam Spotankski, Private First Class Gregg Rauwolf, Begaye, Private First Class Kyle White, and Private First Class Sean Langevin.

First Sergeant Scott Beeson

Specialist Kain Schilling

Sergeant First Class Shane Stockard

BELOW: Private First Class Joe Lancour cooking up one of his specialties at OP1 above Bella.

Private First Class
Sean Langevin

Staff Sergeant
Kyle Silvernale posing
with a feathered friend
at Bella.

*From left*, Specialist Pruitt Rainey, Specialist Jonathan Ayers, Specialist Jason
Bogar, Specialist Gunnar Zwilling, and Specialist Chris McKaig

Sergeant Brian Hissong (left) and Specialist Mike Denton at OP1

Sergeant Mike Santiago behind a
.50-caliber machine gun at OP1
above Bella.

Paratrooper mascot
Peanut at OP1

Sergeant James Takes on November 9, 2007, the day of the ambush

Specialist Kyle White takes a break along the cliff trail minutes before the ambush.

Minutes before the ambush, three paratroopers take a break; *from left*, Sergeant Jeff Mersman, Private First Class Joe Lancour, and Private First Class Scott Derry. Note the steep cliff.

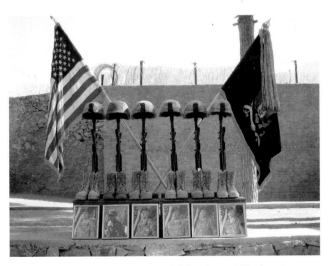

Six combat crosses at a memorial for those killed at the November 9 ambush

Emotional paratroopers at memorial service for Sergeant First Class Matthew Kahler; *from left*, Staff Sergeant Lucas Gonzales, Sergeant Ryan Pitts, and First Lieutenant Jonathan Brostrom

Looking southwest over Wanat. Note the agricultural terraces to the west, the flat area within the village where Combat Outpost Kahler would be built and the road running south toward battalion and company headquarters at Blessing.

Captain Matt Myer (left) with First Lieutenant Jonathan Brostrom

Grease board list of personalities Chosen Few paratroopers picked to star in a movie about the anticipated battle to come in Wanat

Specialist Sergio Abad near the 120mm mortar at Wanat

Looking northeast into Topside a day or so before the Wanat battle, the mulberry tree (center) that enemy fighters targeted with RPG rounds. To the right is the LRAS surveillance device and the enclosure where Sergeant Ryan Pitts made his solitary stand. Behind and to the left of the mulberry tree is the sleeping terrace (where Specialist Jason Bogar is shown napping) where at least five paratroopers were killed.

A photo taken before the battle of what would become the casualty collection center in the southeast corner of Topside. This was originally Specialist Jason Bogar's fighting position. His SAW (squad automatic weapon) is set up to the left.

Looking west across Combat Outpost Kahler toward 2nd Squad's position after the battle. The bazaar, still burning, is in the background with the agricultural terraces beyond where Topside was located.

The burned-out carcass of the armored TOW-missile truck destroyed by enemy fire at Wanat.

In the days after the Wanat battle, a grieving Sergeant Mike Santiago preferred to stay off to himself, avoiding others.

Staff Sergeant Erich Phillips shown here receiving the Distinguished Service Cross. The Chosen Few received an extraordinary number of valor medals: 2 Medals of Honor, 2 Distinguished Service Crosses, 12 Silver Stars, 34 Bronze Stars, and 66 Purple Hearts.

forms and wreak havoc on anything moving in the dark. But given the possibility that Mersman, Roque, and Lancour might be out there alive and together, the pilots couldn't take the chance of killing their own men. Shane Stockard raised this concern over the radio. Unless Begaye and his men could provide explicit directions on where renewed enemy fire was coming from, air crews would be advised not to shoot at figures moving through the canyon.

"The three MIAs could be walking around as a group right now," the platoon sergeant warned.

As the medevac helicopters headed back to refuel, Begaye's worst fear seemed to be unfolding. Ever since sundown he had worried that the enemy might come sweeping through to finish them off. Earlier, when the copters were overhead, he spotted a figure armed with an AK47 approaching from the east. He summoned Rohrs, but the gunman receded back into the darkness. Then when the aircraft departed, the armed figure approached again, this time waving a flashlight, and Begaye could see he wasn't stopping.

*Oh crap, here we go. . . .*

The paratrooper called over to Rohrs a second time. "Hey man, there's this dude coming."

Begaye yelled out a warning. The man was answering something back, but they couldn't understand him. More importantly, he wouldn't drop his rifle as he walked up on them, despite their commands.

"If he comes any closer, shoot him," Rohrs told Begaye.

"Get down! Get down!" Begaye yelled at the gunman.

From where Albert was lying nearby, he could barely see Begaye pointing his rifle at someone and heard the man answering in his foreign tongue. Albert couldn't see much of anything and didn't want Begaye to take any chances.

"Shoot! Shoot! Shoot!" Albert yelled.

Begaye fired a round. Rohrs thought he actually shot the man, but Begaye was certain he only fired over his head. The Afghan dropped onto the ground in a sitting position.

Rohrs moved out to him, took away his rifle, searched him, and checked him for wounds. He had a gunshot in the lower abdomen. Rohrs worked to control the bleeding and then dragged the man back into the perimeter, where they put flex cuffs on him.

At White's location up on the trail they had their own intruder—an old man with a full white beard and a bald head had climbed to their position. Wearing a vest full of ammunition and armed with a rifle, he proceeded back down the trail toward Aranas, literally stepping over Schilling, who was certain the old man would execute him with a few shots. The radio operator closed his eyes, tried to appear dead, and hoped for the best. Within seconds Ferrara's interpreter, Alex Drany, who was huddled nearby with some Afghan soldiers, shot the insurgent to death with his AK47.

Down at the river bottom Rohrs kept caring for his wounded, moving from one to the other, listening and lending comfort. In many ways it was the purest combat medicine he'd ever practiced. He was the only medic—in fact, the only man on the battlefield who wasn't wounded. They were all exhausted, bleeding, and cut off from the world, more than aware that the medevac helicopters had come and gone. Rohrs realized his job was not only to care for their wounds but also to keep reassuring them that help would return.

Rohrs asked Takes if he was in good enough shape to lend a hand.

"Yeah, I'm good."

It wasn't until later that Rohrs spotted the blood on Takes's shirt and, stopping to examine him, was shocked by what he saw.

"Dude, you're shot twice."

"Yeah, I kind of figured that."

The hardest part for Rohrs was denying the wounded the painkillers they kept asking for. Rohrs had given Kalenits that shot of fentanyl, but that was because he was about to be airlifted. There on the battlefield nothing was settled, and if they came under attack before the medevac copters returned, every one of them would need to be alert enough to fight. Rohrs did the next best thing: he pulled out a can of mouth tobacco his wife had sent him. He could see their eyes light up. He passed it around and they all took a dip.

Then gunshots rang out from the mountains above. Begaye was certain it was the enemy trying to goad them into firing back so their muzzle flashes would reveal their position. He made sure his men held their fire. The shots seemed to be coming from the old Afghan security post known as Lone Ranger, tucked high on the ridge over their heads.

Back at Bella they were starting to zero in on the security post with 120mm mortar rounds. At about 7:15 P.M. a single shell arced across the valley and landed short, just below the cliff-side trail where White and Schilling were holed up. It hit about one hundred yards away from where Begaye and his wounded team were huddled down on the stream bed. It was so close that White could hear the hiss of the round just before it detonated in a massive explosion against the mountain. The rock face of the cliff below White absorbed most of the impact, but he could still see shards from the splintered shell, the size of his hand and red hot, shooting through the blackness right past him.

Neither he nor Schilling were hit, but the explosion was so close that the concussive wave knocked White to the ground and left him feeling dizzy and sick to his stomach, symptomatic of a brain concussion—potentially his second of the day after losing consciousness early in the fight from the too-close blast of an RPG.

Begaye felt it too. His first thought was for White—he knew it had to have been close and tried to make contact by radio. Several disturbing seconds passed before White's voice came online. He sounded shaky. Forty seconds after the explosion Begaye was the first to notify headquarters.

"Somebody just dropped a fucking round on us! You just hit 1-6 Romeo!" he screamed, referring to White's radio call sign.

The paratroopers at OP1 immediately called on the mortar crew to cease fire and radioed White, asking if everyone was okay. White reported no one was hit, just woozy. Snatches of his radio transmission at times carried as far as Blessing, where Ostlund and his officers listened, riveted. How does the twenty-year-old paratrooper sound? Is he still with us? Can he manage this crisis all by himself?

At 8 P.M., more than four hours after the start of the ambush that left every American on the patrol dead, wounded, or missing, the refueled medevac helicopters, which had already delivered Kalenits to a field hospital, closed in to try to retrieve the remaining casualties. Kain Schilling was sliding in and out of consciousness, his breathing labored. When he was awake he begged to know how much longer before the medevacs arrived.

Salazar, back on the radio up at OP1, heard the aircraft fly past Bella and put out a call to the men at the ambush site.

"Birds just passed me. Hang on just a little bit more."

→  ←

For the medevac crews the fiercest enemy was the clock. By now the pilots knew the precise location of the two groups of casualties and the burning bush would help guide them in. The problem was that White's group up on the cliff was almost directly above where Begaye's group was waiting on the valley floor below. What separated them was about six hundred feet of sheer vertical rock face.

Routine procedure would have been for one medevac Blackhawk to go in and collect all the casualties from one location and then have the other aircraft do the same for the second location, operating consecutively. But conducting multiple hoist missions at two locations one helicopter at a time would have made an already awful night go on forever. By the time the first aircraft finished its work, so much time would have passed that both aircraft would again be required to refuel. That would mean leaving the second group of casualties to wait even longer before being rescued, which was unthinkable.

The only other alternative seemed more like a movie stunt than a strategy—do both missions simultaneously, with the Blackhawks literally stacked one on top of the other. Nothing like it had ever been imagined, much less tried—the crews had no training for that kind of rescue. The hazards were legion. The helicopters might collide. The one on the bottom would have to hold steady for an hour or more, hoisting casualties while relentlessly buffeted by rotor wash from the Blackhawk hovering above. Both pilots would need to stay right up against the mountain, their rotor blades mere feet from boulders and rocks. Any uncontrolled drift would be catastrophic.

And all of it would have to be done in a hot zone under the threat of enemy fire, with Apache helicopters circling above, looking for targets. The pilots—Horney, Ryan, Carson, and Doe—weighed their options as they headed back to the Waigal Valley after refueling.

"What's the plan, boss?" Ryan asked over the radio as they flew.

The captain was the first to broach the idea of simultaneous hoists. He couldn't see any other way if the wounded were to have a chance.

"How would you feel if I let you go in first to get set up at the bottom, and then I'm going to go get set up above you?" Horney asked Ryan.

Chief Christopher Ryan was the most experienced pilot among them, with more than two thousand hours of flight time. Clayton Horney and Chris Carson had several hundred hours each. And Eric Doe was the least experienced, with only a few hundred hours. The logical choice to handle the more difficult lower hoist, the one that would be tossed by rotor wash, was the Blackhawk piloted by the two Chrises—Carson and Ryan.

Ryan thought it best for Horney to go in first and take the high position, and then he and Carson would follow and position underneath. Once there, Ryan would have to hold the aircraft steady in a constant downdraft. Allowing it to drift even five or six feet in any direction would be dangerous.

As they re-entered the narrow valley, Clayton Horney was the first to fly into position, hovering over Kyle White on the goat trail, the rotors of the helicopter no more than five feet from the side of the mountain.

"Hey Chris, okay, I'm set," he told Ryan over the radio.

"Okay, I'm coming in."

With crew chief Johns guiding him from the back of the aircraft, Chris Ryan very slowly moved—"snuck in" was how he characterized it—the seven-ton Blackhawk until it was hovering directly over the creek-bed casualties. Right away the aircraft started to vibrate, and he knew what he was in for. It was pitching like an airliner in turbulence.

The wind shear coming off the blades of Horney's Blackhawk, buffeted by the uneven surface of the mountain and the winds coming down the valley, created an erratic pattern of turbulence that would ebb and spike, but never subside. Still, after several seconds Ryan felt he had enough control to hold it steady.

"Okay, I think I can do this," he said out loud.

Recovering casualties is slow and methodical work under the best conditions. For Rohrs, working in the creek bed, and medic Shon Crowley, up on the trail site, each wounded man or body had to be "packaged," prepared with the horse collar, and then carefully hoisted into the waiting aircraft. The lift collar then had to be removed and lowered back down. Each extraction could take fifteen minutes. With the number of dead and wounded, the process would easily run two hours.

Both medevac crews were so absorbed in their strange, double-decker hoists that they were utterly oblivious to what was happening in the black skies above them, where Apache helicopters and an Air Force AC130 Spectre gunship orbited like sentries, picking out targets in the darkness and blasting away.

On the cliff Kain Schilling had just emerged from a state of wooziness when flight medic Crowley, working with Kyle White, wrapped the horse collar around him and under his arms. He felt flush with joy as the cable pulled him skyward. Down at the creek bed Rohrs fixed the horse collar on Takes, his last patient and "package," then clipped himself onto the cable and the two rode up together.

Crammed with wounded and dead, along with bundles of weapons and gear that no one wanted to leave behind for the enemy, the two Blackhawks peeled off toward Asadabad, where they would deliver nearly all the casualties to a forward surgical hospital more than four hours after the battle began.

→ ←

The Ambush, as it would come to be known, was over for them. But not for dozens of others. Jeff Mersman and Joe Lancour were still missing. Derry had not mentioned to anyone seeing Roque's dead body. So the medic remained unaccounted for as well. Lieutenant Colonel Bill Ostlund, waiting anxiously back at Blessing for word, would remember this as the longest night of his life.

The medevac crews turned right around and headed back to the Waigal Valley. Patrols from Bella were only just getting to the outskirts of the battlefield, where several of their allied Afghan soldiers were huddled somewhere waiting to be found. Staff Sergeant Christopher Choay and his scout team had by then joined up with Staff Sergeant Kyle Silvernale and his men, and their two teams started moving together up the same trail that Ferrara's men had been walking when they were attacked. A key concern for Silvernale was whether they could find the Afghan soldiers in the darkness and make contact without being accidentally shot by them in the process.

But more than anything, Silvernale was angry at delays. He had been ready to lead a quick-reaction force out to reach his men hours earlier, but command kept him waiting, concerned about an enemy attack on Bella. By the time he was finally approaching the ambush site, he could hear over the radio that the last of the Americans had been evacuated. He knew he was getting close to the battlefield because Silvernale had heard about the burning bush over the radio, and there it was, off to the side, still refusing to extinguish, continuing to throw off light they needed for their night-vision goggles in a moonless world.

"We're coming up onto friendlies. Make sure you know what you're shooting at when you shoot," Silvernale told his men.

As he and Choay and their teams made their way along the goat trail, they came across the first real evidence of what had happened there, an abandoned squad automatic weapon lay in the middle of their path. They would learn later that it was probably Langevin's. They secured the gun and pushed on.

About another sixty-five yards down the trail they found Lester Roque's body. The medic had been shot through the head. All his medical gear was still packed away. Silvernale left part of his team to watch over Roque's remains and continued forward, intent on finding the rest of the missing.

Within another eighty yards they saw Joe Lancour. There was no doubt the lanky Michigan native had gone down fighting. Spent brass shells carpeted the ground around him. He had found a small bit of cover near a tree sprouting down off the trail, and from there he had blazed away with his beloved light machine gun, Reese Witherspoon. The enemy had tried mightily to silence him. The soldier was taking fire from at least two directions—from across the valley and from behind and above. A gunman shot Lancour through his left leg right below the knee. The paratrooper managed to apply a tourniquet to himself to stem the bleeding and keep fighting. But the enemy was relentless. He was shot through the left shoulder. An RPG exploded close enough to send shrapnel into Lancour's face, and a third bullet grazed his neck. The twenty-one-year-old soldier, evidently ignoring his wounds, fired his weapon so furiously that it finally jammed and he couldn't clear it. A fourth enemy round struck him in the right shoulder from above, and this one Lancour couldn't ignore. The bullet drilled through his right lung and his heart. It was fatal.

Silvernale and his men carried their friend's bullet-ridden body up to the goat trail to a broader area on the path where the medevac helicopter could reach him with a hoist.

Meanwhile paratroopers from Chosen Company's 2nd Platoon had been flown in from Bella along with Captain Matt Myer and First Sergeant Scott Beeson. When the men up at OP1 got word, they couldn't help rolling their eyes over the arrival of a company commander they sometimes saw as a bit too "Hooah," too soldier-serious on missions.

When Specialist Turner asked who was leading the 2nd Platoon troopers, Specialist Tom Hanna, then manning the radio, sighed and said, "Take a guess?"

"Chosen 6?" Turner asked, using Myer's radio call sign.

"Mr. Billy Badass himself," Hanna replied

Myer set up a field headquarters at the bridge that crossed the Waigal River where the goat trail from Aranas ended. He sent out Staff Sergeant Jonathan Benton and his squad to assist Silvernale and Choay on the trail and then dispatched Staff Sergeant Sean Samaroo and his squad to work their way upstream along the creek bed at the bottom of the canyon.

→ ←

By the time Horney and his medevac helicopter platoon landed at Asadabad and unloaded their casualties, they had already gone far beyond normal mission length for medevac crews. For Johns, treating or working with six casualties at once in the middle of a live war zone with mortar and RPGs exploding nearby and the enemy taking potshots, the experience was physically and emotionally draining. Once the helicopter touched down and the wounded and dead were unloaded, the veteran medic walked out behind the aircraft, took off his helmet, and took a knee on the tarmac. Shon Crowley, the medic from the other Blackhawk, soon joined him.

The reality was that they weren't finished. There were still American dead on the battlefield who needed to be recovered, and Horney and his crew were best positioned to respond and most familiar with the terrain. The platoon had exhausted all usual extensions dictated by protocol. So the commanding general of US forces in eastern Afghanistan, Major General David Rodriguez, got on the radio.

"Okay, you're extended," the two-star told them. "Stay on mission until mission completes."

For the third time the twin copters lifted off and turned toward the Waigal Valley. Chris Ryan's aircraft took the initiative on recovering the dead paratroopers, while Clayton Horney and his crew concentrated on picking up bundles of abandoned equipment. As Ryan once again held his Blackhawk in a hover over the now-familiar battlefield, Peter Rohrs prepared Lester Roque's body to be hoisted.

Rohrs was back on the ground minutes later doing the same for Joe Lancour. It was challenging because Lancour's body had been found curled around a tree and rigor mortis had set in. His arms were frozen in awkward positions. His body was hoisted to the open door of the Blackhawk piloted by the Chrises, and Johns, the crew chief, could see that the remains were slipping out. He moved quickly to grab the handle on the back of Lancour's body armor and caught it just in time, but the weight of his remains, coupled with the armor, was just too much for Johns, who was already exhausted.

"I can't hold him! He keeps falling! He's slipping! He's slipping!" Johns yelled at the top of his lungs into his headset, but he lost his grip, and Lancour's body disappeared into the darkness.

"Oh, God!"

The commotion startled Ryan and Carson, and over the intercom Ryan asked what was wrong.

"I had my hand on the strap on his body armor. But he just fell out, and I couldn't hold him."

Johns was devastated, aware of the pain it would cause the other soldiers, not to mention the difficulty of relocating the remains. The aircraft were running low on fuel, so they headed back to Asadabad. Ryan kept what happened to Lancour's remains within his aircraft, not even notifying Horney in the other Blackhawk. He was nervous that soldiers on the ground might overhear the radio conversation—that kind of news would be hard for them to take. Back at Asadabad they discussed a fourth mission to recover the dropped body. Ryan felt strongly it was unfinished business. But the medevac teams were clearly played out, and Horney decided to let a fresh crew handle it later on. By the time they arrived back at Jalalabad, they had completed more than ten hours of flying.

→  ←

Staff Sergeant Jonathan Benton from 2nd Platoon managed to push beyond where Roque and Lancour had been found. He linked up with the stranded Afghan National Army soldiers and Alex Drany, Ferrara's wounded interpreter, who had killed the old man insurgent. Two Afghan soldiers had died in the ambush.

Samaroo and Sergeant Jacob Walker, working their way up the cliff from the creek, finally spotted Jeff Mersman's body with the help of an infrared spotlight that the orbiting AC130 gunship shined down on the battlefield like some kind of midnight sun. The twenty-three-year-old Mersman, who had taken a bad fall during the outboard leg of the mission but soldiered on without a complaint, had apparently been blown off the goat trail during the ambush, possibly by an RPG, and tumbled several dozen yards down the steep cliff.

When he finally had come to a stop, the tough soldier—who had to have been badly beaten up by then and possibly wounded—appeared to have still been alive and took steps to help comrades find him. He'd pulled off his assault pack and cracked several chem lights to activate them, scattering them around his location. But no one came in time to save him, and he was shot to death by enemy gunmen. He managed to get off only three rounds from his M4.

When Samaroo and Walker scaled the cliff to reach Mersman, they were surprised by how peaceful he looked, with his eyes closed, as if he had simply laid down and gone to sleep. It was so deceptive that Samaroo called out to him. "Hey, Mersman, you all right?" And Walker moved closer, saying, "Hey, you okay?"

An Air Force Special Operations command helicopter arrived and dropped off two pararescuers, specially trained in medical and rescue operations, but they were lowered to the wrong location, the pilots mistaking a bundle of dropped ammo for Mersman's remains. It was hours before they finally reached his body, prepared it to be hoisted, and pulled it up.

Meanwhile Ostlund was finally notified about Lancour's body being dropped, and word reached the men in the field who had first found him. They all were stunned by the news. Shane Stockard, who had joined Silvernale up on the goat trail, was furious and exploded over the radio.

"Are you fucking kidding me?!" he raged, demanding to know why they hadn't been told sooner. It was an unusual display for an otherwise stoic platoon sergeant, borne of frustration, exhaustion, and the loss of his men. Ostlund had to come up on the radio and tell him to calm down.

It was sunup before Chosen Company First Sergeant Scott Beeson finally spotted Lancour's remains from a distance through a pair of binoculars, wedged between a couple of rocks. Beeson directed Silvernale and Stockard down the cliff so they could recover him. The body was coming apart from the beating it had taken. Silvernale's heart sank at the sight of it. He was so overwhelmed that he had to take a knee, and it felt like he was suddenly out of breath. Lancour had held so much promise. Silvernale was certain he was destined for promotion and leadership. He was one of the staff sergeant's "elites."

*Fuck, this is really what war is—right here.*

Silvernale had to use his M4 carbine to pry the body free. They wrapped it in canvas and carried it up two hundred feet of mountain to get back to the goat trail. Lancour's remains, along with those of two Afghan National Army soldiers, were finally airlifted off the battlefield in the daylight hours of November 10, and weary Chosen soldiers made their way back to Bella.

→ ←

It still wasn't over. In the hours ahead, Army and Marine Corps officers would fan out to homes across the United States notifying loved ones about the ultimate sacrifice made by their sons and husbands somewhere in northeastern Afghanistan. When two officers knocked at the home of Jessica Langevin's parents back in Pittsburg, California, where Jessica was staying during her husband Sean's deployment, she was cooking a spaghetti dinner. Before the officers told her anything, one of them, a female chaplain, noticed that Jessica was seven months along with Zoe.

"Oh my God, she's pregnant," the chaplain blurted out.

In each case where families were notified, there would be little or no detail about what had actually happened. Relatives were desperate to know more.

That was a task left to Matt Myer. Barely twenty-nine years old, he had never lost a man under his command. He knew—Ostlund had already instructed him on this—he was obliged to call each family and answer every question they might have. But it was very tough to be completely honest about some things. There was the sensitive issue of Lancour's body being dropped. Even beyond that, Matt felt very uncomfortable about the responsibility. He had to keep telling himself their need to know was more important than any personal distress he might feel. As company commander, he served not only his men but their families as well.

*Get over yourself. Buck up and do it.*

One by one he made satellite phone calls, standing outside the TOC back at Bella, leaning up against a wall near the landing zone. Beeson insisted on being nearby, if for no other reason than to lend moral support. Matt Myer began each conversation the same way.

"I'm Captain Matt Myer. I was your son's company commander. I'm just calling you to offer my condolences and answer any questions you might have about the circumstances of his death. I know it's a lot to deal with. But I'm here to answer your questions until you don't have any more questions to ask."

He tried to brace himself for the question he dreaded most, the one they always asked: "Why did my husband die?" or "Why did my son die?"

Myer knew no one could really explain why one person dies in combat and another survives. He decided to be straight with them: "I don't know why this happened. I don't understand either. It doesn't make any sense."

First he called the parents of Matt Ferrara. They were mercifully gracious. They even asked how he was dealing with it. It turned into almost a conversation. The father sounded slightly upset, the mother calm. They asked about the patrol: How many were on it? They wanted to know where on his body their son was wounded and if it was possible he died quickly. Myer assured them he believed it was nearly instantaneous. They talked about Ranch House, and Myer told them something they didn't know—that Matt had been recommended for a Silver Star for that battle. The parents mentioned that their son's grandfather had received a Silver Star and was buried at Arlington National Cemetery.

Myer took notes. He wanted to pass the information along to Ostlund, who would also be calling each family. His boss would want to know what ground had been covered.

The calls continued. Jeff Mersman's wife, Lynn, sounded at peace with what had happened. The conversation with Lester Roque's family was tougher. Because they were from the Philippines, there was a language barrier, and Myer wasn't on the phone for very long. Sean Langevin's mother, Roxane, was worried about the state of his body and wanted to know where the bullets struck him. Sean's pregnant wife, Jess, was teary, but understanding, and she wanted to extend condolences to the family of Joe Lancour.

But when it came time to call Lancour's mother, Starla Owens, Myer couldn't bring himself to tell her the truth. She had heard from the casualty assistance officer that her son's body was badly damaged. She wanted to know what happened and, most importantly, whether he suffered. Myer told her he thought Joe died quickly, but that his body had fallen. He neglected to mention, however, that the body was dropped from a helicopter. She said it was important that the family learn the details for closure.

"I wasn't prepared to tell her," Myer wrote in his notes for Ostlund. "But I believe it should be clarified for her."

→ ←

In the weeks before Matt Ferrara was killed on the goat trail he spoke with military historian Dave Hanson about bravery and the kind of men he served with in Afghanistan.

"One thing you never really realize until you get into a big fight is the human will," the lieutenant had said. "Everything these guys learn in training—and when they apply it to something real and do things that are way beyond anything that's expected of a human being, it is incredible. . . . It's incredible to be with soldiers of this caliber.

"It's a big part of history, just like World War II, the Greatest Generation. I think it's not much different now, from what some of these guys go through. It's extremely difficult to operate in this area. And they do it day in and day out across the battalion and the brigade."

→ ←

For his actions during the ambush Specialist Kyle White—in a 2014 White House ceremony—became only the seventh living recipient of the Medal of Honor from the Afghanistan War. A Distinguished Service Cross was awarded to Sergeant James Takes. Staff Sergeant Conrad Begaye and Staff Sergeant Peter Rohrs each received a Silver Star. A Bronze Star for valor was awarded to Staff Sergeant Christopher Choay and posthumously to Private First Class Joseph Lancour and Specialist Lester Roque.

# 9

> > > "IT MIGHT BE DANGEROUS"

*Chris McKaig felt cast adrift* as he stood alone in the Venice Marco Polo Airport. It was November, and he had just arrived as a replacement for the hard-hit Rock Battalion, assigned right out of airborne training at Fort Benning and sent by commercial flight to Europe. But he had no idea how to get to Camp Ederle in Vicenza. By recruitment standards he was an old man, having turned thirty-three the previous July. But he still had his boyish looks, and most of the paratroopers he met and formed friendships with didn't realize initially he was a dozen years their senior. McKaig was from New Jersey, the older of two sons of a mail carrier and his wife. Chris idolized his father, Patrick, an Army veteran who started taking him bow hunting when he was just eight years old. The father dreamed of moving out west to the broad, green valley region of La Grande, Oregon, and that wish finally came true when his boys were in high school. The family fell in love with north-eastern Oregon.

All Chris ever wanted to be was a soldier. He soaked up the war stories of relatives and family friends who served; he watched everything he could find about the military on television. At night he even had dreams of being in combat, and sometimes those dreams turned into nightmares.

Still, he felt the Army was his destiny, and Chris enlisted right out of high school, serving four years, including a stint in South Korea. But

194

it was peacetime, the military was downsizing, and he was denied his request to go through airborne training and become a paratrooper—there were no available slots. So McKaig mustered out and went back to La Grande. He pumped gas, worked in a factory that made trailers, and served in a volunteer fire department. And when the country went to war in 2001 McKaig began a long internal struggle with whether to serve again. When George W. Bush launched the surge in 2007, McKaig couldn't sit out any longer. He went back to the same recruiting office in La Grande he had visited in high school.

Now, finally, he was at war. But standing in an Italian international airport, McKaig wasn't exactly sure how to get to it, at least not until a soldier from the 173rd Airborne Brigade approached. The soldier and his wife had just flown in and were driving back to Vicenza. They offered McKaig a lift.

It was a forty-minute drive, and the soldier, who was behind the wheel, seemed like a tough character—calloused, like he'd seen some things. McKaig never did get his name or rank, but he could tell by the way the man carried himself that he was a noncommissioned officer. He asked McKaig which battalion he was joining. The 2/503, McKaig told him, not yet knowing he was headed for Chosen.

The driver started filling him in on what to expect in Afghanistan, what a tough time the Rock Battalion had endured. A new replacement would be tested, he said. From the backseat McKaig could see the guy was studying him in the rearview mirror. "You're going to either get killed or wounded," he blurted out all of a sudden. "Definitely wounded. High possibility of getting killed."

McKaig thought the guy was joking, maybe messing with him. He looked over at the wife, expecting to see her chuckling. But she was as stone-faced as her husband. They were serious.

*You gotta be fucking kidding me.*

→ ←

A memorial service for the six who died in the November 9 ambush was held on a sun-dappled courtyard back at Camp Blessing, the survivors of 1st Platoon barely filling two rows of folding chairs. Six combat crosses were arrayed before the somber attendees, the arrangement combining a muzzle-down M4, with a helmet perched on the butt end, and a pair of the dead man's boots. One by one, people walked to a podium for a few words. Specialist Gregg Rauwolf said, "Most of us knew and loved Corporal Langevin." An Army medical captain praised Lester Roque's quiet professionalism. Gabe Green recalled the way Jeff Mersman spoke so often about his mom and dad and how Lancour "always tried to make you feel better when you were down." A Marine lieutenant said Phil Bocks "had more initiative than anyone I ever met." Matt Myer read prepared remarks about the unpredictability of war and "how we never truly know what will happen on the next night or the next patrol."

The most touching eulogy came when Shane Stockard walked up before the group, his head and shoulders barely clearing the podium. Fighting back tears, he memorialized his dead platoon leader in plain-spoken remarks made even more poignant by Stockard's Texas twang. "Matt Ferrara was a true friend and a fearless leader. . . . I knew the first time I saw him. I saw how short he was, and I thought, 'Man, it's going to be awesome to have a short platoon leader like myself.' . . . Matt never got worked up over anything. He was as calm as anyone could ever be. . . . He was more hard-headed than me.

"Matt, rest in peace, and watch over the rest of the platoon. God bless you."

→ ←

In the opaque world of the insurgency in the Waigal Valley, it never became clear exactly who led the ambush on November 9. The only certainty was that it was an unusually well-planned attack. Even Bill Ostlund admired its execution.

Somebody with very good military training did that ambush. It was exactly what we would do in our operations.

The only intelligence on enemy activity had surfaced seven weeks earlier with reports that a crucial militant leader in the valley, Mullah Maulawi Muhammad Osman, was assembling hundreds of fighters from villages throughout the area and planning an attack on Bella. Whether Osman viewed the Ferrara mission to Aranas as a target of opportunity that fell into his lap may never be known. To the extent he may have been involved, the success was evidence of skills that Osman, his lieutenants, or his accomplices could bring against Chosen Company in the Waigal Valley. Given the volume of enemy fire and the many locations it came from, as many as fifty to seventy insurgents may have been involved. There was no indication that the enemy had suffered any casualties in what proved to be a lopsided fight.

Battle-damage assessments were always extremely hard. When artillery missions were carried out, it was often difficult to go and see the results of a bombardment because of the vertical terrain. It could take a day or two to reach the place where shells landed. And these jihadist fighters were highly disciplined at recovering their dead and wounded. It often amazed the Americans how a battlefield could be swept clean except for blood trails.

Chosen Company First Sergeant Scott Beeson was growing to admire the caliber of enemy fighters they faced, their physical toughness and skill at moving so effortlessly in harsh terrain. They weren't weighed down by the heavy body armor the Americans wore, and Beeson knew this made them faster and more nimble in a fight.

*Those guys are awesome. I think if you put two of my soldiers with all their gear that they wear against two of their soldiers, I'm not sure who would come out on top.*

One thing was sure: the level of combat in the Waigal Valley was defying its data-driven evaluation. In counting the number of troops in contact, or TICs, Ostlund's staff gave every incident equal weight. So an exchange of gunfire for several minutes over several hundred yards of territory was counted the same way as an incident where six service members were killed. By that measurement the Waigal Valley still showed very little combat. The battalion was still counting eight times more TICs in the Korengal Valley than in the Waigal Valley. Yet with the November 9 ambush alone Chosen Company had suffered nearly as many troops killed in action as Battle Company in the Korengal.

It was becoming increasingly clear that there were very different enemy command styles between the two valleys. Whoever was running the insurgency in the Waigal was more disciplined and patient, biding their time, assembling forces and carefully planning attacks over weeks, with the idea of not just harassing the Americans but annihilating them. Ostlund could see now that the fight in the Korengal was largely more mercenary. Moneyed interests—whether they were Al Qaeda or wealthy businessmen who felt cheated out of their timber profits—were paying local young men $5 a day to go shoot at the Americans, and this was enough to maintain a steady drumbeat of attacks. But north of the Pech Valley, in places like the Waigal, the enemy seemed more fanatical in Ostlund's view. True believers. A committed enemy who was better trained than in the Korengal, more deliberate, pragmatic, and willing to wait for the right opportunity to cause the greatest harm.

The analysis added even greater urgency to Ostlund's now-six-month-old push to pull back out of Ranch House and Bella and set up a new base in Wanat. They had finally burned down Ranch House and left it. But they were still in Bella with no firm commitment from higher-ups for the necessary air assets and approval to abandon that base.

Colonel Chip Preysler, commander of the 173rd airborne Brigade, showed up to celebrate Thanksgiving with the 2nd Platoon paratroopers at Bella and kept remarking with an air of astonishment how they could be defending such an inaccessible base—"What are we doing here?" It rankled Ostlund.

*Motherfucker, you're the one who allocates resources. I've been advocating to get them the hell out of here for months. Just do it.*

He actually pulled Preysler aside and pressed him politely not to make such observations in front of soldiers who would be more than happy to leave this place behind if the command would make it happen.

A week after Thanksgiving the now-emboldened enemy resistance, coming off the US closure of Ranch House and the November 9 ambush, began probing the defenses of Bella. For three straight days beginning November 29, Chosen Company's 2nd Platoon—now having shifted out there from Blessing—fought off incoming-fire attacks, the enemy pausing now and again only to refit, regroup, and continue to attack. In addition to rifle and machine gun fire as well as RPGs, insurgents began targeting Bella with Chinese-made 107mm rockets. One of the deadly workhorses of low-tech militia around the world, the rocket is nearly a yard in length and a little more than four inches wide—a lunatic's idea of a July 4 bottle rocket, but one that can travel five miles with three pounds of explosive. It is designed to be fired from a wheeled launcher. But in truth it could be launched from almost anything. It could be propped up on a mound of dirt or against a stone. The enemy in the Waigal would rig one up pointed at Bella with a bottle of water hanging from the fuse, and then they'd leave it there. The water would eventually evaporate and lighten the bottle so that the fuse would ignite and launch the rocket with no one around to catch any counterfire. During those three days one rocket managed to explode inside Bella just ten feet from the front door of the base headquarters, but no one was hurt.

The three days of fighting began when militants positioned south of Bella tried to shoot down a Chinook helicopter negotiating the narrow canyon as it flew out of Bella. They missed, although one RPG nearly struck the aircraft's tail section. Return fire erupted from the paratroopers at Bella and from the weapons-bristling observation post the soldiers called OP1, which sat high on a western ridge two hundred feet above the main base. It went on like this for two days. When the platoon leader, Lieutenant Jonathan Brostrom, led a patrol south of Bella on Friday, November 30, he came under attack, and when he and other soldiers were climbing down from OP1 on Saturday, December 1, they came under fire. Each time Bella and OP1 would erupt with return fire as paratroopers tried to pin the attacking militants long enough to destroy them with 120mm mortar fire or air support. Combat grew so intense that even Bella's cook managed to get behind a .50-caliber machine gun and lay down fire. The sole casualty during the three days of fighting was an Afghan security guard who suffered a gunshot wound to the stomach. Brostrom was certain they had killed several enemy fighters during the exchanges and was particularly proud of his forward observer, a tall New Hampshire native, Sergeant Ryan Pitts, who would stand out in the open up at OP1 to better spot targets and direct artillery and air support.

"Pitts ignored bullets impacting around him," Brostrom wrote in an after-action report, adding that the soldier "was personally responsible for causing most of the enemy casualties through his effective employment of indirect fires."

Another trooper who distinguished himself was Sergeant Brian Hissong, who directed much of the soldiers' return fire from OP1, even grabbing an AT4 on occasion—kind of a modern-day bazooka developed for defeating tanks—and cutting loose with a round at suspected enemy positions.

Hissong was a fair-haired farm boy from central Illinois. His family owned three hundred acres in St. Joseph, not far from the University of Illinois in Champagne, where they grew corn and beans. Brian was the youngest of two and had dreamed of joining the Army since he was thirteen, and seeing the destruction of 9/11 made him even more certain. He enlisted at nineteen in early 2004 and found himself headed for Italy. The following year he deployed with Chosen Company to Zabul Province in the south, where there were moments of intense combat. Hissong was among the Chosen paratroopers who charged into a basement where their friend, Staff Sergeant Michael Schafer, had been killed so they could finish off the Taliban fighters responsible. He killed one who was only a few feet away by managing to get off the first shot. And Hissong was on a detail assigned to recover five burned bodies of Americans killed when a Chinook helicopter was shot down. After returning to Vicenza he couldn't stop thinking about Schafer and the burned bodies, and he was diagnosed with posttraumatic stress disorder. He discreetly visited a counselor at Camp Ederle and entertained thoughts of leaving the Army. But Hissong, by then a sergeant and team leader, stayed on for the Waigal Valley.

During the winter of 2007–2008 enemy operations in the valley didn't stop. Reports were coming in that insurgents had set up a roadblock near a bridge south of Bella on a road that ran east to the village of Muladish and was used to tax locals passing through. Brostrom saw a chance to take the fight to the enemy.

By January the weather was freezing, with snow and ice on the ground. He devised a pincer-like movement to trap the enemy fighters at the roadblock. He'd lead about two dozen of the Chosen Few south of Bella along the western bank of the Waigal River, approaching the enemy checkpoint from the northwest, while sending a half dozen other soldiers across the river and up over the heights southeast of Bella in a blocking maneuver.

It would be a night-long mission in the cold so they could have their ambush positions set up as the sun was rising. Platoon Sergeant Matt Kahler tapped Brian Hissong to accompany the six-man element. But Hissong was exhausted and asked if he could beg off.

"I'm fine," Kahler said. "I'll just go instead."

Brostrom led his twenty-two Afghan Army soldiers and fourteen US troops south out of Bella shortly before 3:30 A.M. on January 26, a Saturday, as Kahler took his six-man element across the bridge and hiked the switchbacks up to the ridgetop. The platoon sergeant was with a group of scouts led by Sergeant Anthony Stamper and Specialist Mike Denton of 1st Squad. They needed to pass through Speedbump, a fortified outpost manned by Afghan security guards (ASGs) that sat atop the east valley ridge opposite the river from OP1.

The nine Afghan guards on duty didn't know they were coming. That was on purpose. Brostrom increasingly worried these local hired men couldn't be trusted. Moreover, they were undisciplined, known to fall asleep at their post or, worse, smoke hashish during long work hours.

The whole point of hiring local guards, a practice begun by the 10th Mountain troops nearly two years before, was to provide fighting-age men in the community jobs as an incentive to keep them from working for or cooperating with the enemy. But particularly after the attack on Ranch House in August, Chosen Company had grown increasingly suspicious of these men.

Certainly they weren't going to give these local men advance notice of missions. They would ask the security guard commander down at Bella to radio Speedbump when the paratroopers reached the outpost. Except that when Specialist Jacob Walker roused the commander shortly after 4 A.M., the man didn't have a radio to call his men. He'd loaned it to an ANA soldier. Walker found a different radio, but the commander said he couldn't connect with Speedbump. The guards couldn't be alerted.

Kahler and Stamper debated whether to just climb around the outpost and continue on. But the ice was so treacherous on the mountain that they didn't think that was a good idea. The outpost had three structures—two guard posts and a living quarters. Kahler led the men to within fifty yards of the outpost, and they started flashing lights and calling out.

"ASG, we're Americans!"

No response. Scout member Brenton Jones, a private first class, was in the lead and started moving toward the concertina wire surrounding Speedbump. Kahler stopped him.

"It might be dangerous," the platoon sergeant told Jones, and he went ahead on his own.

Kahler crossed the wire and moved closer, calling out, "ASG, we're American!" over and over. Approaching from the south, he walked past the first guard post and got within about twenty feet east of the structure, still loudly calling out that he was an American. There was almost a full moon, and the twenty-nine-year-old Kahler was standing behind a rock visible from the hips up when someone in or near the bunker opened fire with an AK47. There were three shots, and one of them struck Kahler in the upper right side of his head and exited out the back of his skull. He slumped to the ground.

The other paratroopers took cover behind rocks and began yelling, "Americans! Americans! Don't shoot!" They called out to Kahler, who didn't move, and started pressing forward when another three or four shots rang out. More yells and angry screams followed until a voice inside finally responded.

"Okay, okay, Americans."

Stamper reached Kahler first and could see right away the platoon sergeant wasn't moving. He had Jones and another scout, Specialist Ryan Schwarz, try to revive Kahler. Jones performed CPR, but there would be no response.

The paratroopers found the gunman, a man they knew as Mohammed Din, a short, light-skinned Afghan with close-cropped hair and a trim beard. He and five others were rounded up and disarmed. Three others stayed hidden inside the sleeping bunker. As the paratroopers worked to gather up the guards' weapons and disable them, Din kept edging over to get a closer look at what he'd done to Kahler. Denton, armed with his squad automatic weapon, walked up and shoved the security guard away. When Din and another guard took off running, Denton raised his weapon and was ready to shoot them down, but Stamper called out, "Denton, don't fire!"

They needed to get their platoon sergeant back down to Bella. It was a long and difficult descent; the snow was deep and icy. They first tried carrying Kahler's body in a tarp, but it was awkward, and the soldiers kept slipping. Stamper finally just lifted the body over his shoulder and took it down that way. Soldiers from Bella met them about halfway and helped carry Kahler's body the rest of the way. A group of soldiers went back up the mountain to gather some of the platoon sergeant's equipment that had been left behind or fallen as he was brought down the steep slope. All they had to do was follow the blood trail back up.

Back at Bella a distraught Hissong returned to his quarters and began smashing personal belongings in anger and anguish over Kahler's death. He had come to a decision: no way was he staying in the Army.

*If they could kill Kahler, they could kill any of us.*

Kahler's death devastated Jonathan Brostrom. Waiting with the body for the medevac helicopter, he called home. He just needed to talk with someone, to vent. He was upset, tears were beginning to flow, and when his mother, Mary Jo, answered the phone, Jonathan asked to speak with his father. Dave Brostrom listened as his son poured out a story of deception and murder.

At Camp Blessing, when word arrived that Kahler was dead, Matt Myer felt his knees buckling and had to sit down. Myer had spent long days with the platoon sergeant on patrols out of Blessing and during stints at Bella. He had come to know Kahler well, and now he was gone.

When the news circulated through the base, Ryan Pitts was up at OP1. He climbed back down a day or two later, and when he walked inside the perimeter, the place immediately felt empty, like a death in the family had changed everything, even the way the physical surroundings appeared. He was feeling rage and loss all at once, and he walked through the headquarters without making eye contact. Brostrom offered solace, but Pitts wouldn't have it.

Captain Myer and First Sergeant Beeson came to Ryan's hooch to check in on him. Pitts finally couldn't hold back any longer and openly wept. They stayed with him for a time, Beeson offering his own form of rough-edged condolence.

Like a lot of them, Pitts and Myer were convinced Kahler's death was murder.

An Army investigation quickly wrapped up in a few days without definitive findings. Two guards had been on duty at the time of the shooting, including one in the first bunker, where the gunman had emerged. The seven other guards were asleep. The security guard identified as the gunman reportedly had a reputation for falling asleep on duty and, when roused, grabbing for his gun to open fire. There were also unconfirmed intelligence reports that the enemy had engineered the shooting.

As part of the investigation, sound tests were done at Speedbump, and an investigator concluded that if the suspected security guard had been huddling near a wood-burning stove inside the bunker—which many of them did while on duty to keep warm—it would have been harder to hear Kahler calling out. "It is inconclusive whether the shooting was accidental or intentional," the report said.

By dawn the morning after Kahler was killed, a medevac helicopter arrived to pick up his body. Brian Hissong was among a small clutch of soldiers who carried the remains to the aircraft. Before stepping away, Hissong placed his hand on Kahler's head. A farewell.

On the Blackhawk helicopter was thirty-three-year-old Justin Madill, an emergency medicine doctor and flight surgeon new to Afghanistan and flying his first medevac mission. Madill had always wanted to be a physician, and the Army paid for his medical degree. By the time he was sent overseas Madill was a captain with the 101st Airborne Division.

As he pulled Kahler's body into the helicopter, Madill was moved by the grief-stricken young faces of the soldiers who had brought their slain leader to the aircraft. Most were ten years younger than Madill. Images from this small event stayed with the captain long after: how the dead soldier's hand had spilled out of the body bag, plainly showing the wedding band on his finger, and how one paratrooper who had helped carry the body laid a hand on the dead platoon sergeant's head. It was Madill's introduction to war.

This is real. Here I am. In Afghanistan.

The soldiers of 2nd Platoon wanted revenge and fantasized about how they would deal with the gunman, Mohammed Din, if they had the chance. Jason Bogar, for one, was sure he would never forget him.

*If I ever see him, I will do everything in my power to kill him, even if it takes my life.*

→  ←

The same month Matt Kahler died, the hearts-and-minds campaign in the Waigal, already on life support, took a deeper hit when a man named Ziaul Rahman became the new Waigal District governor operating out of the district headquarters in Wanat. The Americans quickly assessed him as a weak, incompetent leader who could bend easily to the pressure of the insurgency. Within a few months Rahman had made the battalion's "negative influencers" watch list.

In March, 2nd Platoon shifted back to Blessing, and 1st Platoon took its place at Bella. First Lieutenant Brostrom returned to Chosen Company headquarters dispirited and convinced that counterinsurgency efforts out of Bella were a lost cause. "That area pretty much turned to crap," he told a military historian a few months after he got back.

They had been able to kill some bad guys, and that was a good thing, Brostrom felt. But little else was accomplished. They certainly weren't bonding with the population. The terrain was too difficult, the area too vast, the people too receptive to the enemy. It took twelve hours to hike to the nearest village from Bella. An ambush on the way or back was not uncommon. And once the paratroopers reached the village, persuading the elders to work against the insurgency and with the Americans and Afghan government just wasn't happening.

Every village had its own culture and even its own dialect. Communicating was a chore, the entire exercise of dissecting each minisociety a huge "pain in the ass." And the young lieutenant was still simmering over Kahler's death. "There was no doubt in my mind it was foul play," he told the historian.

It was amid these frustrations that Matt Myer recommended the next step for withdrawing farther from the Waigal Valley. Ranch House had from the very beginning been seen as too risky. The way he saw it, operating deep within the valley to frustrate the influence of terror groups such as Al Qaeda and Lashkar-e-Tayyiba was not worth the risk.

Even NATO's broad, counterinsurgency goal of extending the Afghan government's reach into these remote areas seemed like a nonstarter in the Waigal Valley because the local government representatives were so ineffective, Myer concluded. He felt like he was spinning his wheels. The only plan that made sense going forward was the one Bill Ostlund had pushed from almost the moment they arrived in Afghanistan: pull back and build a new base. The best location would be the Waigal District headquarters in Wanat, a village near the mouth of the valley that was connected by a gravel road to Blessing just over five miles to the south. Unlike the mountain hamlet of Bella and the town of Aranas, Wanat actually had some semblance of government structure with the district center and its own police department.

They would finally jettison the strategy advanced by Chris Cavoli and the 10th Mountain Division soldiers the year before of setting up outposts deep in the valley system and pulling roads, services, and governance to places like Aranas. Instead, Ostlund and Myer thought it was better to push those resources—roads and so forth—out to these hinterlands from a base closer and theoretically safer to operate from, like Wanat.

Here they had a strong ally in Major General Jeffrey Schloesser, who commanded all ground forces in eastern Afghanistan. Schloesser had taken over in April for David Rodriguez, who had allowed the rescue helicopters that responded to the November 9 ambush to work extraordinarily long hours pulling wounded paratroopers out of that battlefield.

The fifty-three-year-old Schloesser had actually flown into Ranch House the year before and visited Bella. He was shocked at how remote and inaccessible both bases were. He could see that they lay along access routes the enemy relied upon for movement from Pakistan to Kabul. Since 2006, when 10th Mountain troops established them, the character of the war had changed. Attacks across the country had increased, including directly into Kabul. Within a few months of taking command, Schloesser would be pushing hard for more reinforcements across eastern Afghanistan. The flow of enemy fighters and materiel toward the capital was only increasing. He knew Chosen Company was operating in a dangerous place along the famed Muj Highway from Pakistan to Kabul.

But Schloesser was learning that closing down bases was a difficult political pill to swallow. Every month he was meeting with top Afghan officials—the minister of defense, the head of the military, the minister of the interior—and they were arguing that these bases should not be abandoned. Nor was withdrawal necessarily palatable with the American high command.

*The United States and NATO don't pull back from things. They move into things.*

The result would be delay in approving resources for the withdrawal from far-forward bases in the Waigal Valley. This would jam the mission to close Bella and open a base in Wanat into the final months of the Rock Battalion deployment. Brigade commander Chip Preysler was adamantly opposed to leaving that tough job to incoming troops of the 1st Battalion, 26th Infantry Regiment out of Fort Hood. They wouldn't have the battle chops that Rock Battalion had earned. His boss, Schloesser, agreed. He thought Preysler's people were the most experienced US troops fighting in Afghanistan.

→ ←

The village of Wanat sat along a bend in the Waigal River where the valley widened ever so slightly and mountains rose to ten thousand feet on either side. Some fifty families lived there, about two hundred people. There was a nearly impassable dirt road running south from Bella about five miles to Wanat, hugging the western bank of the river. As the road reached the outskirts of Wanat it crossed a bridge that the

Americans built in 2006. The roadway then cut south again, this time along the eastern side of the Waigal. There was a driveway off to the right that led to the Waigal District Center and police station located on an isthmus, gifts from the United States. It was a picturesque spot right along the river.

The road from Bella continued south, crossing a second bridge over the Wayskawdi Creek—yet another American bequest, built like everything else to promote commerce and tug these remote people into the twenty-first century. From there the roadway ascended up a short hill to the village center made up primarily of a mosque, a two-story hotel, and a long bazaar that paralleled the road as it continued out of Wanat and south toward the Pech Valley. The bazaar was really just a series of connected, single-story structures where shop owners sold wares during the day. There was a collection of tables and chairs out front for folks to relax under an awning in the steamy summer heat. Directly across the street from the bazaar a new sellers' market was under construction—single-story, mud-brick buildings arranged in a diamond shape. Behind the old bazaar and east of the roadway was a series of agricultural terraces rising several hundred feet before giving way to trees and scrub brush blanketing the rising slopes of the eastern flank of the valley. Here and there along those hillsides were private homes, cottages, and other structures looking down on Wanat.

To the west, between the village center and the river, was a bluff on which sat several relatively lavish homes built for a few of the more prominent members of the community. Haji Juma Gul was one of the wealthier people of the hamlet, moneyed enough to afford a trip to Mecca in Saudi Arabia for the annual hajj. There was a large, flat area of ground that looked like a big dirt parking lot that sat south of the village center, between the road and the bluff of mansions. This stretch of ground was where Rock Battalion chose to build a new base of operations in the Waigal Valley. The base would be in the center of Wanat with the bluff to the west, the mosque and a two-story hotel and restaurant complex immediately north, and the bazaar along the eastern flank.

For the Chosen Company commander, Captain Matt Myer, it would be the first time in his career he had set up a combat outpost from scratch. The Americans made several trips up from Camp Blessing by road to Wanat in March of 2008. On a straight line the distance between Wanat and Blessing was only about four and a half miles. By winding road it was upward of six miles. The highway was narrow, and there were places where rock outcroppings on the uphill side of the road came close to scraping the side of the gun trucks. Soldiers had to pull in their side mirrors to avoid having them ripped off. The journey could be a one- to two-hour trek, given the slow process of checking for roadside bombs. Lieutenant Colonel Ostlund led a trip to Wanat with Matt Myer and Chosen Company paratroopers, handing out stuffed beanie toys, blankets, and little Etch A Sketches to children. One of the troopers snapped a photo of a sober-looking boy holding a couple of stuffed toys in his arms, and Ostlund saved the picture in his files under the heading, "The future."

Wanat had once been a slice of hope for the US military efforts to defeat the insurgency in the Waigal Valley. When Chris Cavoli of the 10th Mountain Division sent his soldiers up to Aranas and Bella in 2006, the only way to link those communities with the world was to build a road up the Waigal Valley, and that meant bridging the river and the Wayskawdi Creek at Wanat. So Cavoli sent an Army engineer company to Wanat to set up a temporary base and ford the waterways. The young West Point lieutenant leading the engineers, Andrew Glenn, worked hard to connect with the population—holding shuras, taking time to share tea, and urging people to visit the work sites. There were a handful of insurgent attacks to try to disrupt these efforts, but they failed. By the time the bridges were finished, Cavoli noticed the residents had a growing affection for the engineers and the work they'd done. When Cavoli visited Wanat, he walked the streets without his body armor.

But times had changed since 2006. Battle lines in the valley were drawing closer to Wanat, with Ranch House closed and a growing number of attacks on Bella five miles up the road. People in Wanat increasingly felt squeezed between the insurgency and the American plan to build a military base in their backyard.

Ostlund and his officers wanted to settle leasing arrangements for the flat land in Wanat, the last hurdle before the new firebase could be constructed, and they journeyed up to the village on May 26 for an 8:20 A.M. shura at the district center. The Americans received a rude reception. The shady district governor, Ziaul Rahman, and other elders held Ostlund and his officers off as they huddled separately for several minutes, something they'd never done before. Their behavior when they emerged was arrogant and hostile. Village elders said they were unhappy about the prospects of a US installation in their town, a clear departure from previous sentiments. They invited Ostlund to stay for lunch. But when he did, the elders left him alone to dine with the police chief and they ate separately—an absolute slight.

When the six-vehicle convoy finally departed for Blessing shortly before 2 P.M., everyone was on high alert. Afghan National Army troops back at Blessing were tipped off that a couple of dozen enemy fighters would be lying in wait for the convoy on the return trip. Meanwhile Wanat was conspicuously empty. Children who always came around for candy or toys were nowhere to be seen, and the shops were all closed.

About a mile south of Wanat, the convoy of Humvees found itself in a crossfire from both sides of the valley as the vehicles entered a deep bend in the road. An IED (improvised explosive device) blew up in front of the truck carrying Matt Myer. Gunmen up in the hills and off the edge of the roadway to the east opened fire with Kalashnikovs, machine guns, and RPG launchers while others engaged from the west side of the valley. Enemy rounds pock-marked the armored shielding on the trucks and cracked layers of bullet-proof windows while paratroopers in the truck gun turrets opened fire with machine guns and automatic grenade launchers.

The firefight went on for another forty minutes. Myer was in the right front passenger seat and saw an RPG that seemed to be flying almost in slow motion right toward the windshield. It fell short, and the explosion blew more dirt into the air. The gunner in Myer's truck, Specialist Ananthachai Nantakul, said his MK19 grenade launcher up in the turret was down, clogged with dust from the explosions. As Nantakul worked frantically to clear the weapon, Myer and his radio operator, Sergeant Erik Aass (pronounced Awes), got out of the truck and opened fire with their M4 rifles. An RPG explosion knocked Aass to his knees, and a small piece of shrapnel struck him in his left forearm. Nantakul took shrapnel in his hand.

The convoy finally began to move slowly to a point farther down the road, and the soldiers now directed their fire back toward the ambush site. Matt Myer was back out of the truck and this time saw something he had never witnessed in more than a year of deployment: two enemy fighters in plain view making their way up a trail away from the ambush site perhaps three hundred yards away.

*That's the first time I've actually seen the enemy.*

He felt a stab of excitement. Finally a chance to shoot and kill these elusive enemy fighters. But there was a Humvee right in his line of fire, and Myer could neither shoot at the militants nor use his tracer rounds to direct others to target them. Before long the two had disappeared around a bend in the trail. Mortar and artillery rounds from Blessing shook the hillsides around the ambush, and before long the shooting was over.

A battalion intelligence analysis later concluded that Mullah Maulawi Muhammad Osman, a militant leader from the village of Waigal—who apparently was seen as a kind of overall commander of enemy forces gathering in the Waigal Valley—was increasingly concerned about American intentions to open a base at Wanat, particularly given the widespread knowledge that Chosen Company was planning to evacuate Bella.

Erik Aass, who was thirty-one, had one of the most unusual backgrounds in Chosen Company. He was Norwegian by birth, born in the capital city of Oslo, the son of a diplomat. His mother was Indonesian and the daughter of a diplomat. Erik grew up attending schools for the children of American envoys in France, Indonesia, and Norway, and he lived for a time with his family in Washington, DC. From early adolescence on, he identified most closely with American culture and a desire to become a US citizen. Unlike virtually every other enlisted soldier in Chosen, Aass had earned a college degree, acquiring a bachelor's in economics and history from Fordham University in New York City. He signed up for ROTC in college and even went through Airborne training, but he was ineligible to receive a commission for lack of US citizenship. When 9/11 happened, Aass watched thousands of lower-Manhattan evacuees streaming north on foot from the area around the World Trade Center. He finally enlisted in 2002 and became a US citizen while serving in the Army.

During Chosen Company's deployment to Afghanistan in 2005–2006, he was shot in the left hand and right knee trying to recover the body of Staff Sergeant Michael Schafer at the bottom of a basement staircase. Aass came down the steps, firing a squad automatic weapon, or light machine gun. He was awarded a Bronze Star for valor. He later served as driver for the 173rd Airborne Brigade's commander, Colonel Chip Preysler. But Aass never liked being apart from Chosen and, prior to the 2007–2008 deployment to Afghanistan, convinced Matt Myer to take him on as company radio man and clerk. His last name was predictably the target of banter in the Army, and it didn't help that Chosen Company's inimitable first sergeant, Scott Beeson, would sometimes summon Aass by calling out, "Aass . . ." and then after a pause, ". . . hole."

Ostlund, Myer, and the others returned to Wanat for a second shura on June 8, once again with the bearded elders and Rahman in the red-carpeted district center. The elders didn't volunteer anything about another ambush but, when asked, admitted there might be militants waiting on the return trip. Rahman was pointedly told that bombers and spy planes would be watching as the Americans drove back to Blessing. This time when the convoy rolled south and gunfire erupted, there was swift, prepared retaliation, with artillery and a B1 bomber pounding the hillsides. The attack petered out quickly. By the end of June the leasing arrangements for the new base were finalized.

→ ←

Each soldier earned eighteen days of leave during the long deployment, and as the casualty numbers mounted for Rock Battalion and, specifically, Chosen Company, that brief visit home was a time to take stock of lives and, in a few cases, make a major course correction.

Lieutenant Jonathan Brostrom took his leave and surprised his mother, Mary Jo, back in Hawaii for Mother's Day. He brought videos of their combat in Bella, which he excitedly showed his father, who in turn was shocked by a level of violence he hadn't expected in that theater of war. On Jon's return to Afghanistan, there was a stopover at a US airbase in Kuwait, and he spotted a woman, a young officer, wearing a 173rd Airborne Brigade patch on her shoulder. Blond and blue eyed—and female—Amanda Wilson was attracting a lot of attention in an ocean of idle men. She was miserable. Wilson was a new captain and company commander. She had gone home on leave to California to celebrate her twenty-fifth birthday and, while there, received news that three of her soldiers were killed in an attack by a suicide car bomber in Jalalabad. She was riven with guilt for being away when it all happened. When Jon Brostrom walked up and introduced himself, it wasn't long before they realized how much they had in common. He had lost Kahler just a few months before and understood what she was going through. The two officers connected over snow cones on the tarmac while waiting for a flight to Bagram. He bought her a cherry-flavored cone and teased her about how it made her lips red. She thought he was handsome and uncomplicated with his kooky aphorisms—"Big players make big plays." His empathy was exactly what she needed. Brostrom, for his part, was smitten, and when he got back to Blessing, he dug up Wilson's email and they started a war-zone relationship by message and phone.

Mike Denton went home in December and screwed up enough courage to call a young woman he knew from high school and ask her out on a date. Christina said yes and stole the paratrooper's heart when she agreed to see the movie *American Gangster* with Denzel Washington.

Sean Samaroo, a squad leader in 2nd Platoon, had dated back in Vicenza a young woman hired as a liaison to assist troops and their families get medical care at an Italian hospital near the base. Her name was Natasha. She had two children from a previous marriage, and Sean had a son. He had given Natasha a promise ring before leaving for Afghanistan. Now, with the dangers of the deployment becoming all too real, Samaroo wanted to get married. Then if the worst happened, Natasha would receive all the benefits he'd earned. During his leave in January they held a ceremony back in Arkansas where her parents lived.

Jacob Sones arrived home in March to marry his girlfriend, Nicole, down at the courthouse in Plano, Texas. He too was driven by the fear of war and its consequences. It was a rushed affair. She was wearing ripped jeans, and he had wine stains on his shirt.

A third soldier in Chosen Company did the same during his leave, only in secret, without so much as a word about it to their parents. His fiancée had witnessed his nightmares during that break from war and worried about what might happen when he returned—whether he would survive at all. Shortly before the leave was ending, they decided to tie the knot down at the courthouse. They had a full ceremony months later when he was home for good. But they never told their families that they were already married by then.

Sergeant Israel Garcia and his wife, Lesly, planned a romantic getaway in Cabo San Lucas during his leave over Valentine's Day in February. They both wanted to start a family and long debated the right time.

He didn't want to miss seeing the baby start to walk, so both leaned toward Lesly getting pregnant upon his return. But Israel decided that during his leave they should just start trying. Lesly knew full well how dangerous the deployment had become. A devout Catholic, she made a pact with God and didn't even tell Israel. If she got pregnant, it was a sign that God might intend to take Israel from her and was leaving a part of him back on earth. If she did not become pregnant, she would take that as evidence that Israel would be coming home safely.

When the leave was over and Garcia returned to war, Lesly wasn't pregnant.

There were changes afoot for the men of Chosen Company. David Dzwik, who had fought at Ranch House and diligently manned the radio at Bella during the ambush, was elevated from squad leader in 1st Platoon to platoon sergeant for 2nd Platoon. It was a delicate move replacing Matt Kahler. Dzwik knew this full well and told his soldiers he was no substitute for the popular slain leader. But Dzwik said he had his own way of doing things and the men would have to accept this. The transition went remarkably well.

Jason Baldwin, who had been awarded a Silver Star for his heroism at Ranch House, had grown disenchanted since then. With Ranch House closed and a battalion mortar crew operating the 120mm launcher at Bella, the Chosen Company mortar team was split between Blessing and a forward operating base in the Pech Valley called Michigan. Baldwin was eager to see more combat, he was upset that he wasn't yet getting promoted, and he was loud and brash about wanting a change, wishing he was with Battle Company in the war-ravaged Korengal Valley. Erich Phillips was soon fed up with his protégé's complaints and engineered a transfer.

In return for Baldwin, Phillips got Specialist Sergio Abad from Battle Company. If anyone epitomized the lost boys of Chosen Company, it was Sergio. As a little boy of Cuban heritage, he grew up with a mother who became suicidal and a drug addict after losing an older son in a car accident. Sergio longed to get away from the world of his childhood and join the Army. With his mother abusing heroin, Sergio went to live with his grandparents when he was six. He later changed homes again, this time taken in by his great aunt, Sorangel Herrara, when he was twelve. Schoolwork was a struggle. But the military was his dream, and Sergio joined junior ROTC at South Miami Senior High School and became a distance runner, running the two and a half miles home from school rather than wait for the bus.

One day when he was fourteen, he solemnly asked his great aunt to look into his eyes. "This is serious," Sergio told her. "I'm going to die young, and when I do, you need to promise me you're going to bury me at Arlington National Cemetery."

That kind of talk frightened her.

Sergio dropped out of high school in tenth grade and earned a high school equivalency credential through Job Corps before entering the Army in January 2006. He deployed with Battle Company, and about the time of his transfer to Chosen Abad went on leave to see his high school sweetheart. He returned to war only to find out that he had left her pregnant, later learning it would be a girl. Abad was ecstatic and began referring to the unborn child as his gummy bear.

→ ←

Meanwhile the plan to evacuate Bella and build a new base in Wanat continued to be delayed. It was finally slated for July, literally within weeks of when Chosen Company would go home in August. It was a complicated mission set to occur at a time when Chosen Company—and the battalion as a whole—was in a period of high activity. Preparations were underway for shipping personal belongings—and eventually the troops themselves—back home, and there was the task of familiarizing the incoming replacement battalion with its new area of operation. That meant going out on vehicle patrols with the new soldiers and riding side by side with them as they visited villages and met with elders.

First Sergeant Scott Beeson thought it was the worst possible time to take on an assignment like setting up an entirely new base, and he hammered Matt Myer about it.

"This is fucked up and a bad idea. And I would really appreciate it if you would talk to your commander, Colonel Ostlund, and tell him that that is a jacked-up idea. Not very smart. I'll do what the hell I'm told to do. But I don't think this is the right thing to do."

Myer listened to his company first sergeant's impassioned argument and always came back with the same logic: How could they leave this unfinished task for their replacements who would be arriving without any experience fighting in the Waigal Valley? Just because the deployment is nearing an end doesn't mean the responsibilities go away, he told Beeson. The Army way is to finish whatever job is front and center.

It's part of our culture.

Undeterred, Beeson went to the sergeant major of the battalion, Bradley Meyers, and repeated his complaint. "I hope you know that someone's going to get hurt, because we're very vulnerable right now." Meyers heard him out but explained that the move was Ostlund's idea, and the brigade commander, Chip Preysler, was on board with it. He told Beeson to drop it.

Beeson, meanwhile, was catching grief about the mission from within the ranks of 2nd Platoon. David Dzwik, 2nd Platoon sergeant, told him his men were very unhappy about it. It was Beeson's turn to listen. He privately agreed with Dzwik, but already had his orders.

"We're on this tour for fifteen months, not fourteen. Not fourteen and a half. So you do what you got to do and bring everything you need to make it successful. I've voiced my opinion to highers, Sergeant Dzwik, and basically they told us we have a job to do and we need to do it, and that, in turn is what I'm telling you. Your job is not to bitch and whine and complain about something that could happen. Your job is to make your soldiers feel secure."

There were several weeks during the late spring of 2008 when it was never clear to the paratroopers of 2nd Platoon whether the Wanat mission was on or off. That they were so close to going home only made it worse.

Matt Myer finally laid it out for them and told them it was a definite. It was June. They were out in the smoking area at Blessing, and the captain acknowleged the risks in the mission. It was possible the enemy was preparing for a fight. But Myer said he was intent on making their position as defensible as possible. There would be Afghan Army soldiers supplementing their numbers. They would take along a 120- and a 60mm mortar, and there would be artillery support at Blessing. A TOW-mounted Humvee (a tube-launched, optically tracked, wire-guided missile launcher attached to the roof of the Humvee) from Destined Company would go along. The high-tech missile was the one the enemy hated most and nicknamed the "Finger of God." The TOW missile had been designed in the 1960s as an antitank weapon. But the soldiers fighting in Afghanistan found it was devastating against enemy fighters.

The battalion intelligence officer, Captain Benjamin Pry, was hoping to get access to a surveillance drone with video cameras to watch for enemy movements. But the US military's conventional forces fighting in Afghanistan had only two Predator drones for the entire war effort in the country, one in the south and one in the east. And there were competing demands—in the Tangi Valley of Wardak Province southwest of Kabul insurgents had tortured, killed, and mutilated three American National Guard soldiers June 26, and there was an operation underway to find those responsible.

What bothered 2nd Platoon most, however, was intel about the enemy digging in around Wanat, and as the weeks wore on, imaginations began to burn bright with ideas of a great, cinematic final Armageddon awaiting the Chosen Few. This naturally evolved into a discussion of how they would one day all be memorialized in some big Hollywood production they would all go see at the nearest Cineplex. The next important consideration: who's going to play whom in the movie.

Up went a grease board with casting decisions listed for the movie about their last battle with the working title: "Too Short for This Shit." The actor Benicio del Toro, who played a drunken bad boy in the neo-noir action film *Sin City*, would play Jacob Sones, who was once roused from a drunken slumber on the grounds of Camp Ederle by Lieutenant Colonel Ostlund only to tell his battalion commander to "fuck off."

Tom Sizemore, who played a stocky, tough Army sergeant in *Saving Private Ryan*, would portray Platoon Sergeant David Dzwik. The list went on from there. *Napoleon Dynamite* star Jon Heder was to be cast as Lieutenant Jon Brostrom. Gunnar Zwilling got Brad Pitt. Mike Denton got *American Idol* host Ryan Seacrest. An eclectic mix of comedians would be drafted for the movie. Stand-up comics Colin Quinn and Dane Cook would play, respectively, Jason Bogar and Ryan Pitts. And *Tonight Show* host Jay Leno would be cast as Jason Hovater.

Still, the silver-screen fantasy couldn't disguise an undercurrent of bitterness over the mission. It was a real pisser to get stuck with this right before going home, and Captain Myer confirmed rumors about how dangerous it might be. But it was Army. All the bitching in the world never changes anything. There would be a grudging acceptance as the same two words rolled around in everyone's head.

Fuck it.

# 10

## >>> UNDER SIEGE

*One morning Sergeant Zaccery Johnston* and Specialist Gabriel Green were enjoying mugs of coffee at OP1, with its spectacular view of the Waigal Valley and surrounding mountains, when, with heat and a flash, a 107mm rocket blew past them and exploded just yards away. It felt like it missed them by inches. They looked at each other, clinked their coffee cups, and let out a cheer. But the enemy was definitely getting a closer bead on the ridge-top outpost.

Reports from the dwindling number of friendly locals and intercepted radio chatter all pointed to plans by the insurgent leader Mullah Osman to launch an attack on Bella and overrun it, much as militants had attempted at Ranch House the previous summer. Only this time Osman was enlisting scores of men from villages throughout the Waigal Valley river system and summoning fighters from the Korengal Valley. He was collaborating with Lashkar-e-Tayyiba, or LET, the Army of the Righteous that would launch the deadly attacks in Mumbai, India, in November of 2008. LET was adept at training local fighters in tactical skills, including zeroing in mortar fire and ambush organization.

LET's growing influence in the Waigal Valley, along with Al Qaeda and other terror groups, was one of the key reasons Chris Cavoli had pushed his 10th Mountain troopers so far up into Nuristan and built Ranch House above Aranas: he wanted to derail their leverage in southern Nuristan. Now, as Chosen Company continued its tactical withdrawal from the Waigal Valley, planning its next move back to Wa-nat, whatever gains had been made against these violent groups in 2006 and 2007 were gone. Intelligence reports indicated LET was bringing in Arabs, Chechnyans, and Pakistanis to fight in the Waigal. Something very big was in the works. Chosen Company was receiving information that anywhere from one hundred to three hundred fighters were be-ing assembled, along with a half dozen men willing to strap on suicide bombs and sacrifice themselves to breach the base defense perimeter. Planning had been underway since May. They were staging out of vil-lages like Nisha to the far west or Muladish to the southeast, where Chosen Company patrols had visited the previous year, providing med-ical and other support for villagers.

From Bella Matt Ferrara's replacement as 1st Platoon leader, Lieu-tenant Aaron Thurman, sent Afghan security guards out to surround-ing villages, inviting elders to come down for a series of meetings, or shuras. But little came of them. Aranas village leaders arrived at Bella for one session. Thurman hoped to reconnect with them and to build a relationship again, but it turned into a shouting match when the Af-ghans denied any responsibility for the attack that killed Ferrara and five of his men on November 9.

Not every town was cooperating with the surge in militants, but there were enough to provide a logistical support network. The insur-gency was distributing DVDs in the Waigal Valley showing the attack on Ranch House the previous August as they ratcheted up their propa-ganda campaign. And there was more: unconfirmed reports of heavy armaments in the area, an anti-aircraft gun north of Bella, and heavy machine guns near Nisha and one near Muladish. There was even word about 75mm recoilless rifles implanted near the villages around Bella. The Americans could glean a sense of the enemy morale by using elec-tronic surveillance to capture snatches of radio communications, lis-tening to battle-damage assessments of Bella after attacks, discussing whether they managed to hurt or kill any of the Americans they called "infidels," listing the number of their own wounded and dead, and even

grousing about the strain of combat like every other soldier in the annals of warfare: "We are tired. Want a break," one of them muttered over
the radio one day.

Bella was peaceful during the latter part of May and the first week of
June. On Monday morning, June 9, there would be some good news for
the 1st Platoon defenders. A Russian-made Mi17 helicopter was arriving
with fresh fruits and vegetables. An American defense contractor called
Supreme Air operated the aircraft using a Russian crew. The produce
they delivered was always a tasty departure from processed Army fare,
but flying into Bella was becoming more and more of a risk.

Any rotary wing aircraft were forced to navigate between mountain
walls that soared three thousand to five thousand feet on both sides of
a narrow approach in Bella—into the bottom of the Dixie Cup. Anyone
with a rocket or an RPG launcher could set up on a ridge top and fire
down as a helicopter carefully approached. American military aircraft
at least had the option of arriving under the cover of darkness using
night-vision goggles—the Russian crew didn't have that choice. On this
day they came in shortly after dawn, and almost as soon they touched
down, with the engines still running, enemy fighters unleashed a volley of 107mm rockets from ridgelines to the east and north. The aircraft was hit by shrapnel from a missile that exploded into the landing
zone less than ten feet away. Shards punctured the outside skin, and
a fountain of fuel started to spew onto the ground as the three-man
crew scrambled toward one of the surrounding buildings. Miraculously
there was no explosion, but smoke belched from the helicopter. The
crew was in such a panic that they hadn't even bothered to turn off the
engine, and the rotary wings were still spinning.

During the same attack another rocket struck near the TOC at Bella,
exploding against a HESCO bastion built to protect the headquarters.
The HESCOs around Bella were largely filled with rocks, and a piece
of the rocket somehow managed to deflect off one of them and blow
a hole through the plywood wall of the headquarters. It flew across the
room and cut a bloody groove across the top of Sergeant First Class

Stockard's shaved head as the platoon leader was tapping away on a satellite communications laptop. A dust cloud filled the headquarters, and Matt Ferrara's replacement, First Lieutenant Thurman, who was seated nearby, went diving for the floor. James Takes, who was on a radio, stood there, mic in hand, with a stunned expression that said, "What the hell just happened?" Stockard, bleeding from the scalp and red faced with anger over the audacious attack, didn't miss a beat as he stared at the lieutenant on the floor.

"Get up, sir."

Then he blew the dust and wood particles off his keyboard and went back to typing. There was much speculation later about how that episode might have ended if the diminutive Stockard had been just a shade taller. Artillery rocketed in from the cannons at Blessing along with an Air Force A10 jet aircraft with the sky-ripping sound of its nose cannon. Apache helicopters pounded the surrounding hillsides with rockets.

Meanwhile there was a touch of slapstick going on outside as Staff Sergeant Kyle Silvernale searched frantically for the missing Russians. Their helicopter was still smoking and leaking a pool of fuel onto the landing zone, and the rotors were spinning. Paratroopers were scattered around in their bunkers returning fire at enemy gunmen and waiting for the aircraft to start coming apart, sending rotary blades flying everywhere. Silvernale suddenly had a mission.

*Someone needs to turn the damn thing off.*

He and Sergeant Zaccery Johnston finally found the three crew members huddling in one of the last huts they searched as the valley gunfight continued. The Russians were shaken up and not about to budge. But with a smattering of broken English, they managed to communicate something about two red switches that needed to be flipped to shut down the engine.

Silvernale and Johnson headed back outside, and as the staff sergeant provided covering fire, Johnston sprinted to the crippled helicopter and assumed the role of Russian flight engineer. He found the switches, flipped them, and the smoke-belching rotary beast shuddered and fell silent. Two days later the wrecked aircraft was lifted out of Bella slung under an Army Chinook helicopter. Bella enjoyed air cover the entire time. Still, the next day a militant up in the hills took pot shots at a Chinook flying in supplies to Bella, even with an Apache riding escort firing back.

In the hours immediately after the Monday morning attack Chosen Company intercepted enemy radio traffic discussing the need for a doctor to treat casualties—good news to paratroopers. But they also overheard another, more defiant—and more ominous—message go out: "We have them surrounded, and they don't have the capacity to fight us."

There were eight attacks on Bella through the month of June as the incoming enemy mortar and rocket fire grew more accurate. Intel officers were guessing that local insurgents were getting assistance from groups like LET in laying down more precise mortar rounds. The mortar attacks were another deadly game of chance for the Chosen Few, who never could be certain whether, where, or when a round would explode inside the base.

A battalion intel report noted that the deadly enemy mortar firing will "continue to be used until discovered or destroyed. As Bella is broken down, insurgents can be expected to increase the number of attacks."

All the while Matt Myer's evacuation plans were underway, with essential equipment getting packed up and built into sling loads to be airlifted out. The base was essentially under siege during the day, so loads had to be prepared and flown out at night. Soldiers were becoming sleep deprived, fighting all day and building loads all night.

What was most maddening was their inability to spot the enemy mortar tube so they could destroy it and its crew. There would be several rounds fired, and then it was as if the launcher vanished. One theory was that it was somehow mobile, maybe set up in the back of a pickup truck or quickly broken down and stored in the vehicle, which would then be driven away along the mountain road leading south from Bella. Crater analyses of the shape and length of mortar impacts on the base suggested the shells were fired from the direction of the roadway.

Shortly before 4:30 P.M. on Wednesday, July 2, the militants' siege of Bella finally drew blood. It was up at OP1. Another attack was underway, and paratroopers manning the ridgetop bastion opened up with their array of weaponry. Mortar teams down in Bella started dropping rounds from their launchers. Artillery fired from Blessing, and an Apache gunship and Air Force F15s flew up to assist.

Up at OP1 Gabriel Green was firing grenades at enemy fighters from a launcher attached to his M4. He had stepped into his barracks to grab a belt filled with ammunition when an enemy mortar round slammed into the wall behind him and blew shrapnel directly into his back, pieces passing clear through his chest. There were more explosions nearby, and a dazed Green nearly walked in front of automatic fire from the outpost's M240 machine gun before Private First Class Kevin Coons grabbed him and pulled him back. Green's chest started filling up with blood; he was straining to breathe. Stockard, down below in Bella, got word about the wounded soldier. He alerted the medics to follow him, and raced up the steep incline to OP1—a climb that could take newbies unaccustomed to the altitude forty-five minutes; Stockard did it in less than ten. Scott Derry was in a bunker at Bella and watched in amazement as the platoon sergeant raced up the mountain under enemy fire.

*God, this guy's a machine.*

As a medic treated him up at OP1, Green begged not to be hoisted out by medevac helicopter. There was still shooting going on, and Green couldn't forget how a medevac crew had dropped Lancour's body during the ambush battle the previous November. But a Blackhawk was quickly on scene, and Stockard told him he needed medical treatment immediately. A flight medic placed Green in a Skedco, a kind of stretcher that wraps around a patient like a taco, and the hoist began like a high-wire act, with the wounded soldier suspended hundreds of feet above the valley floor. With the Skedco spinning and bullets whizzing past, Green was hauled inside the aircraft. Helping to pull him aboard was Captain Justin Madill, the flight surgeon whose first mission in Afghanistan during his deployment was to collect the remains of 2nd Platoon sergeant Matthew Kahler the previous January. Green was struggling to breathe, and on the flight to a military clinic in Asadabad, Madill performed a pneumothorax decompression, inserting a needle into Green's chest cavity to release air collecting there that was crushing his damaged lungs. The process worked, and Green immediately began to breathe easier. He was flown out of Afghanistan to an Army hospital in Germany, where his lung collapsed more than once during treatment. Several pieces of shrapnel had passed through his upper chest and left arm. Surgeons later removed most of his left lung.

On the day Green was wounded, the leader of the Afghan security guards working at Bella, a man named Abdullah Hamid, demanded his monthly payment then walked off the base, taking fourteen guards with him and further creating a growing sense of alienation between Chosen Company and the local population. They left with an assortment of weapons, their uniforms, and security badges, and there were reports later of Hamid collaborating with militants, turning over the guns and advising them that it was a good time to attack the Americans.

Tensions were rising at Bella. The fact that Green was nearly killed demonstrated that enemy mortar operators could strike with precision. Intel reports were flowing in that Mullah Osman would launch his attack to overrun the base any day. A battalion intelligence analysis fleshed out what was believed to be Osman's strategy—he wanted to take advantage of the planned American withdrawal to make it appear as if his assault on the base, even if it failed, had forced the US military to flee. It would be a propaganda coup. The report even outlined a potential coordinated attack plan that would begin with 107mm rocket fire on Bella from the north, mortar fire from the northeast and west, and an assault with RPGs to destroy OP1 from the southwest. A separate group of militants would try to concentrate gunfire on the Speedbump outpost to keep paratroopers there pinned down, allowing fighters to approach Bella from the south and lay down automatic weapons suppressive fire directly on the fort while a ground force attempted to sweep in from the opposite side, stepping off from the Bella bazaar just across a stream to the west of the base.

→  ←

Matt Myer went into Bella to manage final arrangements before evacuating the base. He worked on setting up air transport, and once the necessary number of helicopters was locked in, the plan was simple: fly everybody out under the cover of darkness while simultaneously sending 2nd Platoon north from Blessing to occupy the flat ground in Wanat so engineers and contractors could begin building the new base there. They'd call it Combat Outpost Kahler in honor of 2nd Platoon's beloved sergeant killed in January.

The new base was an exposed piece of ground. The valley walls on each side rose ten thousand feet. But the hope was that by building the base virtually inside the village, they could effectively interact with the population and draw them within the influence of the central government. Rock Battalion had succeeded at this with bases farther west in the Pech Valley.

Now if the move to simultaneously evacuate Bella and occupy Wanat went off according to plan, the militant leader Osman and his forces would have no one to attack in Bella, and Chosen Company would have occupied Wanat, all in one fell swoop.

Events were speeding up.

The day after Green was wounded, 1st Platoon's leader, Lieutenant Aaron Thurman, ordered the remaining Afghan security guards to leave Bella. He met with local elders, who told him they were worried about the battle to come and thought it wise to get their families out now. That afternoon mortar fire from Bella, artillery from Blessing, and an Air Force B1 unloading nearly a dozen laser-guided bombs pounded the hills to the east of Bella following reports of enemy movement in the area. According to intel, as many as fourteen insurgents were killed and nine wounded. Thurman agreed with the elders and urged them to spread the word that all residents should temporarily vacate the hamlet. Chosen Few soldiers watched them leave town early the next day.

Mullah Osman's attack was expected as soon as Saturday, July 5. But on Independence Day the actions of the Chosen Few made unexpected international news. It began in the early afternoon when a spectacular round of enemy mortar shells loaded with white phosphorous hit around Bella and OP1 just as Matt Myer and two squads of reinforcements from Battle Company disembarked from Blackhawk helicopters and the aircraft began to take off. It was the same burning material the Americans used against insurgents in the Pech Valley and elsewhere to force them out of their hiding places during barrages. These enemy rounds fell too far from the Americans to cause any harm, but the dramatic sight of the explosions and the smoky tendrils arcing into the sky were sobering nonetheless. They had never seen the enemy use the burning chemical before.

This time, though, Staff Sergeant Joshua Salazar up at OP1 spotted a pickup truck speeding south along the valley road and could almost swear he saw two men in the back of it with a mortar tube—the mobile mortar team they'd long suspected was harassing Bella; Sergeant Jackie Lofton saw it too. Salazar opened fire on the truck as it sped off down the road and disappeared. Apache helicopters were called in to attack, and by the time they arrived, the pilots could see a truck heading south at a point about a mile and a half farther down the road from where the OP1 paratroopers had lost sight of the vehicle with the mortar tube. An Apache pilot saw about five men come out of the bed of the truck as he hammered it with 30mm rounds from a chain gun under the nose of his aircraft.

Then the pilots spotted a second truck on the road. Matt Myer approved a second strike, and cannon fire also raked that vehicle. The pilots didn't see anyone in the bed of that truck.

In the hours after the attack eight wounded men were brought to an aid station at Camp Blessing for treatment. One died; two others tested positive for gun residue on their hands, evidence that they were enemy combatants. Even more intriguing to the Americans were enemy radio messages intercepted immediately after the Apache attack. The voices sounded panicked; "Situation is fucked—six dead, ten wounded . . . two martyrs died in the trucks . . . Marwan [Mullah Osman] is injured."

Within twenty-four hours the district governor at Wanat, Ziaul Rahman, who Rock Battalion leaders were already convinced was colluding with the enemy, was telling reporters that the United States had killed twenty-one innocent people in a helicopter airstrike, including women and children. Associated Press and Reuters broke the story. "The civilians were evacuating the district as they were told by the US-led troops because they wanted to launch an operation against the Taliban," Rahman was quoted in the *International Herald Tribune* on Sunday, July 6. Stone-throwing demonstrators gathered outside the base at Blessing. The narrative of innocents slain by errant US bombing raids was only just becoming a sticking point between the Afghan president, Hamid Karzai, and NATO forces operating in his country. It would escalate in years to come, with Karzai making ever-greater demands to restrict bombing operations. But Karzai had not quite reached that point of frustration in 2008, and when the Nuristan provincial governor, Tamin Nuristani, repeated claims on Al Jazeera Arabic television that civilians were targeted in the Apache attack, the president summarily removed him from office. Karzai did, however, call for an investigation into the attack, which the *New York Times* reported in a story the next Monday.

The NATO-led International Security Assistance Force, or ISAF, which was running the war in Afghanistan, put out word that the strike killed fifteen enemy fighters and no civilians. The Rock Battalion launched an immediate investigation, and efforts were made to interview Ziaul Rahman, but he refused to meet with investigating officers. The results were a mixed bag. The brigade deputy commander who ran the probe, Colonel Mark Johnstone, said there wasn't enough evidence to verify that innocent civilians were killed, but it couldn't be discounted either. Moreover, there had been a failure to maintain continuous observation of the target from the moment it was first spotted until the Apaches attacked. If the 173rd Brigade had Predator drones assigned to it for observing the enemy, Johnstone complained, they could have tracked those trucks all the way from Bella and been in a better position to know whether there were civilian victims. "Unlike all the combat brigades in Iraq, the brigade does not have its own Predator," Johnstone wrote in a report finished in late July, highlighting the battalion's lack of resources and support in the valley.

The same day the New York Times story ran, final approval came down from the US forces command for eastern Afghanistan to evacuate Bella and build a new base at Wanat. The go-ahead was ordered by Brigadier General Mark Milley, who served as deputy commander for operations under Major General Jeffrey Schloesser, the overall commander of US forces in eastern Afghanistan.

Following the destruction of the fleeing trucks, with the exception of a few RPG rounds fired over the next few days, enemy attacks at Bella fell to zero. Rock leaders felt certain that between the precision bombing runs on July 3 and the Apache air strikes on July 4, Mullah Osman's plans to hit Bella may very well have been frustrated, at least temporarily.

→ ←

The much-delayed double-axle mission to withdraw from Bella and occupy Wanat had originally been set for Wednesday, July 2. But the battalion couldn't line up all the air assets, so it was delayed one more time to the July 8–9 time frame. For the men of 2nd Platoon the longer the delay, the less sense it made to do it at all. They were literally on the verge of going home. Some members of 1st Platoon would start flying out of the country by the middle of July. Orders had come through to pack up personal belongings so foot lockers could be shipped back to Vicenza. They would each take only an assault bag filled with personal items with them to Wanat.

Much as the men of Matt Ferrara's patrol had done before their November 8 mission the previous year, 2nd Platoon soldiers began calling home to speak with loved ones before they were to move out to Wanat, particularly since they wouldn't be able to make any calls for days or weeks as they established the new base there.

Specialist Jason Hovater called his best friend—his sister, Jessica— to say good-bye. The usually charismatic soldier was in a very dark place. His young marriage had faltered under the strain of a long separation, and he and his wife, Jenna, were talking about a divorce. And now he felt certain he wouldn't survive Wanat.

"I want you to know how much you mean to me and how good of a sister you are," he told Jessica. "Please make sure you tell Mom and Dad how much I love them."

Jon Brostrom couldn't stop thinking about Amanda Wilson. They had agreed to start seeing each other outside of war and even made plans for a Mediterranean cruise with friends. Before that, though, they would grab some one-on-one time together. Amanda would come to Vicenza for a few days. "Bring your A-game," he wrote in an e-mail. The day he left for Wanat Brostrom knew Wilson was in Bagram, and he left a message for her at the brigade office there. She called back. Brostrom told her the Wanat mission was a definite go and that either he'd call her first thing when he got out of it, "before I even get my hands on a bar of soap," or she'd get a Red Cross message with bad news. It was dark humor and she didn't like it, and there was an unmistakable note of fatalism that was troubling.

Specialist Jonathan Ayers called Georgia and spoke with his mother, Suzanne, to let her know there was a mission coming up that was dangerous and that none of them wanted to go. "We don't have a choice," Ayers told his mother.

The six-foot-one Georgian was one of the quietest members of the weapons squad. He was born in Atlanta, the younger of two sons in a family that could trace its roots back to the Revolutionary War. As a child, he had a beautiful singing voice and performed with a choral group called the Young Singers of Callanwolde; he also played the cello in a middle school orchestra. Ayers joined the Air Force Junior ROTC in high school and in drill competitions was named commander of the year for the state of Georgia in 2002. But he dropped out of college after about a year and a half and drifted. His parents thought he was trying to find himself. Ayers got a commercial driver's license and drove long, lonely tractor-trailer routes for a trucking firm.

He finally joined the Army in 2006, finished Airborne training, and headed to Italy. He was only twenty-three when Chosen Company deployed, but with rugged looks and an early receding hairline, most of the guys saw him as the "old man" of 2nd Platoon. It was so unfair because his M240 machine gun teammate, Chris McKaig, was ten years older—in the ballpark for truly earning the label "old man"—but looked so much younger that few of the soldiers realized McKaig was in his midthirties. It really bugged Ayers that he was already showing some age.

*I look like I'm thirty and have a really hard time picking up girls my age.*

Others in the platoon shared Ayers's trepidations about the Wanat mission, but for Jason Bogar, twenty-five, it bordered on an obsession. He called his mother, but he didn't say much. It was a strange, one-sided conversation with Jason mostly listening to news of the family. Somewhat abruptly, he said he had to go. "But I want you to know that I love you, Mom."

Rather than alarm her, Jason chose to pour his feelings into a letter he stored on the desktop of his computer. "I feel my days are numbered, so I want to say this while I still can," he began typing on his laptop. "I pray to God no one will ever have to read this. But as death is all around me, if it falls upon me, you will understand my recent feelings on this madness we call life."

He wrote that he believed he was in the right place doing the right thing and that, as a result, death was "easier to accept." He was a young man confident in the choices he'd made and at peace with the fate he sensed awaited him. "Being back here in Afghanistan is exactly where I was supposed to be and where I wanted to be," he said. "Know that you all are the reason I am here, and to give my life for that is nothing to me."

There were preparations for the hereafter, and then there was the more immediate task of preparing for the fight to come—small, busying, hands-on chores that actually were therapeutic. Meticulously cleaning the M4 rifle. Stocking twelve magazines, thirty rounds each, of 5.56mm ammunition. Ensuring fragmentation grenades—four of them—were secured with the safety pins in place and duct tape around the safely lever. Restocking the night-vision goggles and laser sites with batteries. Topping off the canteens and CamelBaks. Breaking down the MREs and singling out favorite meals and snacks—the M&Ms, if you could find them, or maybe Reese's Pieces.

Bogar and McKaig, both in the weapons squad, checked one another's gear because they were close friends. McKaig's team leader, Pruitt Rainey, swung by to do his own review and ensure his two men, McKaig and Ayers, were good to go.

McKaig actually found the whole process relaxing. He laid a rag out on his bed and broke down his rifle, oiling each of the individual parts and carefully fitting everything back together so it operated with that reassuring, smooth action. He took the RJ Martin fighting knife his father had given him, with the four-inch fixed blade, clamped it into the small vice from his Lansky tool-sharpening kit, ran the rod connected to the sharpening stone into the 25-degree slot on the vice setting, and, putting oil on the blade and stone, started wearing down that edge. He worked the stone back and forth, almost lovingly, for a half hour or more and then turned the knife over to do the other side of the blade.

This would be his weapon of last resort. He'd keep it hidden in the webbing of his vest. It felt very good to be ready.

The night before they left was Chris McKaig's thirty-fourth birth-day, and that made him the subject of one of their ritual birthday beat-downs. They caught him in a lower bunk in the barracks, a horde of young, muscled paratroopers in GI-tan T-shirts and shaved heads descending to twist the birthday boy like a pretzel, expose his belly, and start smacking. Platoon Sergeant David Dzwik yelled out a mock caution to the attackers: "We need him for Wanat."

Twenty-four hours later, on Tuesday evening, July 8, Bogar captured the frustration over the Wanat mission when his squad was packing up for the road trip out there. Sitting up in the turret of a Humvee, he flipped on his camera and turned the lens on himself: "Here we are getting ready to go to Wanat. It's the last two weeks of our tour that we've got left in Afghanistan, and from the intel there should be . . . over a hundred [enemy]. They got fighting positions set up. We're going there. We got two weeks left. It's bullshit."

→ ←

It was misery sitting in the five gun trucks that pulled into the field southeast of the village center at 9:30 P.M. It was pouring rain and water washed into the gun turrets of each vehicle and soaked everyone inside. Whoever was on duty in the turret wore a poncho to keep water from streaming down the back of his neck and soaking his clothes. They tried to cover the turret hole with the poncho, but it inevitably shifted at some point, dumping a bucketful of collected water down on an un-lucky comrade, who responded with a torrent of obscenities.

One of the vehicles was from Destined Company—the Humvee with the TOW missile launcher that Matt Myer had told his men was so vital for augmenting their defenses, the one the enemy called the "Finger of God." Part of the equipment included the Improved Target Acquisition System (ITAS), a thermal imaging system that could be used to scan territory for enemy movements and generate targeting grids.

Destined Company was the heavy weapon element of the Rock Battalion, and much of it had been assigned to the Kunar River Valley on the far southeast edge of the battalion's area of operation along the Pakistan border. But one platoon—the soldiers in it called themselves the Dragon Platoon—was left in the Pech Valley, operating out of a base called Michigan. The three paratroopers manning the TOW Humvee heading to Wanat were from the Dragon Platoon, and their weapon had been used to destroy at least one hundred enemy fighters over the course of their deployment. It was a surgically precise and elegantly simple killing tool. Once fired, an explosive charge launched the missile out of the tube, and then wings popped out and solid-rocket fuel ignited, driving the missile forward. The missile was guided by signals along a wire connecting it to a launcher, unwinding as the projectile flew. All a soldier had to do was keep crosshairs on the target, much like a video game.

Staff Sergeant Justin Grimm led the three-man element. He was twenty-four and from Mattawan in southwest Michigan. Justin made Eagle Scout in high school and was an avid reader of the nineteenth-century science fiction master Jules Verne, as well as military fiction. When he was a kid he would draw an image of a paratrooper on his forearm with an indelible magic marker. Grimm turned eighteen just five weeks after 9/11 and was determined to enlist. By the time he deployed with Destined Company, he'd already done two combat tours with the 82nd Airborne to Iraq and Afghanistan. But he saw more combat in his first week in Afghanistan with the 173rd Airborne than in both the other deployments combined.

Also in the TOW Humvee with Grimm on the trip to Wanat were two Army specialists, Mathew May and Aaron Davis. When the convoy reached the village, a few paratroopers got out and worked in the downpour. Erich Phillips and his men set up the 60mm mortar, and up on the terraces Lieutenant Jonathan Brostrom, Sergeant Ryan Pitts, and Specialist John Hayes struggled in the deluge to erect a spiraling communications antenna. Platoon Sergeant David Dzwik sent some of his men out for rain-soaked guard duty.

At sunup on Wednesday, July 9, as paratroopers unfolded themselves from the cramped quarters of the Humvees, the job of staking out Combat Outpost Kahler began. The battalion had made plans, once heavy construction equipment arrived, to build out the fort with a stone-wall perimeter, an interior line of HESCOs, billets, a landing zone, guard towers, and a potable water system with a pump house, showers, and laundry facilities. All the necessary building material was stacked down at Blessing. But because the mission date had been pushed back, the Afghan contractor who would haul the material to Wanat, along with the heavy equipment necessary to construct the fort, couldn't reschedule until July 13.

This had complicated the mission because to conduct the night helicopter flights for extracting 1st Platoon from Bella required lunar illumination, and the cycles of the moon made July 9 the best shot. The whole point was to abandon Bella and position troops in Wanat all at the same time. Despite this new delay in the heavy equipment, Ostlund chose to have 2nd Platoon go ahead and arrive on July 9. He knew infantrymen were needed to secure the engineers' move to Wanat, improve the road to Wanat, and build up the base. Ostlund believed the paratroopers could manage their defenses until construction work was underway. His intel people said that any enemy movement on Wanat would likely be a gradual escalation of violence as happened at Bella, allowing time to improve defenses.

For now, what constituted a new Combat Outpost Kahler remained largely a muddy, dirty parking lot where the paratroopers would begin building fighting positions here and there and eventually stake out rows of razor-wire coils along the perimeter.

The weapons squad slogged up the slurried terraces northeast of where the trucks were parked to find a good place for an observation post overlooking the new base. Lieutenant Jonathan Brostrom hashed out locations with the other troopers who would man it: Sergeant Matthew Gobble and Sergeant Ryan Pitts, the forward observers; Specialist Pruitt Rainey and the two specialists on his M240 gun crew, Chris

McKaig and Jonathan Ayers; and three other Army specialists—the unofficial company videographer Jason Bogar, Tyler Stafford, and Gunnar Zwilling. The platoon sniper, Specialist Matthew Phillips—who had bachelor partied his way through Vicenza before the deployment wearing a used wedding dress—was there too, also assigned to the observation post.

There were a lot of factors to consider. It was always a good idea to have an observation post on the highest vantage point so the enemy couldn't fire down into it. But here, where there were a series of gradually sloping agricultural terraces before escarpments rose sharply, that would require setting up a location several hundred yards up the ridge and isolated from the main base. They all remembered that fight in the Korengal the previous fall when the enemy bound up the mortally wounded Sergeant Josh Brennan and tried to drag him away. If the observation post were too remote, the rest of 2nd Platoon would be too far away to come to their aid in case of an attack. Building the OP closer would make it far easier to reinforce, but it would also lose the advantage of elevation. The rising ridges to the east were dotted with mud-brick buildings that looked down on the location, some of them only several hundred feet away. Even the two-story hotel in the town center rose higher, though no one viewed that as a threat. There was even thought of placing the observation post on the roof of the hotel, but that was jettisoned as too intrusive on the local residents.

So making the OP defensible was crucial. A small Bobcat bulldozer that was being flown up to Wanat that day to help fill HESCOs would not be able to make the climb up the terraces to the observation post site. Without HESCOs, one possible alternative was a cropping of large boulders northeast of the new base under the shade of some trees, including a large mulberry. The rocks could be tied together with sandbag walls to form a small fort. There were also trees there to provide shade and concealment. The only downside was that about thirty feet to the northwest was a deep ravine where Wayskawdi Creek ran west to the Waigal River. From the lip of the ravine down toward the creek the ground was thick with trees and brush. This was dangerous dead space—ground that was lost from view, allowing the enemy to approach with stealth. That risk had to be weighed against the advantage of the rocks as defensive walls. There was simply no perfect solution.

It was almost a communal choice. Brostrom seemed open to hearing what the men had to say. They would build at the boulder site and call it Topside, after the high point on the Philippine island of Corregidor where paratroopers of the 2nd Battalion of the 503rd Parachute Infantry Regiment dropped in 1945. For these latter-day paratroopers Topside would at least be a temporary choice for an observation post until they had time to scout out a better and higher location.

The decision these troopers weighed in the mud on the agricultural terraces above Wanat would be pivotal in the days ahead. Even more remarkable, given what would play out for Chosen Company, was how the placement of Topside—and of the entire base, for that matter—would be studied and debated by military scholars and young officers in training for years to come. The events about to unfold for 2nd Platoon not only would be fodder for classroom discussion, but also mapping software would allow military instructors to take ROTC classrooms from universities across the country on a virtual tour of where the Chosen Few were encamped and where the weapons squad debated an observation post. Just as military teachers for decades strolled with students across the battlefields of Gettysburg, Shiloh, and other famous engagements to learn the art of war, they would also virtually tour Wanat in the years ahead. Because what would happen here was such an accessible example of contemporary warfare and the kind of small-unit action distinctive to American combat in the twenty-first century, the virtual tour of the violence that was about to be unleashed in Wanat—along with side-trip discussions of the Ranch House battle, the ambush of November 9, and the siege of Bella—would become the most popularly requested battlefield tour by ROTC programs across the country.

But that was not on their minds as they considered the options that morning.

In early July of 2008 the men of the weapons squad did the best they could with their decision on Topside, stringing a single strand of coiled razor wire around a portion of the outpost—they couldn't get more of it—and two sets of Claymore mines to the southeast where the terraces continued to step up the hill, with two more to the north facing into the draw. They also stocked up well with fragmentation grenades they could lob into that dead space.

They wanted some trip flares to put down into the draw, but they couldn't get those either. They continually improved their defenses, raising sandbag walls two or three bags wide. Topside was spread across three farming terraces, each about five feet higher than the next. The lowest terrace was where the men set up their sleeping bags with pop-up mosquito netting. The only protection was a giant boulder ten feet high on the northeast edge of the terrace. A tall, spindly communications antenna was set up there.

The main part of Topside was one terrace up. There the paratroopers built positions between three large boulders, tying the rocks together with sandbag walls. They set up an M240 machine gun on the northeast end, oriented toward the ravine and the structures built farther up the hillside. The boxy Long Range Advance Scout Surveillance System, or LRAS3, was positioned there on a tripod. Through that Raytheon device Pitts or Gobble could scan the hillsides for thousands of yards, looking for enemy movement during the day and with heat-sensor equipment at night.

On the southwest end was Bogar with his SAW; Phillips was nearby with his sniper rifle. A kind of communal area was in between the two fighting positions. Each machine gun nest was sectored off with sandbag walls so that shrapnel from any incoming grenades would theoretically be confined. That was Bogar's idea.

The final gun position was one more terrace up—a half-moon of sandbag walls where another M240 machine gun was oriented to the southeast. Rainey and his gun crew, Ayers and McKaig, were positioned there. Troopers called it the Crow's Nest.

At the base of the terraces below Topside, between the observation post and the main base, was the single-story row of shops that constituted the town bazaar, a place where young men gathered to sip tea and watch the Americans work so hard in the heat and sun.

→  ←

When Matt Myer stepped aboard a Chinook at Bella in the dark midweek, he became the last man off that base. The decision had been made to leave Bella largely intact, and it was now completely empty. There was no fanfare of plywood hooches set on fire for all the world to see, as had happened at Ranch House. This time they just left it all. To hell with it. Myer knew there was no way to avoid handing the militants a propaganda coup, allowing them to video a triumphant march into the vacated operating base. But when he lifted off from Bella, the captain felt a wave of relief wash over him. Certainly what seemed the riskiest part of this double-hinged operation—the evacuation of Bella and the occupation of Wanat—was now behind them. They had escaped the siege of Bella and could start clean with the new Combat Outpost Kahler.

→  ←

By Thursday morning, July 10, the rough outlines of a new military base at Wanat were beginning to take shape. A mortar position and ammunition depot were fashioned along the western border. It would be surrounded by HESCOs. Just across the perimeter were dense trees and shrubs running north and south. On the bluff behind the trees was a large structure the troops called the blue house because of its color, and to the southwest was the home of wealthy local resident Haji Juma Gul.

Clockwise from the mortar position following the base periphery were three sandbagged positions along the northern end of Kahler where Afghan National Soldiers were dug in. Their Marine Corps mentors, three enlisted men, were nearby.

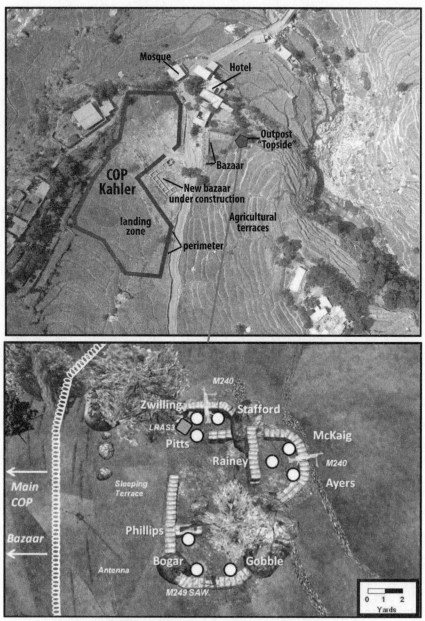

**Wanat, COP Kahler and surrounding area**
**Bottom: Outpost "Topside"**
*Courtesy US Army*

Directly behind the Afghans, 3rd Squad started digging in. Sergeant Israel Garcia—who had wanted so badly to conceive a child with his wife, Lesly, during his leave in February—was the acting squad leader. Right across from them and just outside the edge of the base was a single-story, unadorned structure that served as the village mosque. Following the base perimeter around to the east Staff Sergeant Jonathan Benton's 2nd Squad was building a fighting position directly opposite the bazaar. Both Garcia's and Benton's bunkers were crude efforts consisting of a shoveled-out fighting hole big enough for several men that was surrounded by sandbags or stunted HESCOs. None of it was ideal considering the potential enemy vantage points high on the rising hillsides to the east and west. In the 3rd Squad position several four-foot-high HESCOs were laid out in an L-shape to the north and west of the position. None of them was filled to the brim with dirt and rocks because the Bobcat had run out of fuel. The dozer couldn't be refueled because of a missing adapter that didn't arrive until later. An armored Humvee with a 40mm automatic grenade launcher protected the east side of the bunker and a modest sandbag wall along the southern edge. The ground was rock hard, and the soldiers were able to dig it eighteen inches deep at best. Sergeant Mike Santiago hated the position and their inability to make it secure against enemy fire from higher elevations. The 2nd Squad position was in similar straits, although it had a retaining wall as part of its defense, and its HESCOs were six feet high.

Almost all the HESCOs in the fort were smaller because the little Bobcat bulldozer wasn't big enough to lift up dirt to the standard size of eight feet. That could be remedied quickly once the heavy equipment to build the fort arrived. It would take several weeks to construct all of Kahler, but one task that could be done immediately would be filling up full-size HESCOs to improve security right away.

All the fighting positions had camouflage netting stretched over the top to obscure views from the surrounding hills and to serve as shade in the oppressive heat. But there was no hard, overhead cover for any of the positions. Dzwik had found some lumber in the new bazaar under construction and was willing to pilfer it, but they decided it would only aggravate their new neighbors.

Staff Sergeant Sean Samaroo, who had just gotten married in January while on leave, had his 1st Squad set up a traffic control post across the street from the eastern entrance to the base along the road running north and south. Their Humvee, armed with a .50-caliber machine gun, was parked on the road oriented south. The 1st Squad bunker was made up of sandbags and small HESCOs and was constructed up off the road on the first agricultural terrace running uphill. There was a second traffic control point on the road about 150 yards south, manned by ten Afghan soldiers.

Known as Sergeant Sam to his men, at thirty-four, Samaroo was one of the older enlisted men in Chosen Company. Born to a mother who was Puerto Rican and a father who was from Guyana in South America, Samaroo grew up—of all places—in Oklahoma. Sean graduated from high school and took a series of jobs. But he was bored with his life, and inspired by the Army slogan of that era, "Be All You Can Be," he enlisted, choosing to be a paratrooper. He served in Iraq with Chosen Company in 2003 and later in Afghanistan.

Samaroo was furious that 2nd Platoon had been handed this mission in Wanat amid reports that as many as three hundred insurgents were filtering down to attack them. But he played down those worries during his last phone call with Natasha before leaving Blessing: "Don't worry about it. I'm going to do what I do best—come home to you and the boys, safe."

The entrance to the new base was just a gap in the razor wire. To the right of the opening was Benton and his team, and to the left was the new bazaar under construction, a diamond-shaped market square with unfinished stalls and one side open to the road. It had a wall around the outside, and along one edge facing the interior of the fort was the base-command post. It really was just a space of dirt with the bazaar wall constituting one side, a Humvee on the opposite side, and

HESCOs and sandbags tying everything together. A couple of foxholes were dug in the center. The Humvee was mounted with a .50-caliber machine gun.

The armored Humvees at the Benton and Garcia locations were each armed with an automatic grenade launcher in the turret. A flat area on the south side of the base was designated a helicopter landing zone, and a fifth Humvee from Destined Company armed with the TOW launcher was positioned just north of there. The truck was moved at various times. Six Army engineers were on hand to help build the first set of defensive works. They used the Bobcat to fashion a small ramp to elevate the TOW-mounted Humvee and make it easier to fire at higher elevation targets in the surrounding hills.

For the next few days the 2nd Platoon paratroopers captured with their video cameras images of comrades in the fetid July heat, miserable under their body armor and helmets, wretched even when they were only sitting in a foxhole, worse when they were digging holes and filling sandbags. "Fucking hot, we're in a dirt hole," said Private First Class James Schmidt, with a listless look and clammy skin. Hovater pointed Sergeant Jacob Walker's camera at the townspeople standing near the bazaar just across the roadway. They had gathered there every day, sipping tea and watching the paratroopers. "See these people up here? They want to shoot at us," he said, standing over a foxhole at 2nd Squad's position next to other soldiers who were digging deeper. "Basically, this is the most sucky thing to do."

The paratroopers were quickly running out of water. Dzwik made sure the trucks arriving Tuesday night, July 8, carried as much as possible, but that was only enough for a few days at best. When helicopters delivered the balance of troops and equipment Wednesday, there was a pallet of water included that provided each trooper a box of sixteen half-liter bottles. In the heat soldiers were going through it fast. The original plan was to have ample supplies arrive slung under Chinook helicopters—twelve trips with two or three slings each. But with all the other demands for air support in the region, that request was slashed.

They only received six helicopter supply trips, and those were dedicated to necessary defense-building supplies such as HESCOs, sandbags, and stakes for nailing down the razor wire. The paratroopers had iodine pills and hand-pump filters to purify local well water, but many of the men didn't want to bother with that and just rationed what they had. Brostrom and Dzwik let them rest during the hottest part of the day and use the mornings and evenings to fortify their fighting positions. But this slowed down the work, a problem made worse because they were also running out of sandbags.

During one of those midday breaks not long after they arrived, Bogar panned his camera across Topside for some day-in-the-life footage. The men were largely motionless in the 90-plus-degree heat. Bogar's lens lingers for a moment on each member of the team, just long enough to capture the mood. The ever-confident Sergeant Ryan Pitts seems most relaxed, even vigilant, up on his feet and scanning with binoculars.

"Got your fuckin' camera working, videotaping this?" he says, grinning at Bogar.

Specialist Tyler Stafford, sprawled nearby, complains about heat rash in his crotch, digging with his fingers. Specialist Gunnar Zwilling sits opposite, waving shyly into the camera with a tight grin. The typically overanimated young private, who so often played the role of platoon jester, reflects the skittishness many felt.

"How's it goin'? Keeping alive. Want to go home."

Over in the southwestern fighting position Sergeant Matthew Gobble and Specialist Matthew Phillips try to relax under the camouflage netting. Each is leaning up against boulders on opposite sides of the position, Gobble twirling a pink fly swatter and ignoring the camera. Phillips, looking exhausted, lolls his head back and stares into the lens.

"Been up for thirty-six hours," Phillips says.

Bogar pans over to the higher fighting position facing southeast, the Crow's Nest. Chris McKaig, recently promoted to specialist, answers the camera with a "caw-caw!" His profile fills the lens, and he offers up his usual bravado: "Kill." Specialist Jonathan Ayers to his left says, "Crow's Nest is where it's at, baby."

The big man, Specialist Pruitt Rainey, lounges opposite the camera, his back against a sandbag wall, looking utterly relaxed, squeezing peanut butter out of an MRE pouch onto an MRE cracker.

"You know what's better than Outback? Peanut butter and crackers from an MRE," Rainey says in his North Carolina twang, adding a cheerful, "Eleven days and a wake-up."

That's how long they estimated before they could all finally go home. Bogar pans away.

"All we got to do is survive Wanat," he says.

It was wrenching scud work in the scorching heat, scraping out foxholes in the rock-strewn earth with small, Army-issued, folding-shovel e-tools. Water was growing scarce. It wasn't until Friday, July 11—four days after they arrived—that hired pickup trucks delivered fifteen cases of water. The plastic shrink-wrapped cases were broken open all over the new base.

→  ←

The paratroopers held only resentment and suspicion for the Nuristani people of the Waigal Valley—even outright hatred—in the wake of the Ranch House attack, the ambush, and the death of Matt Kahler at the hands of a local security guard, all in the span of less than a year. Now those feelings were reaching a crescendo. They were particularly wary of the fighting-age men who lounged in the bazaar watching the soldiers labor in the burning sun.

Matt Myer was back at Blessing building a case for how these people couldn't be trusted. The Army had quickly launched an investigation into the Apache attack after all the bad press, and the Chosen Few commander was on the list to be interviewed. His words to the investigator, Colonel Mark Johnstone, were like a sad list of bitter regrets after fourteen months of trying to make things work. He complained of how the valley people "undoubtedly [had] linked closely with the enemy" over the last year. The plans by Chosen Company and the 10th Mountain troopers before them to pull people away from the insurgency by hiring local men to be security guards or day laborers had utterly failed, Myer told him.

Rather than gravitate to the Americans, the locals they hired "would report on the layout of our bases, patrol movements, and directions of patrol." He ticked off a litany of actions to prove his point: how security guards fled their post during the Ranch House attack; how the commander of that enemy assault, Hazrat Omar, had acquired a detailed map of the base; how the ambush on November 9 occurred even after Matt Ferrara's good-faith effort to meet with Aranas elders; and how Matt Kahler was gunned down by a security guard at the Speedbump outpost. "I am convinced from other intel reporting that [the guard's] intent was to murder him," Myer said.

"Seven of my soldiers have died because of the reporting and actions of local people that are linked to and work for the enemy," he told Johnstone.

→ ←

By Saturday, July 12, a sense of alienation from the townspeople was palpable. Elders and the local police chief had walked over to the new base to make a show of complaining about its presence. There was a pervasive feeling of being continuously watched. And then word arrived that the district governor, Ziaul Rahman, and the town fathers were holding a shura without inviting Brostrom to attend—an unmistakable slap in the face. The lieutenant and Staff Sergeant Benton took five paratroopers; Alex, the interpreter; and some Afghan soldiers. They hiked about 150 yards over to the police station on the other side of the small town center and found the gathering of elders. Rahman presented the Americans with a "night letter" that had been circulating in the bazaar. It was from the insurgency, threatening to kill any civilians cooperating with the Americans. Brostrom was livid about the snub and, when he got back to Kahler, stormed into the command post and threw down his helmet.

"These motherfuckers were doing a meeting without inviting us over there, and when I walked in there they just shut up and ended the meeting," he said to Dzwik.

Early that afternoon Captain Matt Myer and his radio operator, Sergeant Erik Aass, arrived aboard a Chinook helicopter with a fuel pump and fuel blivets. They were the only two passengers aboard. Climbing to Topside, the captain checked the defenses and suggested moving the position higher up on the hill, but Brostrom and the men felt that his suggested location was too exposed; they wanted to tie the boulders into their current defenses. Myer said he wanted it moved once a prefabricated bunker was airlifted in from Jalalabad. The Chosen Company commander planned to stay in Wanat until they all went home, which he expected to be about mid-August, although the command was preparing plans for them to leave earlier, by the end of July.

Myer spotted Haji Juma Gul during the day and later received an invitation to dinner at his home up on the small bluff overlooking the new base. The captain headed over that night, and while Chosen Few paratroopers stood security outside, Myer, Brostrom, Aass, Specialist John Hayes, the platoon radio operator, and Myer's translator sat down on the floor with Gul and enjoyed an evening snack of chicken, naan, and sweet tea. Gul was welcoming, and his demeanor struck Aass as not unlike a small-town politician, a man with perhaps competing agendas. Gul warned that there were insurgents in the nearby villages. He told Myer to expect an attack in Wanat at some point—he just didn't know when.

"That's obviously going to happen," Gul said of the attack, through the translator.

→  ←

At battalion headquarters in Blessing intelligence officers continued to receive reports from spies within the Waigal Valley saying Mullah Osman, the field commander for enemy forces in the area, had devoted some of his fighters to Bella and sent others to Wanat, worried about the coalition plans to build a base there. "The future construction of a base in Wanat was a significant concern for Mullah Osman because a base established at this location would severely disrupt the AAF's [Anti-Afghanistan Force's] freedom of movement throughout the valley," according to an analysis written a few weeks later. Throughout the day, Saturday, July 12, bits and pieces of information kept coming in from the field that Osman was planning to attack the base within a week after construction started. A key spy for the Coalition forces was an Afghan they'd nicknamed Rudy, who operated north of Wanat. Up through Saturday Rudy reported in twice, and he sounded agitated. He was surprised enemy fighters had not yet attacked 2nd Platoon.

The battalion intelligence officer, Captain Benjamin Pry, would debate Matt Myer about what kind of attack Osman might throw at Wanat. Myer seemed convinced it would be harassing fire and probing attacks. That didn't make sense to Pry because of how close the town bazaar and the mosque were to the new base: Why would the enemy risk damaging those buildings and alienating the residents? Osman liked large, unexpected attacks, Pry thought. He had a hand in the effort to nearly overrun Ranch House the previous August. Some intelligence suggested his men were involved in the ambush on Lieutenant Ferrara's patrol on November 9. Osman's attacks were always well planned and deadly, Pry knew.

The Rock Battalion had managed to win use of one of the US military's few surveillance drones in Afghanistan to watch for enemy troop movements around Wanat. But it was for only part of the time—about half of each day during the first three days 2nd Platoon was building Kahler. Even when a Predator drone was spying from overhead, it could be hit and miss. The aperture for watching for people on the ground

was limited, like "looking through a soda straw," a surveillance officer would later say. Spotting small groups of men moving stealthily
through the hills would be tough, and what surveillance they received
showed no enemy movement in the days after 2nd Platoon arrived in
Wanat. It had been quiet in the Waigal Valley since 2nd Platoon arrived
in the village, and there were plenty of other demands on the surveillance aircraft in east Afghanistan. By Saturday, July 12, higher command
pulled the Predator out and sent it elsewhere. Pry complained angrily
about losing the surveillance, but it was to no avail.

Back at Blessing Lieutenant Colonel Bill Ostlund sat down to type
out some candid thoughts after nearly a year and a half of fighting in
northeastern Afghanistan. He was drafting a memorandum for General
David Petraeus, whom he had known for years and who would soon
take over Central Command, which would include Afghanistan. He
wanted to tell the four-star what he'd learned.

"I have a history of being straightforward and opinionated," Ostlund
tapped out on the keys of his laptop. He began by saying he didn't feel
the circumstances in Afghanistan were as dire as the media portrayed.
"I am not sure who is selling the doom and gloom," Ostlund wrote,
adding that the bad press over the Apache attacks in the Waigal Valley
should not cause leadership to restrict how the war was waged.

"We fight a close, consistent, brutal fight. True light infantry mountain warfare. We need the tools to fight this fight," he wrote. "There are
enemies in these remote valleys who would never negotiate a peace and
have to be destroyed as they won't be defeated."

Ostlund ticked off what wasn't working and needed to be improved:
"Aviation assets are incredibly lacking in numbers and ability." The brigade had six Apache attack helicopters, and at times as many as four
were down for maintenance. It was taking way too long to get the
wounded off the battlefield.

US forces shouldn't shrink from using more devastating tools in the
American arsenal to defeat the enemy. Right now two-thousand-pound

bombs were at their disposal, and the battalion had used them often. But if authorized, there were fifteen-thousand-pound "daisy cutters" available to level real estate and rapidly produce more landing zones. The key problem was the enemy's skill at using the harsh terrain to their advantage and burrowing under rocks and boulders to protect themselves against conventional munitions. They could and should employ napalm-like bombs, Ostlund argued. "If it is legal, we should be using it in this terrain," he told Petraeus. "It would transform areas of our battle space, further pushing the [enemy] to irrelevancy."

Ostlund was willing to use almost anything to kill every last one of them—the hardcore fighters, the dead-enders, the fanatics who refused to give up.

→  ←

On Saturday evening, July 12, Specialist Sergio Abad from the mortar crew was taking a turn at the Destined Company missile truck, scanning the hillsides with the thermal-imaging ITAS device. Suddenly he got excited. He could see a small crowd of men walking up on the ridge to the west, and he alerted Specialist Aaron Davis, who took a look and counted as many as fifteen. He'd never seen that many before while doing surveillance with the ITAS. He thought they might be carrying weapons, but at that distance, he wasn't 100 percent certain. Still, it was a terrific target.

*Oh my God, we're about to catch these motherfuckers with their pants down.*

Davis was the only African American soldier on the base, a twenty-one-year-old native of East Texas who grew up in the oil town of Kilgore, about an hour west of Shreveport, Louisiana. He decided to enlist after a recruiter working the hallways of Kilgore High School, where Davis was a senior, stopped him for a chat. Davis bunked next to Mike Denton during basic training, and they got to be close buddies. Both wound up in the Rock Battalion, but in separate companies.

Staff Sergeant Grimm thought Davis was the best soldier he'd ever had.

Word of the sighting that night was passed along to the sergeant of the guard, Israel Garcia, who alerted the commanders. The decision came back to hold off. Garcia was pissed and Davis was surprised.

*People don't climb mountains at night for leisure.*

An odd thing had happened at Topside that afternoon. A small irrigation ditch that ran along the northern edge of the outpost suddenly began to flow with water. The men joked that maybe it was the enemy trying to cover the sounds of their movement in that deep draw.

That aside, the men had finished much of their work to improve their defenses, and Pitts offered to spring for dinner so the troopers had something other than MREs. One of the interpreters went into the village with cash to buy lamb and rice, with some naan bread from the locals. While a few at Topside stood guard, the rest settled in around the sleeping terrace and ate hot food. The topic of conversation turned to favorite foods and which gastronomic craving they would satisfy first when they got home. There would be money to burn after fifteen months at war, and they talked about motorcycles to be purchased and Las Vegas excesses to be enjoyed when they got home. It was a combat version of the family gathering around the table for what they couldn't know would be one last meal together.

The moon had been setting within an hour or so after midnight every night that week, leaving the sky brilliant with stars and the valleys black with darkness. Sometime after midnight on the Sunday morning of July 13, Ryan Pitts walked the perimeter near the concertina wire and shined his infrared flashlight down into the ravine—the dead space they always worried about. He saw nothing.

About 2 A.M., down below on the main base, Staff Sergeant Erich Phillips roused Specialist Derek Christophersen from sleep; it was time for guard duty over at the command post. Christophersen was one of six Army engineers at the new Kahler combat base. He had been operating the Bobcat every day, filling HESCOs. He and Specialist Joshua Morse had been bunking at the mortar pit with Phillips and his team mostly because they seemed like a tough crew and there was a good chance a fight was coming. In the wee hours of this Sunday morning Christophersen made his way across the base and climbed into the turret of a Humvee behind the .50-caliber machine gun. The sky was completely clear, even beautiful. Marking time for the next two hours until his shift ended, Christophersen counted fourteen shooting stars.

# 11

> > > COMBAT OUTPOST KAHLER

*They were up there on the ridgeline again.*

This time it was Specialist Mathew May with the Destined Company TOW truck crew who spotted them. He was surveying the hills with the thermal-imaging ITAS device and saw three figures at 3:30 A.M., tracked them, and saw five total about twenty minutes later. The figures looked like they were carrying assault packs, and this time it seemed very possible they had weapons. At the command post Matt Myer had been sleeping fitfully in one of the foxholes during his first night on the new base and awoke shortly before 4 A.M. to the news of the sighting. Myer walked over to the TOW missile truck, where Staff Sergeant Justin Grimm explained that the figures were a little less than a mile away in an area high on the ridge where villagers had said no one should be.

*They are definitely not sheep herders. . . .*

May was ready to fire the wire-guided missile, but the captain was worried that the target was too high on the ridge for the TOW truck to reach and thought it would be wiser to do a simultaneous double strike with both the missile and the 120mm mortar. Erich Phillips's mortar crew started working up targeting coordinates for the big launcher.

The entire base had come to alert status as they did every morning by 4 A.M. It was called stand-to, and it had been protocol since the Ranch House attack showed how these predawn minutes were the most likely time for an enemy assault. All across the new post were the small sounds of men assembling themselves with body armor and weapons as the sky, just less than an hour before sunrise, went from dark to a deep cobalt blue. Some paratroopers were queueing up for a patrol to scout out locations for a new Afghan National Army outpost up in the hills. At Topside the guys started warming up the big green LRAS3 surveillance box to get their own eyes on the insurgents, but it was taking forever. Sergeant Ryan Pitts was impatient and told the missile-truck soldiers to give him coordinates so he could work up the fire mission for Erich Phillips's team at the 120mm mortar position.

Back at the mortar pit, as they readied the mortar tube, the men were excited about leaving soon. This would be the mortar team's last day living in the dirt in this wretchedly hot weather. A new team was coming in by helicopter, and Phillips's people would ride the same aircraft back to Blessing. Abad, whose girlfriend was expecting a baby girl—his "gummy bear"—was actually supposed to leave Blessing on a helicopter, fly to the sprawling US military installation over at Bagram north of Kabul, and take a jet home. He would be the first team member to head back to the States. Phillips reminded him that as soon as they touched down in Blessing he needed to grab his gear and get ready for the helicopter flight to Bagram.

Staff Sergeant Sean Samaroo wanted to wash up after four days of heat and muck. He was tired of "whore baths," where they just sponged out their crotches and back sides. He wanted to get clean finally. There was a town water pump right next to 1st Squad's position at the traffic control point. During the water shortage soldiers had drawn from the well and used iodine tablets to purify the water, even if it tasted like something out of a swimming pool. Now Samaroo asked one of his team leaders, Sergeant Brian Hissong, to stand guard so Samaroo could scrub and get a decent shave. Hissong was annoyed that the order hadn't yet been given to attack the men spotted up on the hillside to the west.

"We'd better fucking kill these guys before we get hit," Hissong told his squad leader.

As the two men strolled to 1st Squad's position, they and the entire force of forty-nine American troops and twenty-four Afghan soldiers were being watched. In the darkness of the night scores of enemy
fighters had all but surrounded Combat Outpost Kahler. They had
set up machine gun nests, piles of RPGs, and teams of fighters with
automatic weapons, boxing every point on the compass except due
south. They were in the hills and ridges that surrounded Kahler like an
amphitheater.

And they had also succeeded in co-opting the entire village. The
perfidy was breathtaking. Villagers who had gone about their business,
albeit in ever-decreasing numbers in the days since the Chosen Few
arrived—tilling fields, selling food to the soldiers, inviting them to dinner—were now gone, almost all of them fleeing as militants came into
their bedrooms and onto their balconies and rooftops, taking up firing
positions. Insurgents had filtered into the area from the north along
the Waigal River and from the village of Qal'eh-ye Gal two miles east,
using the Wayskawdi Creek ravine. There was a machine gun set up in
the home of Haji Juma Gul, and men with RPGs and AK47 rifles were
in the trees and hedgerows right along the western perimeter of Kahler.
There were even gunmen at the police station a few hundred yards to
the northwest along the river. Militants were posted in the mosque just
across from 3rd Squad's bunker and in the two-story hotel structure
in the village center. They were in buildings high up on terraces to the
northeast and the southeast looking down on Topside and Kahler. And
they had reached the base of the draw directly adjacent to the observation post in the dead space where the soldiers couldn't see them. They
had shown extraordinary discipline in fanning out to their sectors without making any noise or disturbance that might betray their strategy.

An analysis of the battle completed two years later by the US Army
Combat Studies Institute at Fort Leavenworth, Kansas, offered high
praise for the enemy, describing its leadership and the core of its
fighting force as "professional and experienced. That attack displayed
considerable planning, effective intelligence, and accurate knowledge

regarding the capabilities and effectiveness of American weapons systems and observation equipment."

It started with a single burst of gunfire at 4:20 A.M. A signal. And then the entire valley erupted. Samaroo and Hissong ran the last few steps to their bunker and dived in.

→  ←

Amid this rain of bullets and RPG rounds, Afghan soldiers at a traffic control point along the road running south soon abandoned their positions and fled into Kahler. But across the rest of the base, Chosen paratroopers' first instinct—as happened during the Ranch House assault in August and the ambush of Matthew Ferrara's patrol in November—was to stand and fight.

They moved like performers on a stage to their assigned places. Specialist Jonathan Ayers took up the M240 machine gun in the Crow's Nest up at Topside. Jason Bogar readied his light machine gun from the southwest bunker. When the very first shots were fired, Specialist Tyler Stafford crouched behind the M240 machine gun in the northeast end of Topside and turned his head toward Specialist Gunnar Zwilling, his assistant gunner coming up behind him, to ask, "Where's it coming from?" Then his world blew apart.

Ryan Pitts was just a few feet away inside the center portion of the post, scanning the western ridge with his binoculars, and was turning his head in the direction of the gunfire when he was suddenly thrown off his feet. Sergeant Matthew Gobble, who was close to Pitts, had just swiveled from the LRAS3 toward the southwest position where he was heading when the force of a blast struck him.

Multiple grenades had slammed into Topside almost simultaneously.

Stafford was thrown back over a rear wall of sandbags into the center of the outpost. The thrust of the explosion against the outside of their post had shoved the M240 machine gun into his face, smashing in his lower three front teeth. But that was the least of it. He had burning shrapnel layered down his body, along both arms, and all the way down to his knees. Zwilling, behind him, caught the force of it and was thrown, winding up on his back, dazed.

A separate explosion had hurled all six-feet-two-inches and 185 pounds of Pitts to the ground, his legs riddled with shrapnel. A hunk of steel drilled into the back of his left foot, nearly severing his Achilles tendon. Gobble, near Pitts, caught a cloud of smaller pieces from his left heel all the way up to the side of his face, and it slammed him to the ground. It felt like someone had taken a sheet of plywood and smacked his entire body on that side.

Yet another RPG blew up against the front sandbag wall of the Crow's Nest, the displaced air knocking Chris McKaig against the rear of the position. He could feel the heat and pressure. Ayers stayed hunkered down at the M240, rode out the blast wave, and began firing back.

Stafford thought he was in flames from the heat of the blast and hot metal pieces in his body, and he started screaming, "I'm on fire! I'm on fire!" until he realized he wasn't.

Pitts found he couldn't move his legs. He stared down at the bloody limbs as a voice in his head shouted "MOVE!" But nothing.

Shrapnel wounds from exploding grenades, if a soldier survives it, are like some kind of medieval torture. Not only did they shatter bones and tear open flesh, but they also laced the wounds with sharp pieces of twisted, burning steel ranging from pepper-sized bits to shards inches long. Pressure placed on an injury site—whether from rolling on the ground or getting bandaged up—wasn't simply a matter of pressing on an open sore; it meant pressing pieces of steel into muscle or bone. Writhing in that kind of pain, Stafford looked over and saw Zwilling on his back, a stunned expression on his face. And then there was another explosion. This one threw Stafford clear out of Topside and onto the sleeping terrace, and his helmet was blown off his head; he saw it laying a few feet away and crawled over to retrieve it.

Gobble dragged himself the rest of the way into the southwest bunker. His wounds were widespread but largely superficial. Still, it felt like his head was scrambled, and he couldn't focus.

Nearby Bogar was blasting away at the enemy with his light machine gun.

→ ←

The first thing Matt Myer saw was an RPG whooshing in from near Gul's house and exploding against the TOW-mounted Humvee. It was one of at least three launched at the vehicle during the first thirty seconds. He knew immediately that this was a complex, coordinated assault, and he radioed Blessing. Bill Ostlund was in the headquarters when Myer contacted him. The Chosen Company commander knew one way to quickly communicate the gravity of what was unfolding.

"This is a Ranch House–style attack," he told his boss.

The missile truck crew were all inside their vehicle during the opening salvos, and Grimm, in the right front passenger seat, was screaming at Specialist Aaron Davis, who was behind the wheel, to start the engine and get the truck moving.

"Back the fucking truck up! Move! Move! Move!"

The vehicle was facing west. Davis got it running and slammed it into reverse. But before he could move the truck, two RPGs from the east hit the driver's door and the engine compartment; a third from the west exploded against the side where Grimm was sitting. Armor protected the men inside. May had dropped down from the turret as the firing began. But the engine, without armor, started burning.

"TOWs are going to cook off!" May yelled.

Grimm didn't need persuading.

"Get the fuck out of the truck!"

→ ←

Down at the mortar pit, in the minutes before the fight started, Army engineer Derek Christophersen—who had counted fourteen falling stars just hours before—was running the Bobcat, trying to dig a ditch to drain water that had collected during the night near the 120mm mortar. He didn't even hear the opening enemy salvos over the sound of the Bobcat engine until another engineer, Specialist Joshua Morse, yelled at him to get down and take cover. Christophersen was in such a rush to reach cover that he left the miniature bulldozer sitting there with the engine running.

The 120mm mortar could do some real damage to the enemy, but Erich Phillips and his crew needed to feed coordinates into the targeting system. He didn't have those coordinates, and there was no one to provide them. The Islamist fighters had shut down Topside. There just hadn't been time since they arrived for Phillips to gather some preset targets as he had done at Ranch House. The mortar was currently set for a location far up the ridge where the TOW truck soldiers had earlier spotted people that morning, so Phillips dropped some rounds there. But that did nothing about the militants attacking them from right outside the base perimeter. He cranked the mortar tube higher to blindly bring rounds in closer, but this was almost wishful thinking. And then the gunfire grew so intense that Phillips finally had to back off the tube. He could see his men putting out rounds, throwing grenades. They were fighting back in unison even without his direction.

David Dzwik, the 2nd Platoon sergeant, had been nearby when the shooting started and raced in to join the defense. In fact all across Kahler, from the Afghan Army fighting positions and the bunker for their Marine advisors in the north to the dug-in locations of 1st, 2nd, and 3rd Squads and the command center, troops were returning fire. But Phillips could see they weren't putting a dent in the volume of enemy shooting.

*We're not even near fire superiority. We're losing this battle.*

At the TOW missile truck flames from the engine were burning back over the driver's side doorway and were clearly out of control. Smoke was filling the inside of the vehicle. The three soldiers inside climbed out the right side of the truck. Grimm ordered Davis and May to head for the command post even as enemy rounds exploded in the dirt along the thirty yards of open ground they had to cover. Both men took off at a sprint. Davis tripped and fell, and Grimm could only hold his breath, waiting for an enemy bullet to cut his soldier down. But Davis got back on his feet and ran, reaching the command center with May. Grimm followed, shocked that he managed to cover the distance unharmed.

Behind him, flames engulfed the missile truck.

→ ←

Back in the center of Topside Ryan Pitts lay in the dirt, surveying his wounds. Even after the bone-crushing attack of RPGs, Pitts was comforted—and surprised, frankly—that he could hear his comrades going about the grim task of fighting back. An M240 machine gun was unleashing rounds up in the Crow's Nest, and there was the sound of Bogar's light machine gun firing. Pitts could see the meat of his upper left thigh was riven with shrapnel and gushing blood. He worried that a femoral artery in there could rupture and kill him in minutes. With his left hand damaged by shrapnel, Pitts began dragging himself into the southwest fighting position.

Gobble was laying there bloody and shell shocked. At the sight of Pitts crawling in, Bogar didn't miss a beat when he saw how badly Pitts was wounded and turned from his weapon. "What do you need me to do?"

First thing Pitts wanted was to stop losing blood, and Bogar reached for the little medical kit strapped to his left leg to retrieve a tourniquet. Pitts almost instinctively corrected him. Use mine, he said. Procedure was to save your own tourniquet—you might need it. Bogar wrapped the Velcro sleeve high up on Ryan's right leg and tightened it down with the windless. Neither bothered with bandaging just then.

"You good?" Bogar asked. He had to get back to his gun.

"I'm good," Pitts responded, and Bogar turned to resume laying down rounds. They had built a gun portal in the center of the sandbagged wall, and Bogar was on his knees there, firing away. There was a building to the southwest high on the terraces where militants were pouring down fire onto Topside. Ryan couldn't help but notice in all the chaos that the young video artist—the platoon's eternal optimist—was now a portrait of focused concentration on the task of killing the enemy.

Down on the sleeping terrace where Stafford had recovered his helmet, he worked to get his bearings. He didn't see Zwilling anywhere. But there was Matthew Phillips over behind a sandbagged wall that tied in the huge boulder to the northwest to the fighting position where Stafford's M240 machine gun was located. Phillips was on his knees priming a grenade.

"Phillips, I'm hit, man. I need help. I'm hit," Stafford called over.

Phillips looked at his friend with a half-smile and nodded as if to say, "I'll get to you in a second," and then he rose up to lob his bomb just as another enemy RPG exploded close by. A tail fin from that rocket ricocheted over and struck Stafford's helmet, leaving him stunned and struggling to refocus. When Stafford finally turned to find Phillips, it looked like someone had released the air out of him. He was collapsed on his knees, his chest on the ground, arms askew, a gaping wound in his right side. Phillips, twenty-seven, was clearly dead.

Stafford could feel with his hand that there was blood pooling beneath his body armor. His friends were dying. His body was wrecked. And the explosions just kept coming. A wave of panic washed over him. He had to concentrate and force himself to calm down. Then he pulled out his 9mm, the only weapon he had left, and crawled back into the northeast fighting position.

Up in the Crow's Nest it seemed like blind firing over the top of the wall was the only alternative, and even then the battle could bite back hard. McKaig was shooting without aiming over the sandbags when another RPG struck, throwing him back a second time and leaving both hands laced with shrapnel. He tried to use his teeth to pull a piece of steel out of one of his knuckles, but the metal was white hot, and he burned his tongue and lips. It was chaos. Some of the assault bags stacked up in the rear of their foxhole caught fire. There was no firing portal in the Crow's Nest. The idea of rising up over the top of the sandbags to take careful aim was terrifying. Incoming rounds were shredding the uppermost sandbags. McKaig had this inescapable fear of taking a bullet to the face. There were stretches when Ayers was firing his weapon so long that Specialist Pruitt Rainey, who left the Crow's Nest to help coordinate defense of Topside down below, yelled back at his soldier to watch his rate of fire. One of the times Ayers rose up to fire he cried out: "I'm hit! I'm hit!"

McKaig looked him over, trying to find blood, but there wasn't any. Ayers said the round struck his helmet, and so McKaig scanned the Kevlar cover.

"Holy shit."

A bullet had grazed the top left side of the helmet, ripping through the outer fabric cover, but failing to penetrate. McKaig told him he was okay—he was a lucky man.

Down below, Stafford reached the northeast fighting position where he was originally poised to fire the M240 machine gun when the battle began. Now he lifted the 9mm over the top of the waist-high wall of sandbags and, like McKaig in the Crow's Nest, fired blindly for a few seconds. Then Stafford recalled how Phillips had tried to lob a grenade at the enemy. If they're within grenade range, they're very close.

The Claymores.

Both Claymores were designed to blast a cloud of steel balls in a shotgun fashion right down into the draw. He reached one clacker and squeezed it again and again, but there was nothing. Stafford assumed the electrical line to the mine had been severed, maybe by the RPG blasts. He reached over for the other detonator and clacked it. This time there was an explosion. But the blast seemed like it was throwing shrapnel in the wrong direction, back over Topside. Stafford wasn't hit, but he wondered whether the insurgents had turned the mine around.

He found Zwilling's M4 and fired the rifle blindly over the sandbag wall. In seconds there was another RPG that struck the outside of the wall and exploded. Again, as happened with McKaig, shrapnel raked Stafford's hands, nearly blowing off his left index finger.

The soldier now lay there on the ground, bleeding from his wounds and feeling spent. The sound of incoming enemy fire had reached a crescendo, hitting the top of the sandbag walls around him. Stafford began crawling into the southwest fighting position, certain the enemy would come plunging into the outpost any moment to kill them all. He found Pitts and Gobble laid out with their wounds and Bogar firing the SAW gun.

"Sergeant Pitts, I'm hit in the stomach. They're on the northern side. They're coming," Stafford said.

Stafford saw trickles of blood running down the front of Pitts's face and watched his expression as the sergeant grew angry. Still unable to use his legs, Pitts proceeded to crawl out of their position and push back up to the northeast end of Topside by himself.

→ ←

In the opening minutes of the attack at the mortar pit Specialist Sergio Abad fell with a wound to the shoulder. It was unclear whether he was shot or struck down by shrapnel. The incoming fire on this bunker at the western perimeter of Kahler was getting worse. Another mortar team member, Staff Sergeant Jesse Queck, moved to help Abad, but the wounded soldier was conscious and his injury seemed manageable, so the staff sergeant told Abad to bandage himself and went back to the fight. Abad even helped pass ammunition to other soldiers. The mortar crew, with David Dzwik fighting from behind the partially filled HESCOs, tried in vain to match the heavy volume of enemy fire, to effectively set the militants back on their heels as infantry doctrine dictated. But there were just so many of them firing at the positions from both sides of Kahler. Dzwik noticed one insurgent behind the trees outside the western perimeter of the base. The man would fire his RPG launcher, and nearly every time the projectile would be deflected off into the wrong direction by some errant tree branch. Sergeant Hector Chavez could see enemy fighters up even in the trees just outside the perimeter and Chavez was certain he'd managed to shoot some of them out of the branches. Queck picked up a shoulder-fired rocket launcher, stepped outside the mortar pit to avoid hurting anyone with the back-blast, and cut loose with it even as bullets impacted close by. He aimed into the foliage along the west side of the base where he saw muzzle flashes.

A few RPGs that missed the bunker flew across the base and exploded into the village bazaar across the street to the east, setting some of the buildings on fire. But one finally whooshed into the bunker and detonated near Staff Sergeant Erich Phillips, who was thrown to the ground. Some boosting charges for the mortar shells caught on fire. The place was stacked with phosphorous and high-explosive mortar rounds, and Phillips and Queck didn't hesitate. They started yelling at everyone to get out. Dzwik, the mortar team, and the two Army engineers in the bunker started out across 100 to 150 feet of open ground toward the command post.

Abad, who was wounded, was struggling. Chavez and Joshua Morse, one of the engineers, fell back to help him, but it was slow going. Enemy gunmen zeroed in with rifle or machine gun fire. Chavez was struck in both legs, and Abad suffered a second wound, this time to one of his legs. Morse started by himself to drag Abad until Sergeant Erik Aass, the company radio operator who was in the front passenger seat of the armored Humvee at the command post, left the vehicle and ran over to help. Together they dragged Abad into the headquarters area. Chavez, despite his wounds, managed to make it almost the rest of the way on his own before he fell, and Erich Phillips stepped out to pull him in. Grimm moved over to treat Chavez, cutting off the wounded paratrooper's pants to examine where he'd been hit on the inside of his upper thighs. The wounded Chavez lay there with only one question.

"Is my junk still there?"

Grimm assured Chavez everything in that department was fine.

→ ←

The enemy was clearly targeting every major weapons system on the base, all the powerful add-ons that Myer had insisted on bringing to ensure security—they were being destroyed one by one. The strategy was working. A deadly shroud of RPGs wreaked havoc at Topside. Destruction of the most feared weapon on the new base—the TOW mounted on the Destined Company's Humvee—was absolute. And the mortars had been neutralized under a relentless deluge of small arms fire and RPGs that threatened a massive explosion and drove Phillips and his men to abandon the mortar pit. Now an enemy shooting from multiple quadrants was concentrating on the remaining big weapons in the turrets of the Humvees.

Over at the traffic control bunker overlooking the main road where 1st Squad was hunkered down, the paratroopers watched in amazement as enemy rounds from hundreds of feet away struck with precision the turret shields around Specialist Adam Hamby, who was manning the .50-caliber machine gun. Sparks erupted as the bullets impacted. The sheer volume of incoming rounds paid off. Hamby, who had been forced at one point to duck when the firing grew hottest, opened the feed tray on the gun to reload it, and the lid was damaged by an enemy round. When Hissong moved over to the truck to try to get the weapon working, a round exploded in the chamber, blowing off the feed tray cover. The gun was now useless.

Enemy bullets also disabled the automatic grenade launcher in the Humvee at 3rd Squad's position, and the other MK19 over at 2nd Squad's position near the entrance continued to jam. The only major gun still functioning with persistence was a .50-caliber machine gun in the Humvee at the command post, manned by a teenager.

Private First Class Will Krupa, not yet twenty, had arrived in January as a replacement and was the youngest member of 2nd Platoon. He graduated from boot camp at Fort Benning around the time Ranch House was nearly overrun. Krupa shook off the intensity of incoming enemy rounds to keep his gun operating, and before long he was almost knee deep in spent brass shells and belt linkage.

Myer wanted very badly to break up the enemy attack with artillery fire from the battalion's pair of 155mm howitzers at Blessing and kept feeding gunners the grid coordinates. But the rounds were so large that he could only employ them at distances of several hundred yards from Kahler, and the enemy was literally at the gates of his combat base. He wanted to use the 60mm to fire on those close targets, but it stood out on the bullet-swept open ground of Kahler like some lone sentry without any fortifications around it. All the work up to that point had gone into securing the 120mm in a bunker, and when Phillips and his men tried venturing out to retrieve the 60mm, the enemy gunfire was just too intense.

Ostlund was on the radio at the outset, promising a B1 bomber in twenty minutes, and told Myer to start sending grids for the laser-guided bombs the aircraft could dispense. He also said that Apache and medevac helicopters were "spinning up" at Jalalabad, and Air Force F15s were on the way. But they could take anywhere up to an hour to get over to Wanat.

→ ←

Up at Topside from the southwest bunker Stafford looked over and spotted Pruitt Rainey for the first time. The big man was in the center of the outpost, leaning up against the terrace wall, using the radio. He was trying to provide the command post with a casualty report, explaining that they had three wounded in urgent need of evacuation—Pitts, Stafford, and Gobble. Stafford yelled over an update to Rainey. "Phillips is dead!" he shouted. Rainey couldn't hear him, and Stafford repeated it.

McKaig left his position in the Crow's Nest at one point and came down to the southwest bunker, but Rainey yelled at him to get back up and support Ayers.

→ ←

Fifty miles southeast at the large US military installation in Jalalabad, twelve-hour crew shifts for the Apache AH64 attack helicopters had just ended. Aviators were back at what functioned as both their headquarters and lounge, discussing the previous work stretch. One of the senior pilots, Chief Warrant Officer 3 James Morrow III, had just volunteered to work an additional six hours because another aviator wasn't ready to start. At 4:37 A.M. the alert phone in the room started ringing, followed by beeping sounds from the portable radios aviators carried with them at all times. Crew members ran the 150 yards to the tactical operations center and found it already bustling with commotion over something happening up in the Waigal Valley. Pilots for Apaches and Blackhawk medevac helicopters, along with other support personnel, filled the room. A new base at Wanat was under a coordinated enemy attack and at risk of being overrun. The base was so new that it wasn't even on the maps.

Morrow was twenty-nine and from Worcester, Massachusetts, where his family for decades owned Guertin's Café on Grand Street. He joined the Army as a helicopter mechanic and later became a pilot. He and his Apache crews were with Alpha Company, the "Spectres," of the 1st Battalion, 101st Aviation Regiment, 101st Airborne Division. It was Morrow's third combat deployment flying the attack helicopters since joining the regiment eight days after 9/11. The battalion motto was "Expect No Mercy."

Alpha Company flew six Apache helicopters out of Jalalabad, and in the months since they'd arrived they had learned to scramble faster with each mission. It was almost like a ballet. Morrow would be the senior aviator on this mission, and because he'd already been flying for twelve hours, he thought it wiser to be copilot and gunner rather than pilot.

While he was getting briefed on the mission, his pilot, Chief Warrant Officer 3 John Gavreau, was already spinning up the rotors and an off-duty airman was in Morrow's seat, warming up all the weapons systems.

By the time Morrow ran out to climb into his cockpit and take off, armed with his usual two water bottles, a can of caffeinated Rip It energy drink and an empty Gatorade bottle to piss in, they were ready to lift off, and with two Blackhawk medevac helicopters were in the air by 4:53 A.M.—sixteen minutes after the alert came.

The bread-and-butter mission for Apache helicopters in Afghanistan, in short order, was to save the day—any day that troops were in trouble on the ground. The enemy called the helicopter the "Angel of Death" or simply "The Monster." A defense industry publication would write about how a Taliban lookout once spotted an incoming Apache and shrieked a warning over the radio: "The Monster is above my head now! Do not move or you will die!" The exquisitely maneuverable aircraft tended to end fights when it showed up. The attacking militants would break off and flee at the sight of them. The only problem was that in 2008 there were never enough Apaches to go around. The other Apache helicopter flying with them this day was piloted by Chief Warrant Officer 3 Brian Townsend, who was working with Chief Warrant Officer 2 Thieman Lee Watkins Jr. as copilot and gunner. The call sign for the two aircraft was Hedgerow.

Morrow loved the Apache—its sparing, sleek design, the way the cockpit fit around him like a glove, and how it struck fear in the enemy. The helicopter looked like a giant dragonfly. The crew was just two people arrayed in stadium seating with the gunner in front and pilot behind and slightly elevated. It was designed in the 1980s as a tank killer, but its capacity for surgically annihilating enemy combatants on the messy battlefields of Afghanistan, where friendly forces or civilians could be in close proximity to a target, made the aircraft indispensable.

And it had so many ways of killing. It had thirty-eight rockets of the point-and-shoot variety and at least two laser-guided Hellfire missiles. And then there was the chain gun slung under the nose of the aircraft. It was armed with three hundred 30mm cannon shells. They were like the ones fired out of the nose of an Air Force A10 jet plane, but with less propellant, so they made a slightly smaller splash. The beauty of the weapon was that it could be digitally directed from any of an array of video screens in the gunner's cockpit. It could even be operated by a screen attached to his helmet. The thermal sighting system keyed on body heat. Wherever the gunner or pilot turned his head, the chain gun would point, and then it was just a matter of pulling the trigger. He effectively could kill people by looking at them.

→ ←

Rainey up at Topside was making it clear they were in trouble. It was a moment of truth for Jonathan Brostrom. His worst nightmare was unfolding up there. The observation post was on the brink of being overrun. It was precisely this scenario that led Brostrom to settle on locating Topside only fifty to seventy yards from Kahler—to be able to reinforce it quickly. The only difference here was the ferocity of the threat. Everybody had expected at least harassing fire from the ridges above Wanat. No one anticipated the enemy would have Kahler and Topside in a vice.

Now the lieutenant had dead and wounded platoon members up at the observation post, and it was time to act. Myer had control of the air and artillery support and was in overall command. Across the grounds of the new base he could see his men pinned down but fighting back. Right there in the Humvee at the command post Private First Class Will Krupa was up in the turret, blasting away at enemy insurgents along the bluff to the west with the big, 50-caliber machine gun.

Brostrom was convinced he needed to get to Topside. Myer stood next to the driver's seat of the Humvee with the door open, talking on the radio. The closest air support they had, a B1 bomber, was still fifteen minutes away. Myer would ask the plane to drop five-hundred-pound bombs on the flat land on the opposite side of the bluff to the west. They couldn't see into that area, and Myer thought it likely the enemy was using it as a means of reaching the west perimeter of his base.

At some point the captain turned from the radio to see Brostrom trying to tell him something about Topside.

"We need to get up there."

Myer could see his platoon leader was determined.

"Okay, just hold on a second."

He was juggling tasks and just needed time to think. There were a multitude of risks. It was unclear just how bad circumstances were at Topside. But Brostrom was insistent.

"I need to get to the OP," he said to Myer. "I think that's where I need to go."

Myer couldn't deny the logic.

"Okay, you can go."

And the lieutenant was gone, running across open ground to 2nd Squad's position near the entrance of the base to find someone to take with him.

→  ←

Four miles to the south at Blessing, Chosen Company First Sergeant Scott Beeson was assembling a quick-reaction force with 1st Platoon leader Lieutenant Aaron Thurman and Platoon Sergeant Shane Stockard. Staff Sergeant Kyle Silvernale, who had led troops up to the ambush site the previous November to find his dead comrades, would also go. They pulled together nineteen paratroopers, gathered as much ammunition as they could grab, climbed aboard four Humvees, and headed up the road to Wanat. There was no time for the arduous process of clearing the roadway of any IEDs. They'd have to gamble the enemy hadn't planted any. Moreover, to head off any ambushes along the way, Beeson instructed the gunners in each vehicle to open fire into the draws along the twisting roadway and just keep blasting as they drove through them. The result was a convoy of armored vehicles barreling toward Wanat like a scene out of *Mad Max*, with weapons blazing at every turn.

→ ←

Ryan Pitts crawled from where Stafford and Gobble lay and where Bogar was fighting and through Topside to the bunker on the northeast end. Enemy hand grenades and RPGs had ravaged all of that area. Equipment was wrecked. The knowledge that Matt Phillips, who was married only last year, was dead, and Zwilling, the soldier they called their "little brother," might be killed as well infuriated him. The enemy was trying to slaughter them all. Two can play the grenade game, Pitts was thinking. He had plenty of the round Army fragmentation grenades right there in the bunker. Sitting with his back against the northern wall of the fighting position, he took one of them, pulled the safety pin, released the spoon, and counted in his head as the fuse burned, "one one-thousand, two one-thousand, three one-thousand, four one-thousand," and he lobbed it in the direction of the draw to the northwest, where it exploded. He had never concentrated so hard on the simple act of counting.

*Longest four seconds of my life.*

He threw another, and another, "cooking" each like that to ensure an enemy so close couldn't pitch them back. They detonated somewhere in the dead space. Then he turned his attention to the M240 machine gun that had been thrown back by an explosion in the initial phase of the attack and busted out Stafford's front teeth. Still unable to move his legs, Pitts pulled himself into a kneeling posture and, with both hands, dragged his right knee up so he was kind of in a lunging-forward stance, braced against the sandbagged wall. This gave him the leverage to push the machine gun up into position and start blind firing toward the enemy. But the gun kept jamming. The ammo belt was coming out of a bag where lengths of the belt were folded. As each fold unwound, the belt grew taut and the resistance jammed the weapon. What he needed was an assistant gunner. It was, after all, a crew-served weapon. But Pitts was alone. So with each snag, a painful cycle began of bringing the weapon back down, clearing the malfunction, and then lifting himself back up to resume firing. Meanwhile, down in the draw, to the extent that Pitts's grenades and gunfire didn't stop or slow them down, enemy fighters were preparing to assault.

→ ←

The most shielded troops at Kahler at the outset of the battle were those at the 3rd Squad fighting position on the north end. This was due entirely to Sergeant Mike Santiago's decision every morning at stand-to to have his soldiers climb inside the armored Humvee at their position and be ready to fire through the windows. He thought their fighting position was wholly inadequate. So this morning, as usual, he directed Private First Class Jacob Sones—Chosen Company's Article 15 champion—and Specialist James Schmidt to climb into the armored Humvee. Sergeant Israel Garcia, the acting squad leader, was already in position behind the 40mm automatic grenade launcher in the turret. They were all in the truck when the shooting started and enemy rounds began pelting the outside of the vehicle and the shielding around the turret.

But Sones, who relished the action, wouldn't stay put. He got out of the truck at one point, and Schmidt followed him. They gathered up more equipment and ammo to bring inside the vehicle. Sones spotted Schmidt's sunglasses and snatched them up so his comrade could fight in style. It was aggravating Santiago, who was concerned for their safety and wanted them to stay inside the truck. When the automatic grenade launcher stopped firing, Sones assumed it was out of shells and once again jumped out to help load the weapon. He hefted one of the large cans filled with grenades onto the hood and then climbed up there in full view of the enemy to hoist the can into position for Garcia to reload. All the while Santiago kept yelling at Sones to get back inside the truck. He could see Sones's legs through the bullet-proof windshield. Sones had one thought in his head during all of that.

*I'm going to get shot in the ass.*

Over at 2nd Squad's position near the entrance to Kahler a soldier in fact did get shot in the ass. Specialist Michael Tellez, one of the engineers, took a round through the fleshy part of his backside. That bunker suffered three casualties in swift succession. The first to be wounded was Sergeant Jacob Walker, the former Mormon missionary who spoke Italian and had helped his close friend Matt Phillips and his buddy Tyler Stafford negotiate Italy. Walker had a light machine gun propped up on the hood of the Humvee and was pouring rounds to the northwest. He had fired about eight hundred rounds when an enemy sniper shot him through the left wrist, shattering bones. Tellez was next.

And then Brostrom showed up on his mission to Topside. He stepped into the bunker and dropped down next to the squad leader, Staff Sergeant Jonathan Benton. The two were close. Benton, who was a month short of his twenty-eighth birthday, was easily the biggest soldier in Chosen Company at six-feet-six inches and 275 pounds. He was an Army brat born in an Army hospital in Hawaii and raised outside Fort Carson, Colorado, where his father retired from the service. Like James Takes over in 1st Platoon, Benton had served in the Old Guard at Fort Myer, Virginia, just outside Washington, DC, after enlistment. Benton had actually been part of the historical Alpha Company patterned after George Washington's personal guard. During ceremonial events the soldiers wore Revolutionary War uniforms and marched with flintlock muskets. He was shipped out to Italy in 2006, and this was his first combat deployment.

Brostrom wanted to take the platoon's medic, Specialist William Hewitt, up to Topside and needed one other soldier to go along. Benton tapped Specialist Jason Hovater, the resident Chosen Company comic who did such a dead-on impersonation of the battalion commander. Hovater, wearing a stone-faced expression, hustled out of the bunker to follow Brostrom out of the base entrance. Hewitt got up to go but was just then struck by an enemy bullet through his right arm, leaving a ragged wound, and then an RPG exploded nearby, throwing him back into the pit. He was in no condition to head up to Topside.

With Hewitt out of action, Combat Outpost Kahler was without a medic. The only alternative was a SAW gunner with medical training, Specialist Jeffrey Scantlin, a replacement assigned to 2nd Squad. Scantlin, who had just turned twenty-four, was a native of Alaska and the son of an electrician who worked for the city of Anchorage. Jeff had dropped out of first one and then a second college before enlisting in the Army and signing up to be a Green Beret medic, part of the Army's Special Forces. But he failed an advanced casualty treatment exam twice—in one instance by accidentally putting a tourniquet over a wound that he'd missed on a simulated patient. He was then dropped out of the course and shipped off to Italy and the 173rd Airborne Brigade. Scantlin joined 2nd Platoon at a difficult time, shortly after Matt Kahler was killed, and the soldiers were in a bitter and foul mood. It had taken months before Scantlin finally felt accepted by his comrades. Now, as casualties piled up in the 2nd Squad position, over at the command post and up at Topside, they suddenly needed him more than ever.

→  ←

Enemy videographers scattered throughout insurgent positions were capturing footage of the battle. Much of it was blurred by camera movement or was out of focus—useless imagery. But some of what they filmed shows, perhaps unintentionally, that the battle wasn't entirely one-sided. From a half-dozen vantage points around the valley the focus is always on the desolate miasma of smoke and dust that is Combat Outpost Kahler, where through the haze can be seen boxy images of the armored Humvees, each marking an American fighting position. Here and there flashes of light signal another RPG explosion. The sounds of weapons firing on both sides bleed together and—amplified and echoed by the valley walls—become a seamless roar that waxes and wanes but never dies down.

In the foreground of each frame is an enemy fighter, often a bare-headed young man clutching a Kalashnikov, lying on a rooftop or amid boulders, taking aim without exposing himself too much or for too long. Commanders on radios or with loud speakers issue encouragements and orders. And then the shaky camera work pulls back at times to reveal the cost of shooting at the outnumbered paratroopers: militants with blood-gushing face wounds or through-and-through bullet holes in a shoulder. Some of the Jihadist fighters nervously stand back out of sight, waiting for a break in the American gunfire. At one point a camera lingers on a scene in the riverbed out of the line of fire. There is the enemy equivalent of an ambulance: one fighter—a man either dead or gravely wounded—draped over the back of another man; the bearer has one of the casualty's arms over each shoulder and is dragging him from the fight. The image helps explain the enemy's discipline when it came to collecting dead and wounded from the battlefield.

The film also shows how thick with bullets the air was where the Americans were fighting. At times paratroopers had no idea from which direction the latest volley of gunfire was coming. Sergeant Brian Hissong was fighting from 1st Squad's position when a bullet traveling right to left in front of his face brushed so close that it literally raised the skin on his nose. He spun and fell to the ground, realizing he was unhurt, then he uttered a short prayer: "If it's my time, make it quick. I don't want to fuckin' die slow."

→ ←

When Jonathan Brostrom and Jason Hovater ran out of the front entrance of Kahler a few minutes before sunrise at 4:48 A.M., they did something that shocked anyone watching, not the least of which was the enemy: they ran right through the middle of the attacking forces.

There were basically two ways to reach Topside from Kahler, both dictated by the location of the town bazaar, a row of interconnected single-story shops running north and south along the west side of the road separating the main base from the observation post. The quickest route to Topside was a left turn out of Kahler and then a few dozen yards to go around the north end of the bazaar and then across an open field in front of a two-story hotel structure and up a few terraces. A longer route was to turn right out of the base entrance, jog around the south end of the bazaar, and then climb the agricultural terraces. Brostrom, leading Hovater, chose the quicker route around the north end. Benton, who had thrown a smoke grenade in that direction to cover their egress, was stunned when he saw them do it. There were enemy gunmen in those hotel windows, including some manning a machine gun, and the two American GIs would literally be running right in front of them.

Brostrom and Hovater sprinted even as bullets flew and RPGs exploded nearby. They cut around the north end of the bazaar and were lost from sight. It's possible the brazen maneuver so stunned the enemy that they failed to react quickly enough to get a clear shot.

→ ←

Not far away Pitts was still struggling with the M240 machine gun when, to his left, over the sandbags, a head popped up. It was so sudden that it startled the sergeant. Seemingly out of nowhere Jonathan Brostrom had reached the sleeping terrace. He was wearing that familiar goofy grin that seemed to fill up half his face.

"Sergeant Pitts, what's up? What are you doing here? Where they at?"

Pitts recovered from the surprise and felt a sense of relief wash over him.

*How did he get here?*

He gave his lieutenant a quick rundown of their plight. He said there almost certainly were enemy fighters down in the draw to the northwest. And he warned that some of them might even be behind the huge boulder to Brostrom's left that sat on one end of the sleeping terrace. The two paratroopers had to yell at each other to be heard over the gunfire. The air was almost suffocating from the smoke and dust of explosions.

Now briefed, Brostrom disappeared down behind the sandbags and went about organizing a defense, realizing almost immediately that he needed more men. He radioed Staff Sergeant Sean Samaroo at the 1st Squad position down at the base of the terraces. "Sergeant Sam, get your ass up here quick!" Samaroo said he'd try. Rainey made contact with Brostrom and began organizing their remaining heavy weapons. He dropped into the southwest fighting position where Stafford and Gobble lay wounded and Bogar was on his SAW. Rainey wanted Gobble's M4, with its attached grenade launcher. The sergeant handed over the rifle along with the ammo rack he wore loaded down with magazines and a dozen or more of the brass-covered grenades for the launcher. Gobble was still struggling to focus. With the outpost constantly under fire, this battle had become terrifyingly different from anything they'd been through before. In the past any shooting exchanges with insurgents usually ended in a matter of minutes. But there was no break in the fight this time. No moment even to gather your thoughts and catch your breath.

*I really want this to just be over. . . .*

Rainey kept moving. He made his way over to Pitts and told him Brostrom wanted the M240 machine gun down on the sleeping terrace. Pitts handed it over, along with bags and cans of extra ammunition, maybe twelve hundred rounds. The big soldier, in turn, gave Pitts the M4 with the grenade launcher attached—the one he took from Gobble. Then Rainey gathered up the machine gun and ammunition and headed down to the sleeping terrace. After all the chaos and death, Pitts was feeling better.

*Somebody's taking charge. We might get out of here alive.*

→ ←

After treating Walker, Tellez, and Hewitt at 2nd Squad's cramped bunker, Scantlin knew he was needed elsewhere. He consigned his SAW gun to another soldier and took a medical bag with extra supplies from Hewitt. The medic still had the bag strapped to him, so rather than wrestle it off, Scantlin just took his knife and cut the straps. Staff Sergeant Benton offered Scantlin an M4 rifle so he'd have at least some weapon, but Scantlin waved it off.

"Everybody else is shooting. I think we have that part of it covered. I need to see what's wrong with people, and I need both hands to do it," Scantlin said, and then he took off for the headquarters compound where there were other wounded soldiers—Abad and Chavez.

In fact two other medics were on their way to the battle: Specialist Nikhil Shelke, who would hitch a ride on the first medevac helicopter headed for Wanat, and 1st Platoon's medic, Specialist Jonathan Kaderli, who was riding along on the furious gun-run convoy driving up from Blessing, blasting into every draw to discourage ambushes. But they were both still a long way off.

Scantlin ran to the command post. Abad, who had tried to get to his feet at one point, was now sitting up with an IV solution that Erik Aass had managed to establish. Abad seemed to be okay, so Scantlin turned his attention to Chavez, placing additional tourniquets on both of his damaged legs over the ones already in place and starting an IV for him too.

Then it felt like the earth moved.

Flames from the burning TOW truck some thirty yards away began cooking off the missiles loaded inside, and the entire vehicle erupted in an explosion. For some it sounded like a series of blasts. A shockwave of displaced air traveling at sixteen hundred feet per second rocketed out in all directions with the unifying effect of focusing every mind. The battle seemed to be going from bad to worse. In a bunker close to the explosion were three Marines who were advisors for the Afghan soldiers. The blast wave walloped all three, leaving them flat on their backs.

No one, thankfully, appeared injured by the explosion, although some were deafened for several seconds. But debris started raining down, and there was the whoop-whoop sound of an object flying end over end, followed by the collapse of the camouflage netting draped over the headquarters. A heavy missile warhead that had been part of the TOW truck's arsenal crashed into the command post. It was packaged in a three-and-a-half-foot tube and weighed about sixty-five pounds—and was smoking. A humming noise was coming from inside. Everyone had the same thought.

*This is going to blow up.*

Some moved instinctively to flee. Others simply braced themselves for the explosion. Aass threw himself across Abad. Only Erich Phillips chose to do something about it.

*It can take everyone, or it can take me.*

He grabbed two empty sandbags and, using them like mittens, picked up the heavy warhead, ran outside the command post, and flung it as far as he could. Scantlin, who by that time had run back to 2nd Squad position, thought it was the craziest thing he'd ever seen.

In fact the warhead never detonated. One terrifying crisis was suddenly over, only to be replaced by another.

Scantlin came back to Chavez then realized Abad was in trouble. The soldier was struggling to breathe and turning blue. Scantlin felt certain Abad's lungs were being pressured either by air or liquid building up in his chest. Effectively, he was suffocating. Scantlin performed a pneumothorax decompression. He pushed a long needle into Abad's side to release any accumulated air. Then he did a second one for good measure. But neither worked, which meant the problem wasn't air, but liquid, probably blood building up internally. Abad would need the surgical insertion of a drainage tube, and Scantlin didn't have the tools for the job.

What he needed was a medevac.

→ ←

Up at Topside Jonathan Ayers and Chris McKaig huddled together in the Crow's Nest, feeling utterly outnumbered. Ayers with his M240 machine gun and McKaig with his rifle were trying to keep up a steady drumbeat of returned fire. But it seemed as if the entire hillside—from several yards away to far up the ridge—was covered in militants firing down at them. When both soldiers had risen high enough to aim over the sandbags they could see muzzle flashes going off like malevolent twinkling lights. Sometimes they'd catch a glimpse of a figure moving in the brush—an arm or part of a shoulder exposed for just a fraction of a second before it was gone. It was hard to get a bead on anyone.

Ayers brought the machine gun up yet again, and this time an enemy round struck him right above his body armor plate. It burrowed through his upper body and exited out his back. Ayers slouched forward with his weight on the machine gun so that the barrel see-sawed upward, pointing at nothing in the sky. His head rested on the gun with his face turned to the left so McKaig could look right into it. He saw his buddy gently cough as blood spilled out of his mouth. His eyes went blank, and McKaig reached up with his fingers to feel a pulse, but there was nothing.

"Ayers is hit! He's dead!" McKaig screamed. They could hear him down below over the sound of the battle. Panic, like bile, flooded up through Chris McKaig. He'd never seen a soldier die before. From the way the machine gun went cockeyed, the enemy must have realized they had a kill, and the incoming rounds only seemed to intensify.

*We're losing.*

McKaig was now alone in the Crow's Nest, and it felt like a whole hillside full of enemy troops would be headed his way. He even thought he could hear them coming. McKaig wanted to use everything he could get his hands on to stop them. With Ayers still draped over part of the gun, McKaig fired the weapon to shoot the last remaining round on a nearly spent belt of ammo. His mind was racing. He didn't think to open up one of the boxes of additional M240 ammo in the bunker and reload. Instead, he grabbed his rifle and opened fire, pulling the trigger so fast that the gun seized up and he couldn't chamber another round. Then he grabbed Ayers's rifle, but there was bullet damage to the magazine and McKaig only got off a few shots.

*What else to do?*

He threw two grenades, one to the southeast and the other toward the draw in the northeast. Enemy fighters were throwing rocks hoping they could frighten the Americans into believing these were grenades and jumping out of their sand-bagged position to become targets. McKaig remembered the Claymores and clacked the detonators, setting them both off. He couldn't resist peaking over the edge of the sandbag wall to have a look. Sure enough, the enemy had been advancing. When one of the Claymores exploded, the blast caught a militant trying to climb across the concertina wire thirty yards away. The man was wearing a blue shalwar kameez—or man-jammies, as the GIs called them—over a military vest. The explosion blew his shoes off, and McKaig saw what looked like sparks flying off the man's chest. His body lay on the wire.

That done, McKaig turned and headed out of the Crow's Nest.

→ ←

At the command post Scantlin was struggling to keep blood pumping through Abad. The father-to-be had stopped breathing and now Scantlin was performing cardio-pulmonary resuscitation in the vain hope that he might live if a medevac arrived in time. Every time he blew into Abad's lungs, he could hear the fluid gurgling down there.

"We got to get a medevac in here now!" Scantlin kept yelling.

The message was always the same from someone on the radio. "Another five minutes out." It fact, it would be half an hour before a medevac finally touched down on the base landing zone. Long before then Scantlin would give up administering CPR, accepting that Abad was dead and covering him with a poncho.

→ ←

The enemy had learned hard lessons fighting Chosen Company in the
Waigal Valley for fifteen months. To prove the insurgency had a future,
they had to succeed, first and foremost, in killing Americans. Nothing
would get the American public's attention or foment misgivings about
the war as much as the sight of American bodies coming home.

The young paratroopers with their body armor and their helmets
and the heavy weapons they carried through the mountains and employed with such swift and precise fire had proven stubbornly difficult
to kill. Their American aircraft—the Apache helicopters and fighter
planes and gunships—could be devastating. There was a window of
perhaps several minutes to an hour or more before these flying mon-
sters would arrive to end the battle in the Americans' favor. If fighters
could find the courage to close in on the US Army positions, the pilots
might hesitate to shoot for fear of killing their own people.

From the enemy's perspective, there had been a good opportunity the
previous summer when the militants massed against the small US Army
mountain outpost above the village of Aranas, a place the Americans called
Ranch House. The allies of the paratroopers—Afghan soldiers and locally
hired Afghan security guards—had melted away at the opening shots and
Jihadist gunmen had fought their way into the center of the base.

Only twenty-two Americans opposed them. And yet despite overwhelming superiority of numbers, despite a deluge of RPGs, rifles, and
machine gun fire, the Americans had fought back fiercely, even calling
down a strafing mission on their own base, and militants failed to kill
a single one of them.

An even better opportunity had presented itself four months later in
the valley southwest of Aranas. It was a perfect trap—a narrow, cliff-side
trail with almost no place to hide. The militants were waiting in positions surrounding the narrow column of fourteen Americans walking
the trail. It was excellent killing ground. Other fighters were positioned
to block reinforcements from the nearest US base at Bella.

And yet once again the paratroopers had bitterly resisted, even after
many of them were forced to jump off a cliff. The Jihadist fighters kept

shooting for hours at soldiers crouched along the trail or seeking cover among rocks and trees after tumbling into the valley below. And most of them survived, in many cases relentlessly returning fire.

The Americans had slipped through the enemy's grasp seven months later, despite hundreds of militants closing in on them at the valley crossroads outpost near the hamlet of Bella. The US Army evacuated their people under the cover of darkness using helicopters.

So the enemy fighters had followed them to Wanat for a last chance at killing them.

To succeed, they knew they would have to get very close, close enough for a sure kill. A few weeks before the attack on Wanat and more than a hundred miles to the west in Wardak Province, insurgents had ambushed an American convoy and tortured, killed, and mutilated three American National Guard soldiers. In Wanat the terrain might just let them repeat that success. From where the Americans had built their outpost, the ground to the northeast fell sharply into a tree-filled ravine where the Wayskawdi Creek ran east to west. Fighters could work their way from the east down the creek bed at the base of that ravine and remain totally out of sight. They could climb up the draw several dozen feet through thick vegetation to a point only several feet from a huge boulder near the observation post.

From there an attack of grenades followed by close-quarter rifle fire could surprise and annihilate any Americans on that terrace behind the boulder. An enemy fighter behind the rock could merely cut left and flank the north side of the terrace where there was a sandbag wall. From that range they might kill the paratroopers, even with all their body armor, helmets, and guns.

→ ←

When the enemy attack came, Brostrom and Hovater were already on the sleeping terrace near that large boulder and below the limbs of a tall mulberry tree towering over that end of the outpost. It was under the branches of that tree in the days before the battle where the paratroopers took their siestas, sitting cross-legged in the dirt or sprawled with their backs against the boulder or the mulberry. Tyler Stafford, Pruitt Rainey, Gunnar Zwilling, Ryan Pitts, Matthew Phillips, and the others would smoke cigarettes and talk about going home.

Now Phillips lay dead there. Rainey stepped down onto the terrace carrying the M240 machine gun by a strap over his shoulder, his arms loaded with ammunition given to him by Pitts.

Suddenly enemies came face to face. Rainey was the first to see them. "They are right behind the fucking rock!" he yelled. "They are right behind the fucking sandbags, right behind the fucking sandbags!"

The sleeping terrace erupted with AK47 fire and explosions, possibly from grenades.

More gunfire. More explosions.

Bogar over in the southwest position had been hunched over, trying to clear a jam in his light machine gun, working with his Leatherman tool. When he heard the violence he moved instinctively. Slinging the weapon, he jumped the sandbagged wall to reach the sleeping terrace and moved toward what was obviously a breach in Topside's defenses.

Rainey was shot several times. One was a gut wound. Another hit him in the upper back and smashed into his spine. Other bullets or pieces of shrapnel also tore into his body, including one that blew a hole through his left jaw. He had just turned twenty-two in February and died with a Chosen Company Punisher tattoo on his right elbow.

Hovater, less than a month from his twenty-fifth birthday, was killed instantly by a bullet that hit the bottom of the night-vision mount on his helmet and deflected into nearly the center of his face. The pathway of the round suggests he was lying prone on the ground in a fighting position. His rifle had no magazine in it, and some soldiers later surmised he was in the process of reloading when he was killed.

Bogar, who chronicled the life of Chosen Company with his ever-ready camera, stepped into the middle of a slaughter. A bullet struck him in the right side of his head and he fell dead. He was twenty-five.

Several feet away Brostrom, the twenty-four-year-old lieutenant, was struck down and killed by a single round that hit him just above his right temple. He might not even have even seen it coming.

All the bodies had cuts and penetrating wounds that could have come from grenade explosions. Their shouts and screams amid the blasts and gunfire could be heard fifty yards away at 1st Squad's traffic-control bunker near the base of the agricultural terraces.

From that position Staff Sergeant Sean Samaroo strained to see what was happening at Topside and spotted an enemy fighter crouched on top of the large boulder on the sleeping terrace. The man had an AK47 and was firing bullets into the outpost as he yelled, "Allahu Akbar!" Samaroo was stunned that the enemy was that close to Topside.

*How is he fucking right there? How did he get inside the wire?*

The staff sergeant took aim and dropped the fighter with four rounds from his M4 rifle.

Ryan Pitts was still alive. A sandbag wall separated him from the fighting on the terrace below and he was using the grenade launcher attached to the M4 that Rainey had given him to drop grenades as close to the draw as he could. He held the rifle almost vertical in the hope that the grenades would not land too far away. The first one he launched looked almost as if it would drop back down on him.

→ ←

On the opposite end of Topside McKaig slid into the southwest bunker to find Stafford and Gobble lying against boulders, facing each other, their legs intertwined. He looked over their wounds. Stafford was covered in blood and looked like he had been blasted by a giant shotgun. McKaig noticed how some of Stafford's front teeth were bashed in.

Bullets were hitting inside their position. McKaig, Gobble, and Stafford were not yet aware that four of their friends had been slaughtered on the sleeping terrace a few feet away. McKaig found another rifle, but it was dicey trying to raise up and fire. He peeked over in the direction of the sleeping terrace and caught sight of an insurgent just behind the left side of the large boulder. The man was holding an AK47 in his right hand and reaching around the rock to fire blindly into Topside, spraying bullets.

Their corner of the observation post was taking rounds from opposite directions, including from a building far up on the terraces about 100 to 150 yards to the southeast. This, McKaig thought, he could deal with. There was a light antitank weapon, a kind of modern bazooka, hanging from the branch of a tree right in the corner of their position. The weapon was a one-shot rocket launcher made up of two tubes, one inside the other. McKaig extended the tubes, pulled the safety pin—or thought he had—and then leaned out around a rock that protected one side of their position and took aim at a window of the structure.

But the launcher wouldn't fire.

The fighting position was cramped—McKaig was on his knees near Stafford and Gobble. Gobble started yelling at McKaig.

"Pull the fucking safety, McKaig! Pull it!"

"I pulled the fucking safety!"

But of course he hadn't. This time he yanked hard and the weapon was armed. He leaned out again, focused where he could see five or six muzzle flashes coming from the building, and fired. The missile was dead on; it exploded against the bondeh, and the gunfire from there stopped.

But they were huddled so tightly together that the back-flash from the launcher scorched Gobble and Stafford. They looked like characters from a Warner Brothers cartoon, with little bits of their uniforms smoking and their faces blackened with soot. Except they didn't sound like a Warner Brothers cartoon.

"You motherfucker!" Gobble said.

"You piece of shit!" Stafford chimed in.

→ ←

Down below in Kahler the one remaining major weapons systems still hammering the enemy was the .50-caliber machine gun in the armored Humvee that was part of the command post defense. Will Krupa was firing it, and the weapon was quickly becoming his all-time favorite gun. He knew he was abusing the hell out of it, putting so many rounds through the barrel that it was red hot. But the gun didn't break down.

Krupa had grown up in New Hampshire, the oldest of two boys. His dad worked for the state, assisting veterans, and his mom managed physical therapists. Will had been a cheerleader at Bishop Brady High School in Concord, New Hampshire, during the basketball season when he wasn't playing football or baseball—he thought it was fun. He joined the Army as soon as he graduated in June of 2007, just weeks after Chosen Company had reached Afghanistan. He chose Airborne, finished training, and was sent to Vicenza. While waiting to join Chosen in Afghanistan, Krupa was assigned the sobering task of helping widows from 1st Battalion pack up their belongings for the trip home to the United States. Like Scantlin, Krupa arrived in Bella to join 2nd Platoon in the days right after Matt Kahler was killed and went through the same difficult period of winning acceptance from the other paratroopers. But also like Scantlin, Krupa finally felt a part of the team by the time they arrived in Wanat. He had been tapped that morning to man the .50-caliber at the command post. The type of heavy machine gun he was using had been a part of the US arsenal longer than almost any other weapon, with origins in its design dating back to World War I. It was efficient and massively deadly, firing rounds nearly four inches long at a muzzle velocity of twenty-nine hundred feet per second to a range of more than a mile.

Krupa was running through dozens of hundred-round ammo cans, loading the rounds and throwing the empty containers out of the turret. He could churn through one hundred bullets in fewer than fifteen seconds. Soldiers kept bringing him more ammo, taking it from the

1st Squad Humvee, where their .50-caliber was disabled. The barrel of Krupa's machine gun needed to be changed out, but it was too dangerous to climb outside the vehicle to make that switch. Krupa tried to stagger his rate of fire so the barrel wouldn't turn white hot and begin to warp.

He was shooting the big gun into the trees and foliage all along the western perimeter of Combat Outpost Kahler and could see branches and leaves disintegrate under the onslaught. Specialist John Hayes gave directions where to fire and Krupa stitched rounds into the far hillside across the river and at the buildings just outside the base that militants were using as gun positions. One of them was the home of Haji Juma Gul, the town father who had begged Matt Myer to spare his house in the event of violence. Now Krupa was putting fist-sized holes in the walls. He saw a figure holding an RPG launcher behind some foliage suddenly disappear under the chug-chug-chug of his machine gun.

*I like the way this feels.*

And the brass just kept piling up.

→ ←

For the first time Topside had fallen silent, and there were decisions to be made. The rocket McKaig had launched at the mud hut high on the terrace seemed to give them a reprieve in enemy fire from that direction. McKaig only had two magazines left. He and Gobble and Stafford needed to do something now—perhaps even get the hell out of there. He looked back at Gobble, the senior man.

"Do you want to fall back, or do you want us to get more ammo?" McKaig asked.

Gobble still seemed out of it. He managed only to nod at McKaig, who had asked an either-or question.

"Who's going to get more ammo?" McKaig asked.

No reaction.

"Okay now, don't all volunteer to go down," he said. "I guess it's going to be me."

Then he was gone. He threw himself through the gun portal built for Bogar's light machine gun, causing some of the sandbags to collapse. McKaig wriggled free and took off running down the terraces, making a beeline for 1st Squad's bunker, zig-zagging as much as possible.

Gobble watched McKaig go and looked at Stafford.

"We got to get out of here, man."

He pushed more of the sandbags out of the way so that he and Stafford could climb out. As Stafford waited by the terrace wall to the left, Gobble crept around the boulder to the right and peered onto the sleeping terrace. For the first time, he realized the awfulness of what had happened down on the sleeping terrace—he could see bodies of dead American soldiers everywhere. An enemy fighter on the west side of the large boulder took a shot at him, and Gobble pulled back.

Were any Americans alive?

"Is anybody out there?" Gobble yelled.

No one answered, and he turned back to Stafford. "They're all dead. They're all gone. We got to go." Stafford agreed, and both men took off south, using the terrace wall to their left as cover until they crossed the concertina wire perimeter, and then they turned west down the terraces.

Stafford got caught in the razor wire and, for a moment, saw a gunman in the window of the hotel to the northwest. He thought any next second would be his last, and he kept kicking furiously until he finally managed to free himself and keep going.

At 1st Squad's position Staff Sergeant Samaroo, who shot an insurgent off the boulder near Topside, assembled a small relief force of himself and two of his specialists, Adam Hamby and Tyler Hanson. They started moving up the terraces when they suddenly saw McKaig coming down to them and, in short order, Stafford and Gobble, looking like bloody, stumbling refugees fleeing some horror. Gobble fell before he reached the bunker, and Samaroo pulled him in.

All three tumbled into the bunker or were dragged inside. Gobble told Samaroo that everyone else up at Topside was dead. McKaig, the only one of the three with a weapon, immediately took a position against the terrace wall facing Topside. He warned everyone to expect an enemy attack at any moment.

"They're coming! They're coming!"

→ ←

Ryan Pitts also noticed the silence over Topside. There was no incoming fire, and even more disconcerting, there was nothing going out. He crawled to investigate, first looking into the sleeping terrace to see the bodies down there. Their sleeping bags, looking like twisted rectangular mounds with their pop-up mosquito netting, had tumbled down to the terrace below. Pitts continued crawling through the position. He snatched a look up into the Crow's Nest where Ayers's body lay. With each new piece of evidence that he was alone, Pitts edged toward panic. Then he reached the southwest position and saw it was empty.

He was all by himself and could now hear enemy fighters calling out to one another just yards away. Why they didn't just come charging in was a mystery. Pitts dragged himself back to the northwest position, trying to contain his fear. He was too badly wounded to flee. There were people just a stone's throw away eager to kill or capture him. They'd already slaughtered his friends.

He keyed the handset on the radio and whispered the call signs for Dzwik, the platoon sergeant; Captain Myer; and his buddy, John Hayes, the platoon radioman: "Chosen six, two-five, two-six-Romeo, this is nine-two." The voice transmission could be heard at all the fighting positions below.

Myer picked up. Pitts told him he was alone and couldn't move. Pitts said he could hear the enemy talking just a few dozen feet away, and John Hayes, the radio operator at the command post, could actually hear those voices in the background as Pitts was whispering. It was one more crisis that Myer couldn't do anything about. He had dead and wounded around him in the operations center. Brostrom had already headed up to Topside with a team, and Myer had no idea what had happened with them. He had no one else to spare just then and told Pitts as much. Pitts knew he couldn't make himself any clearer about how dire it was. He told the Chosen Company commander that Topside would fall without reinforcements and that this was his last transmission.

Others who heard those words down below couldn't stand by, however. Two Marines named Jason, fighting in the north part of the base, were galvanized by Pitts's words. Corporal Jason Oakes and Corporal Jason Jones had been busy. One of the Afghan soldiers they mentored had been wounded out in the open, and they had left their bunker to drag him behind cover and treat him. Now the Marines heard Pitts over the radio and started preparing to head across the base to offer their services.

Nearby, at the 3rd Squad bunker, enemy fire had disabled the automatic grenade launcher, and Santiago was in the turret, firing a squad automatic weapon he got from one of the engineers. That's when the radio crackled with Pitts whispering his dire circumstances. Sones knew he had to act. Armed with his SAW gun, he and Garcia ran toward 1st Squad's position, moving in the direction of Topside. It all happened so fast that Santiago, who couldn't hear the radio, wasn't even sure at first why the two soldiers were suddenly gone, leaving him and Schmidt behind.

→ ←

Jimmy Morrow and his Apache helicopter crews had opted to take a direct route from Jalalabad to Blessing. A common pattern was to fly northeast through the Kunar Valley and swing due west through the Pech Valley. But this crisis didn't allow time for that, so they went into the clouds at ten thousand feet to clear the mountains north of Jalalabad and then cross the deadly Korengal Valley. The medevacs took a more circuitous route to avoid the clouds, but they generally kept to the same bearing. By the time everyone converged over Blessing, the air traffic was hectic. The soldiers manning the artillery were preparing to hold their fire to make way for the Apaches, which had been orbiting briefly.

Soon the medevacs showed up and proceeded to land in order to top off their fuel tanks. The twin Blackhawks were part of a platoon that, like the Apaches, was with the 101st Aviation Regiment. After arriving in Afghanistan in January, the medevac pilots and crew members decided the platoon needed a motto to boost its image, and several possibilities were tossed around. There was, "The louder you scream, the faster we come," but that was an unmistakable double entendre. "We don't come until you bleed" was rejected out of hand as unintentionally misogynistic. Being based in Jalalabad, they thought about "Jalala-Bastards," but finally agreed on "Burning gas to save your ass," even managing to find someone who could draw a cartoon for an emblem showing a muscle-bound Blackhawk hoisting a donkey.

→  ←

At Topside Pitts was growing increasingly lightheaded from the loss of blood. The tourniquet on his leg was causing blood to accumulate in his upper right thigh above the bind, and it hurt. The sergeant nonetheless tried to clear his thoughts. He'd be goddamned if the enemy was going to take him alive. He knew what Al Qaeda was capable of. No one could forget the cold-blooded, theatricality of Wall Street Journal reporter Daniel Pearl's execution by the terror group in 2002 or how the Al Qaeda henchman Abu Musab al-Zarqawi personally beheaded freelance American worker Nick Berg in Iraq in 2004. That wasn't going to happen to Pitts. He still had 40mm grenades and raised the rifle again to almost vertical to start lobbing the explosives somewhere near those voices he heard. What else to do? He radioed 1st Squad, and Brian Hissong picked up. Pitts told him to lay down fire directly over the observation post.

"If you see my position, shoot over the top of the sandbags."

That way any insurgents trying to charge in and kill Pitts might be cut down by a canopy of lead. Hissong obliged and sent a stream of rounds over Topside. Captain Myer came up on the radio again to tell Pitts that the Apache attack helicopters were just minutes away. He asked for guidance on where those aircraft should lay their rounds. Pitts urged that they attack from west to east and concentrate on the draw to his northwest.

For Pitts the news was encouraging. But it was a solution minutes away or more. He was living in the moment, and right now there were no other options but to prepare to be overrun. Still in the northeast bunker under the limbs of the big mulberry tree, he sat with his back propped against the earth wall of the terrace to the east. He held the M4 with the launcher in his lap. With any luck, the enemy wouldn't know exactly where he was when they came. If they climbed up from the sleeping terrace, it might take them a second to see him tucked in the corner.

*I want to kill at least two or three of them before they finally kill me.*

So this would be the end.

→ ←

Fifty yards away Garcia and Sones reached 1st Squad's bunker, and with no immediate enemy assault as McKaig had feared, Samaroo was ready to finally try to reach Topside. This time the team would be him, Garcia, Sones, and Denton. Suddenly drafted for the mission, Denton was ready but convinced they were headed into a nightmare.

*I'm scared shitless.*

They chose to climb the terraces by using a series of cut-throughs, or drainage sluices, carved into each wall of dirt. This way they wouldn't have to scale each terrace wall and the cut-throughs might offer cover from enemy fire. In short order they reached the same terrace level as Topside and turned north toward the outpost. Samaroo got there first.

Garcia vaulted the concertina wire where Stafford had gotten stuck several minutes before and then lifted the coil for Sones and Denton to crawl under.

→ ←

Pitts heard voices. Samaroo was calling his name. His buddies had come. They were climbing into the southwest position. Sones, unsettled by the sight of his dead comrades on the lower terrace to his left, pushed through the small fort until he reached Pitts. Garcia was right behind him. Sones fell to his knees and immediately began working to treat Topside's last survivor. He saw the tourniquet on Pitts's right leg and started to cut away his trousers to get a better look at his wounds.

"You didn't have to get shot for me to take your pants off," Sones said.

The sergeant smiled back at him. More and more, Pitts's ability to focus was slipping, his head was swimming, and he was tiring of Army protocol bullshit. He took off his helmet.

*Fuck this.*

But Sones wouldn't have it. "Sergeant Pitts, you gotta put your helmet on. The Apaches are coming."

*Fine.*

Pitts obliged. Denton had jumped down to the sleeping terrace, and from where he stood among his fallen friends, he could read the battlefield, how the enemy must have assaulted from the low ground behind the boulder. For good measure he stepped around the west corner of the big rock and started shooting down into the draw. They'd have to get ready for another assault, and Denton turned to the difficult task of gathering spare ammo from the dead. He first went to Hovater, the friend whose religious counsel had helped strengthen Denton's faith.

"I love you," Denton said out loud, tears in his eyes.

Then he policed up his friend's M4 magazines and a belt of 40mm grenades Denton could use because he was carrying a rifle with a grenade launcher attached. He took more rifle ammunition and a radio off of Brostrom's body and gave the radio to Samaroo. Then Denton made his way up to the Crow's Nest and found Ayers, still slumped over the M240 machine gun there. He gently lifted Ayers off the gun, apologizing out loud about having to move him like so much baggage in the way.

"I am sorry, buddy."

Denton oiled the weapon, looped in a new belt of ammunition, and opened fire on the upper windows of the same structure that McKaig had targeted with the light antitank weapon. Insurgents were back there again, firing from the building. Denton paused long enough to lob grenades with the launcher attached to his M4 into the draw to the northeast.

He was looking in that direction when he saw the orange flash of an RPG coming straight at him. It wasn't the only one. Another volley was descending on Topside; the enemy was attacking once again. Denton could only manage to turn his head at the last second as the RPG exploded, launching the big man out of the Crow's Nest and down into the main portion of Topside, where he hit the ground head first. A hunk of steel had blasted into his right hand, causing a compound fracture; he could see the bone sticking out the back. Other large pieces of shrapnel struck him in the right foot and left hip, leaving his entire left side numb. Small pieces of steel raked much of his body. The pain was excruciating.

Sones was thrown back within the bunker. A large piece of shrapnel blew clear through his left shoulder, in one side and out the other. Another hunk of metal was lodged in his right calf, and there was shrapnel layered down his left thigh. It felt for a moment like his left leg had been blown off, and Sones didn't even want to look at what his mind's eye told him was a bloody stump. Pieces of steel peppered the length of his left arm all the way down his hand, and his left wrist was broken. Shrapnel had actually penetrated a bracelet he wore in honor of Matt Kahler, the twisted edges sticking into his wrist.

Samaroo had been on the radio giving Myer a status report that only Pitts was found alive. "I'm not a fucking medic. But I'm pretty sure everyone else is dead," he told the captain. Then Samaroo's world seemed to evaporate around him, lost in a white-hot explosion. When his senses refocused, Samaroo heard himself screaming. Blood was spurting from an open head wound to his right temple, and he was sure he was dying. The radio he'd been using was stuck on voice transmission—it was hot micing—sending his anguished cries to radios across Kahler, where stunned Chosen Company soldiers could hear Samaroo bawling that he loved his wife, Natasha, and his son, Dylan. Brian Hissong, who felt helpless down at 1st Squad's position where he had three wounded men who couldn't be left behind, finally couldn't stand listening any longer and switched the radio to a different channel.

The worst of the attack was what happened to Garcia. An RPG hit him straight on. The rocket impacted the soldier's pelvis just above his left thigh and exploded, blowing a hole through his body nearly a foot wide. His entire backside was gone. The son of immigrants, who had worked to become an American citizen in time to volunteer to fight his new nation's wars, had been nearly cut in two.

He was thrown over the rear wall of the northwest fighting position and landed in the center of the outpost, where his insides spilled into the dirt. Pitts caught some bits of shrapnel but managed to shake it off and immediately crawled into the center of the post. He was horrified by the physical damage Garcia had suffered. His friend was on his stomach with his head turned to the side.

And he was still alive.

# 12

> > > "PRAY TO JESUS"

By the time the twin medevac flights were busy refueling at Blessing, waiting for the green light to fly to Wanat, dire word had come through about more casualties. Combat Outpost Kahler was reporting ten wounded and eight dead. Even though the battle still raged, given the volume of wounded, the first medevac lifted off and headed directly for Kahler at 5:45 A.M. with orders to touch down on the new landing zone despite the danger and collect the wounded.

The second helicopter was piloted by Chief Warrant Officer 3 Chris Hill and his copilot, Captain Ben Seipel. On board was the crew chief, Sergeant William Helfrich, and the flight medic, Staff Sergeant Matthew Kinney. A fifth man with them was a flight surgeon, Captain Justin Madill, whose first mission the previous January was to help pick up the body of 2nd Platoon sergeant Matt Kahler. Now Madill would be flying up to a new base named in honor of that slain soldier.

→ ←

At the Kahler command post Matt Myer realized he had a disaster on his hands up at Topside. The original garrison for the outpost had been all but destroyed and two successive relief forces annihilated, or nearly so. His men knew the savagery of the attacks all too well. They heard the horrors on the open mic. But there was only one thing to do—send yet another team.

Myer turned to the men huddled in the command post.

"We need to get up there."

Nothing. No one said anything. No one moved. The captain understood the hesitation. He could hardly blame them. Nevertheless, he repeated it twice more.

People were stirring. A group began to form. Staff Sergeant Erich Phillips would lead them. Sergeant First Class David Dzwik would go, along with Staff Sergeant Grimm and Specialist Davis from the blown-up TOW truck; Sergeant Erik Aass from platoon headquarters; Staff Sergeant Jonathan Benton, the 2nd Squad leader; the two Marine Jasons, Oakes and Jones; and two more men from the mortar team, Staff Sergeant Queck and Sergeant Jared Gilmore.

Gilmore was a twenty-five-year-old former high school track star from Mandeville, Louisiana, just across Lake Pontchartrain from New Orleans. He was a state champion in the mile and two-mile as a freshman at Northlake Christian School until a damaged Achilles tendon ended his competitive running. He was raised on family crawfish broils and, while deployed, sorely missed such Louisiana cuisine as jambalaya, crawfish étouffée, and deep-fried alligator. Gilmore enlisted in 2003 and went to Afghanistan the first time in 2005–2006 with the 173rd Airborne Brigade. On this July morning in Wanat he was in the biggest battle of his life, and by the time he and the other mortar team members were forced to flee their bunker, Gilmore was fairly certain he would not survive the day.

Smoke grenades were thrown to obscure their movement as the group reached Hissong and his men in the traffic control point bunker. Gobble by now had completely regained his faculties and was furious to learn that he had left Pitts behind. With his pants cut away by soldiers trying to treat him, Gobble demanded to go with this next relief force, but he was told to stay put.

→ ←

As the Apache helicopters approached Kahler at 5:22 A.M., Matt Myer came up on the radio.

"Be advised, we are in a bad situation," he told the pilots. "There's an OP that is just east of my location. . . . They should have smoke out and [you should] continue gun-runs outside of their location to get the enemy pushed back."

The first order of business was getting those attack aircraft up to Topside.

"I need you to come in hot immediately," Myer told them.

Brian Townsend, at the controls of one of the Apache aircraft, already had a sense of how bad things were because the battalion commander, Bill Ostlund, was on the radio minutes before telling them how close the enemy was to overrunning Topside. "They're within hand grenade range at this time," Ostlund had said.

Townsend's nickname was Tizzle, and his Indiana twang gave his voice a sense of authority and confidence over the radio. Brian got his airplane pilot license at eighteen and, after graduating from Purdue University with a degree in aviation administration, wanted to fly helicopters for a living. He settled on Army Aviation and picked the Apache. This tour in Afghanistan was his second combat deployment.

As the Apaches rounded a bend on the Waigal River, the pilots came onto a landscape of ruin. There was a dark haze blanketing the valley floor, and an oily column of smoke churned out of the flames from the burning remains of a Humvee. Civilian buildings were on fire and a stack of HESCO liners was in flames. There was very little discernible US military structure down there. The sun had come up just a half-hour before, and the morning rays made it difficult to distinguish details with the naked eye.

"Damn, it's hard to see," Townsend said to Watkins, a six-feet-five-inch member of the Texas Army National Guard who had volunteered to go along on this mission.

A fear swept over Townsend, not for his own safety but for the safety of the Americans on the ground. He and the other aviators were flying into a battlespace where they had almost no idea where friends were versus foes, and Townsend was terrified that he might kill the wrong people. Enemy gunmen along the perimeter and in the ridgelines were firing, and their muzzle flashes looked like fireflies blinking on and off.

"Tiz, oh fuck, there's muzzle flashes all over the place," Watkins told his pilot.

The air crews could get a general sense of the main base because they could see Humvees set out on a flat field adjacent to what looked like bunkered positions under camouflage netting. But there was radio chatter about an outpost somewhere to the northeast that was in deep trouble. People were giving them lines of attack based on billowing clouds from colored smoke grenades, but in the slanted rays of dawn it was hard to recognize the colors. And certain key reference points kept cropping up on the radio, like a hotel and bazaar, as if the pilots could recognize those buildings from the air. Everything down there looked like a mud hut.

And there was no time to waste. They already had the grid location for Topside.

"All right, Jimmy," Townsend radioed Morrow, "we're on the west-hand side, left-hand side of the valley approaching Wanat. We're going to look for the green smoke, and we're going to lay some fucking thirty down."

Townsend decided to take control of the 30mm chain gun on this first pass and almost immediately had a brush with his worst nightmare. Searching through the haze for Topside, Watkins mistakenly fixed on 1st Squad's position at the traffic control point. The bunker sat up on an agricultural terrace just as they were told, and they could see figures inside. There was also a figure running along the eastern edge before disappearing under a tree canopy.

"Hey, right there," Watkins said.

"Where?"

"I'm trying to make sure he's not in the OP. There's a guy just on the other side of those trees."

The crew could not have known that the figure Watkins saw was actually Sergeant Brian Hissong just outside 1st Squad's position, trying to find a place to fire in support of Topside. Fortunately Townsend's attention was fixed elsewhere as he hammered at enemy positions to the northeast with cannon shells.

→ ←

Up at the observation post the second rescue team led by Garcia and Samaroo had been reduced to a writhing mass of very bloody young men. Somehow Denton and Samaroo found each other and wound up outside of the observation post to the south. Samaroo had a head wound and blood all over his upper legs. Denton worried Samaroo might have a slashed femoral artery, something that could kill him quickly. But the staff sergeant was more concerned about his genitals and wanted Denton to check him out.

"Dude, I'm not worried about your dick—I'm worried about your arteries," Denton said.

Samaroo insisted, and as Denton cut open his pants to survey the wounds, he finally reached in with his hand and checked the vitals. "Okay, man, you're all right." Denton explored the wounds and concluded that no major artery was cut. Then he searched around for a weapon and found a jammed M4. Because his right hand was fractured, Denton moved awkwardly to clear the weapon with his left hand, with the rifle tucked under his right arm. He managed to get it working, then helped Samaroo back inside the southwest fighting position, which seemed a good stronghold with two boulders on opposite sides. Sones had already made his way in there.

Pitts still lay in the center of Topside next to Garcia, holding his hand. There was nothing Pitts felt he could do to treat his friend. He was almost afraid to touch Garcia, fearing he would only make the soldier's agony worse. Garcia wanted to get his face up off the dirt, and Pitts tried to help, rolling him slightly and attempting to prop him up with a rock under his body armor. But it was causing too much pain, and Pitts pulled the rock away. Samaroo caught Pitts's eye, trying to get a sense of how Garcia was doing. Pitts looked over at the squad leader and just shook his head. Samaroo felt Pitts and Garcia were too exposed to enemy fire in that center section of the outpost. They didn't feel they could move Garcia, so they pulled Pitts inside their southern position. There were Apache helicopters overhead by then firing into enemy positions, and medevac helicopters were entering the far side of the valley.

Samaroo, Pitts, Denton, and Sones felt helpless about Garcia; words of encouragement were all they could offer. "Just hang on, brother," Denton said. Samaroo told him to "pray to Jesus." Now and then they heard Garcia say, "Yeah." Samaroo was certain he could see Garcia hold his hands in front of his face, as if to begin praying.

Pitts took Samaroo's open-mic radio and fixed it. Denton got to his feet and, with his rifle, kept an eye on the area around the huge boulder to the northwest where the enemy might attack.

For Sones the wrenching wounds he'd suffered, along with the sight of Garcia, had drained away much of the fight and spirit that had driven him to volunteer for this mission. Stunned and bleeding, he tried to watch for anything coming from the south when he spotted a crouching figure moving across the terrace. Sones recognized Staff Sergeant Erich Phillips moving with vigor and determination toward their position. The sight instantly filled Sones with relief.

He looks like a fucking war god.

"It's our guys!" Sones started yelling.

Phillips climbed into the southwest bunker, the others following behind, and took stock of the bloody survivors.

"Garcia is pretty messed up," Samaroo said. "You need to get him first."

When Phillips reached him, Garcia was still in agony and just kept repeating how much he hurt. The physical carnage shocked Phillips. With help from others who arrived, Garcia was gently moved out of the south end of Topside.

Phillips turned back to the fight. Others filed into the post, moving past Garcia and reflexively turning to look at him. It was jarring for Aaron Davis.

*God, let him go. He's suffering.*

Dzwik paused with Garcia for a moment and could hear him murmuring a prayer in Spanish. "Hail Mary, full of grace, the Lord is with thee. Blessed art thou amongst women, and blessed is the fruit of thy womb, Jesus. Holy Mary, Mother of God, pray for us sinners, now and at the hour of our death. Amen."

Garcia lost consciousness and died not long after.

→ ←

At the command post during a lull in the fighting Matt Myer decided to see for himself what happened at Topside. He had given Aaron Davis his M4 because the paratrooper had left his rifle in the burning missile truck. Armed now with only his 9mm pistol, Myer took the quickest route, which was the way Brostrom and Hovater had gone. By that time Apaches had been hammering the bazaar and hotel structures with 30mm fire, but enemy fighters would keep using the buildings for fighting positions. Still, running as fast as he could, Myer managed to reach Topside unscathed.

The first thing he saw were the bodies of his men on the sleeping terrace. The sight of them became a kind of information overload for the company commander, triggering a cloudy, half-formed logic that made Myer feel like he somehow needed to make things right. He started to drag the body of Jason Bogar, but then stopped and just stood there, a figure of despair in a state of semishock.

*What am I doing? Why am I trying to move him? He's not alive!*

As if to refocus his thoughts, Myer reached over and felt for a pulse on Bogar. There was nothing. He saw Brostrom and was struck by how different the platoon leader looked in death, though Myer didn't know exactly how or why. He could see Jason Hovater, the terrible wound in the middle of his face, and he flashed on the graphic image of old Civil War battlefield tintypes and the carnage those communicated, except that this was *right here, right now.*

Myer let loose with a kind of primal shriek.

"FUCK!"

He said it a few more times.

Aass was right there. He was surprised to see his company commander suddenly show up and asked Myer how he got there. The captain turned and pointed his 9mm toward the hotel complex. Then he told Aass to take the weapons and equipment off the dead so they would be ready for evacuation. Myer heard the voice of Staff Sergeant Samaroo, who was nearby, a strangely calm admonition in all the madness.

"Hey, sir, you're on the wrong side." He meant that Myer was standing on the less-defensible sleeping terrace. "That's the side they're coming from."

The captain moved inside the bastion. Aass collected the M240 machine gun he found slung over Rainey's shoulder and took Bogar's SAW. It was clear from the shell casings all around that both men had fought to the last. As the troopers tried to clear debris, someone spotted an enemy grenade that had failed to detonate. Myer reached down, picked it up, and lobbed it into the draw. Then he headed back down to the command post to coordinate the air missions.

Meanwhile a few soldiers started caring for the wounded while others took up fighting positions. Erich Phillips tried to organize a defense. Benton made Denton sit down so he could be treated. Samaroo was on his feet refusing him, ignoring his wounds, telling people not to worry about him, "storming around," as Aass saw it. But he was weakening and finally lay down while Queck cut his pants to examine the damage. As Staff Sergeant Benton held Denton still in a kind of octopus grip, Grimm started stuffing battle dressings into the large wound in Denton's hip. Grimm did the same with the hole in Sones's right leg. Scantlin, who had assumed the vital role of platoon medic, made his way up to Topside and moved from Pitts to Samaroo to Denton to Sones, checking to see if they were alert and responsive, if the bandages and tourniquets were working and adequate.

Marine Jason Jones joined Jared Gilmore to crew an M240 machine gun. The other Marine, Jason Oakes, took the position where Pitts had been ready to make his last stand and opened up with a light machine gun. Topside was back in business.

→  ←

Back at Blessing, after some confusion about whether to load up a medevac with ammunition supplies for the battle, the helicopter piloted by Chris Hill was ready to lift off for Kahler. The crew was nervous. Their mission was to use their hoist to retrieve casualties from Kahler's embattled outpost, Topside. Such missions were dangerous enough when not under fire, and it was clear from radio transmissions that this battle was far from over.

Even before leaving Blessing they could hear how their sister ship had reached Kahler and was forced to abort its first landing attempt when they came under enemy fire. The Blackhawk had circled around and touched down, taking on paratroopers Tyler Stafford, Hector Chavez, Jake Walker, and William Hewitt as well as Michael Tellez, an engineer.

Chris Hill's helicopter finally took off shortly before 6 A.M., and Seipel, the copilot, established radio contact with Matt Myer, who sounded exasperated. The copilot, who turned twenty-six the week before, had grown up on a Missouri farm and graduated from West Point in 2005. One of the top students in his class was a Californian named Matt Ferrara. Seipel was fully aware that his classmate had died fighting in the Waigal Valley region the previous November. On the radio as he spoke with Myer, Seipel could hear Krupa's .50-caliber machine gun blasting away in the background. The copilot said they'd need to have the observation post marked by colored smoke. Myer told him it was already being done.

The aircraft entered the valley and began searching for Topside. They could see both Apache helicopters firing at targets northeast of the base. They spotted the signal smoke, and Chris Hill flew one pass over Topside before noticing a flat area on one of the terraces to the southwest, just outside the coil of concertina wire.

"Chris, I think we can sit on that terrace," said Seipel, who spotted the same location.

"That's exactly what I'm going to try to do."

They wouldn't have to take on a dangerous hoist mission after all. As the aircraft swooped in for a landing, Madill, who was in the back, suddenly caught sight of an Afghan squatting on a boulder up on the hillside where enemy fire had been reported. The man was maybe six hundred feet away, and the surgeon could actually make out what he was wearing—a light-colored shalwar kameez with a brown vest overtop. He was watching the helicopter approach and had no weapon, though Madill felt somehow certain he was an enemy fighter. At the last second, as if in some gesture of defiance, the Afghan rose to his feet and locked eyes with Madill. Then he passed out of view as the helicopter touched down, sending up a cloud of dust. On the right side its rotors were only a few feet from the next higher farming terrace. Right in front of where the helicopter came to rest, almost under its nose, was the perimeter razor wire for Topside. There were two levels of terraces below that separated the helicopter from the outpost. Lying adjacent to Topside were Americans' dead bodies, and the pilots could see one of them was horribly mangled, looking as if his lower body was gone.

The paratroopers in Topside were ecstatic to see the medevac unexpectedly land so close to them. It was 6:05 A.M., more than ninety minutes since Ryan Pitts had been wounded. He had lost a lot of blood since then and was growing pale and weak. His right leg was raked with shrapnel from hip to boot. One hole in the back of his leg was slightly smaller than his fist. His left Achilles tendon was partially severed. His ass was in terrible pain. A hunk of metal had somehow embedded up into his crotch, into the perineum, narrowly missing all the male vitals.

The flight medic, Kinney, was quickly out of the helicopter and over the coiled wire on his way to the outpost. Helfrich, the crew chief, had stepped out with his headset still wired to the aircraft, as protocol required, to assist in loading the medevac while remaining in contact with the pilots. But Seipel could see the wounded and those soldiers helping them—specters caked with black dirt and blood, all wearing body armor—already struggling to climb the terraces. He told Helfrich to go help. The crew chief immediately disconnected and was on his way. Seipel said the same to Madill.

Madill disconnected and left. Soldiers were working to get Pitts, Samaroo, Sones, and Denton to the aircraft. Aaron Davis was assisting Denton. Both had gone through basic training together and were longtime friends. In Denton's mind the two of them—Denton is white, Davis is black—reminded him of a scene from the movie Forrest Gump, where Forrest carries his wounded battle buddy, Buford "Bubba" Blue, off the Vietnam battlefield. Only in this battle of Wanat it was the other way around—Davis helping Denton.

Aass was trying to get Sones to the aircraft, but the wounded soldier hesitated: "Wait—where's Pitts?" The sergeant was, after all, the reason they'd fought their way up to this wrecked place. He sure as hell didn't want to get on the medevac without him.

"He's right behind you," Aass said.

Pitts at first insisted he could make it to the aircraft on his own, even though he knew this was just foolish pride—he couldn't even walk. Two soldiers had to half-carry, half-drag him with his arms around their shoulders. Climbing the terraces was a challenge. They were five to six feet high, and everyone was reduced to clawing, pushing, and pulling up the loose dirt and rock walls.

Madill made his way toward the outpost. He was stunned to see a single coil of razor wire as their only perimeter defense.

*That's it? Wow, these guys are really exposed.*

Madill could see a soldier and a Marine—it was Gilmore and Jones—down on or below the sleeping terrace manning an M240 machine gun. A stocky senior noncommissioned officer approached him—Dave Dzwik—and Madill asked if there were any other wounded. Dzwik told him no. Madill pointed at the bodies lying outside the outpost.

"Are they dead?"

They were talking into each other's ears over the background noise.

"They're gone!"

"Are you okay?"

Dzwik said he was. Madill turned and, with Kinney, helped the wounded finally reach the medevac. The pilots could hear enemy rounds snapping overhead. Dzwik, back near the bodies, motioned to the pilots to be sure to come back and pick them up. Chris Hill revved up the engines, lifted off the terrace, and banked hard to the left. As the helicopter made a sweeping turn over the base, the four wounded paratroopers inside watched the smoking, burning panorama flow past.

It was a cramped area for Madill to work in. He leaned down and yelled a question to Pitts about morphine. Ryan told him he'd already had one shot. The injection had been below his tourniquet, however, and seemed to have no effect. He remained in great pain.

"Do you want morphine!?" Madill repeated.

"Yeah!"

For Pitts the shot felt like butter melting in a skillet. Warm relief pulsed through his body.

*This is good.*

→ ←

The four-truck Mad Max convoy from Blessing made the trip that normally would take two to three hours in fifty minutes. By 5:30 A.M., approximately an hour and fifteen minutes after the attack began, the reinforcements from Chosen Company's 1st Platoon rolled up from the south.

When the column of trucks rounded the last bend, the smoky pall cast over the valley ahead told the whole story; the images only got worse as they got closer. There was a lull in the fighting just then, and Kyle Silvernale thought maybe the battle was over. His truck pulled up to the traffic control point where 1st Squad was bunkered down, and Brian Hissong stood there waiting to meet them, his face pale and his features drained of expression.

"Hey, where they at?" Silvernale asked him about the enemy.

Hissong's voice was flat. "They're everywhere."

Silvernale needed him to snap out of it and start making some sense, so he smacked Hissong in the shoulder with his hand and repeated the question.

"They're fucking everywhere!"

"Well, where do you need me?"

"I don't know."

Silvernale could see that the road ahead led to a cluster of buildings a hundred yards to the north. "Is there a blocking position to the north? Is there anyone to the north?"

Hissong said there weren't any paratroopers positioned there. So after Silvernale checked in briefly at the command post and left two soldiers with Hissong to help defend that bunker, he led the first two trucks up the road where insurgents almost immediately opened fire.

As Silvernale and his men pushed into the village, Beeson and Stockard reported to Myer, who said he wanted them at Topside. Both headed up there.

Beeson arrived and could see that one of the sergeants who had come up to relieve the outpost was in tears and almost hysterical. He believed the Apache helicopters had made a terrible mistake.

"They killed everybody. The birds came in, the helicopters, they came in and they shot through the thing. They killed everybody," the sergeant said.

Beeson couldn't let this go on.

"Whoa! Whoa! What are you doing, brother? You're the fuckin' leader! You chill out. Number one, no birds fired in here. They fired close. I heard the radio transmission. They fired close. And they may have zipped along through here. But none of their rounds hit our guys.

"Look around here, brother. There's all kinds of your soldiers looking at you right now, freaking out 'cause you're freakin' out."

The admonishment stopped the sergeant cold. He turned to see the faces staring at him.

"Sorry. Sorry, First Sergeant. I gotcha."

Stockard brought along Sergeant Zaccery Johnston, who had braved enemy fire during an attack on Bella the month before. Specialist Jonathan Kaderli, the first platoon medic, and Private Second Class Matthew Young went up as well. Meanwhile another medic from Blessing, Specialist Nikhil Shelke, had arrived on a medevac flight into the landing zone at Kahler and also made his way up to Topside. Suddenly 2nd Platoon had plenty of medics.

The look of the embattled outpost was almost too much for Beeson to bear. The dead bodies, the wounded, the blood-smeared gear. The look in the eyes of those who were alive and manning Topside. Everyone seemed emotional.

Stockard reached Erich Phillips, complimented his defense efforts, and asked how he could best help. Phillips wanted men up in the Crow's Nest. Johnston and Young headed up there. Ayers's body was removed and brought with the others. The M240 that Denton had used had been ruined by the RPG that wounded him, and Johnston needed another gun. Phillips passed him a second M240. Johnston started firing on a building up on the terraces to the northeast and was certain he managed to kill an enemy fighter who was preparing to launch an RPG from one of the windows.

At one point Stockard and Dzwik were on the sleeping terrace among the bodies of the dead. The 1st Platoon sergeant was curious whether his 2nd Platoon counterpart had any idea where his leader, Brostrom, was. In all the confusion Dzwik had lost track of the lieutenant and wasn't even aware he had headed up to Topside to help reinforce the position.

"Do you know where the hell your PL is?" Stockard asked.

Dzwik said he didn't. Stockard reached over with his boot and turned one of the bodies. It was Brostrom. Dzwik was shocked and knelt down beside his platoon leader. He studied the eyes that were expressionless and saw that his mouth was open. Dzwik flashed on how many times he had poked fun at Brostrom for being a mouth breather, always with his mouth open, even when he wasn't saying anything. He reached over and gently closed Brostrom's mouth, told him he'd stay and protect him as the fight continued—"I got your back one last time"—and then took up a position nearby to return fire.

The arrival of 1st Platoon reinforcements buoyed Erich Phillips.

*Fuck, this might be over.*

→  ←

Between the gun-runs near Topside the Apache helicopters were constantly hunting enemy fighters in the surrounding hills. It was tough work; the daytime warmed up the rocks in their thermal sights, and militants using them as cover sometimes blended with rocks into a single shape on the screens in the Apaches. Much of the time the pilots or gunners simply fired weapons aiming with the naked eye.

The skies over the narrow valley teemed with aircraft: Apaches, medevac helicopters, an Air Force B1 bomber, and Air Force F15 Eagle jet fighters. Later Air Force A10 jets would show up, along with a

Predator drone, and by early the following morning an AC130 gunship. Townsend had already complained about one of the F15 Eagles dropping down to his altitude when they should have been no lower than eight thousand feet.

The sleek jet fighters, unable to conduct attacks with all the helicopters working below them, were performing "show of force" flights with the idea of intimidating the enemy. Townsend chuckled about that over his intercom, skeptical that this enemy—who had already defied convention by continuing to attack even after the Apaches showed up—was paying attention to the fighter planes.

"We've been shooting the shit out of them," Watkins said, "and they don't care about it. They're not going to care about a plane at eight thousand feet."

Minutes later Townsend and Watkins were rolling up the left side of the valley when Watkins spotted three figures on their bellies along a ridge overhanging the west bank of the Waigal River.

"Make sure that's not the OP, bro," Townsend warned.

"That should be too far away."

"Are you on 'em?"

"Roger," Watkins says.

"Hit 'em."

At the last second the three figures appeared to turn away from their fighting position, perhaps after realizing the Apache coming up from behind them was closing in. But it was too little too late, and they were consumed in fountains of 30mm explosions.

→ ←

A new battle was being waged inside the village of Wanat. Silvernale and Specialist Tyler Kuhlman had followed the trucks on foot, using one of them as a shield until they took up a position in front of the one-story mosque that was on the west side of the road. There was clear evidence from the spent brass shells all over the front entryway of the mosque that enemy insurgents had used it as a fighting position.

It was there that they fired on 3rd Squad's position where Garcia, Santiago, Sones, and Schmidt were hunkered down when the battle started. Silvernale waved through the first truck, and as the second one drove up, RPGs exploded between the two vehicles. The trucks moved on, and now Silvernale and Kuhlman were pinned down by enemy fire in front of the mosque. An insurgent with an RPG launcher stepped out from between the hotel and the bazaar about fifty yards away.

The man fired, and the rocket exploded along the side of the mosque about a dozen feet from the two paratroopers. Suddenly a quick-draw contest was underway. Silvernale, shaken by the blast, was down on a knee trying to slam in another magazine and come up ready to kill that fighter when he ventured out again. But by the time Silvernale rose up with his rifle, the man was already standing there with another loaded RPG launcher pointed at the mosque.

Oh shit.

This time the RPG whooshed in and exploded only a few feet around the corner of the building, knocking Silvernale to the ground with a four-inch-long piece of shrapnel sticking out of the back of his left hand. Kuhlman was hit by flying glass from a mosque window. Silvernale tried to pull the steel out with his fingers, but the pain was too much, and he couldn't get a good grip. He reached for his Gerber hand tool, grasped onto the hunk of steel with it, and gave a good yank, pulling it free. Then he bandaged up his hand.

→ ←

Now there were a dozen or more soldiers defending Topside, and for several minutes it seemed as if the worst was over. Dzwik, set up near the large boulder, wanted a dip and called over to Phillips for some of his Copenhagen. The staff sergeant tossed over his can.

Gilmore, armed with an M240 machine gun given to him by Corporal Jones, moved to a couple of different fighting positions before setting up the gun in one of the most exposed sites—just on or below the sleeping terrace where at least five soldiers had died. From there Gilmore could fire directly into the hotel and other two-story buildings at the center of Wanat less than fifty yards away. The enemy fighters, in turn, could plainly see the paratrooper and the Marine with him, prone with the M240 machine gun. Rounds whizzed past the pair. Gilmore concentrated his fire on the upper windows.

When others at Topside saw what he was doing, they directed their weapons at the same location. Gilmore was certain he was wounding or killing enemy fighters. The rate of fire from the militants was slackening off.

Stockard was throwing grenades from the Crow's Nest down into the ravine, and he wanted to venture out and set up new Claymore mines. Beeson wouldn't let him risk it. Private Second Class Matthew Young, who had just turned nineteen, offered to go. He said he was "expendable," and Stockard looked at him.

"What the hell do you mean, *expendable?*"

He told Young to stay put.

The enemy had begun firing RPGs into the branches of the mulberry tree with the idea of showering the defenders with shrapnel. Both Marine Corporal Oakes and Army Specialist Davis caught bits of metal; both kept fighting.

Gilmore's machine gun was overheating. Erich Phillips came to assist and started sprinkling water down the barrel from a plastic bottle punched with holes. It was an air-cooled gun, and doing this could crack the barrel, but they were in a hurry and it worked—they got the weapon back in service.

Beeson worked with Aass on the radio to call in targets for artillery and air support, taking direction from Stockard, who wanted that large compound on the terraces three hundred yards to the northeast, from where enemy fighters relentlessly kept pouring fire into Topside, reduced to rubble. It looked like it was about three stories high.

"Tell them to make it one story," Stockard yelled.

Grimm, fighting from Pitts's last position, was amazed the enemy continued to attack, even with American air support overhead. He had never seen that before. The fighting at Topside now took on a kind of rhythm. The paratroopers and Marines behind the sandbags blasted away at the hotel, or down into the draw, or toward the building on the terraces across the creek that Stockard wanted demolished. When the enemy responded with machine guns and RPGs, the paratroopers would duck down and start throwing grenades. Then they would rise up to open fire once more. When the Apaches started coming in close to target the draw, someone would be alerted and tell everyone to get down while the earth shook. It was always stunning how close the Apaches could fire without hurting any of the Chosen Few.

At one point Grimm tried to detonate a Claymore mine set up to explode down into the ravine. It was the same mine that Stafford had tried to set off. Now Grimm wanted to see if he could repair it and, during a lull in enemy fire, jumped over the sandbag wall and crawled several feet out in the open to inspect the wired connection. He found it in shreds and pulled back into the outpost. Benton looked at him.

"You feel stupid now?"

"Yes, I feel pretty fucking stupid now. That was the dumbest thing I ever tried to do."

The two men got a brief respite from the combat when they spotted a pack of Camel Light cigarettes amid all the used bandages, blood, and spent brass. There were two cigarettes inside, and Benton had a lighter. They both took long, luxurious drags, and it felt like the heavens had opened up and the angels were singing.

Scantlin had set up medic shop just outside the southwest gun position where every so often Hayes and Hanson showed up with more ammunition. At one point there was a lull in the fighting, and he suggested they both take a break and have some water. Enemy fire started up again, and they both begged off, heading back down to Kahler. Almost the moment after they left, an RPG exploded where they had been standing, and Scantlin was left briefly unconscious, although the shrapnel somehow missed him entirely.

Meanwhile Phillips kept moving around the base, directing fire, shooting his own weapon, and delivering ammunition. Gilmore, down on the exposed sleeping terrace with Jones, kept hammering the hotel windows with the M240. He was cranking out thousands of rounds and had to keep shoveling away the spent brass shells. Someone delivered an extra barrel that allowed him to finally change out when the weapon got too hot.

An RPG exploded in the branches of the mulberry tree and Dzwik caught a piece of shrapnel in his left arm. He screamed out for a medic. Nikhil Shelke came to his aid. Everybody could hear Dzwik cry out when he got hit, and Phillips couldn't resist the opening.

"Dzwik, you scream like a bitch when you get hit."

"The joke's on you," Dzwik replied. "I got blood in your Copenhagen."

"Keep it."

At one point an RPG fired from the hotel slammed into a boulder near where Beeson had taken cover and knocked him onto his knees. At the sight of the first sergeant going down, it was almost as if the entire force of defenders gasped at once.

"Hey, First Sarge, you okay? I thought they killed you!" Benton yelled.

But Beeson was only stunned and straightened himself back up.

"The fuck they did!"

→　←

Chris Hill was flying four of the wounded from Topside to a base at Asadabad, which was close and had a small treatment clinic. But while in route word arrived that the Asadabad clinic was already overflowing with casualties, and Hill diverted to his home base in Jalalabad, arriving there at 6:40 A.M. The wounded paratroopers were offloaded and Hill and his crew started toward Blessing, but before they got there, news came of another casualty back at Topside, and they headed back to the battlefield. Seventy minutes had passed since the medevac left Topside, and yet clearly the battle there was still raging. This time, as the medevac touched down on the terrace, the fighting looked even more intense than before. The pilots could see an Apache only about 150 feet overhead firing rockets into buildings north of the outpost. The rockets were loaded with phosphorous that exploded and sent up large plumes of white smoke. The panoply of images reminded Seipel of old Vietnam combat footage.

The medevac had carried up a load of ammunition from Blessing, and the crew dropped the ammo and took on the casualty. Kaderli and Shelke, the two medics, helped Dzwik to the helicopter. Seipel was surprised to see it was the same soldier who had motioned to him about the dead bodies during the last trip. Madill was shocked as well. This was the man he had spoken with the last time, the guy who told him he was okay. Now Dzwik was being evacuated. He lay down inside the aircraft, and Madill came over to check his bandages. The intensity of all the fighting and dying finally caught up with Dzwik, and he became emotional. Madill took his hand.

→ ←

Minutes after Hill's Blackhawk helicopter lifted off from the terrace above Topside with Dzwik aboard a new volley of RPGs descended on the position. Aaron Davis was firing Bogar's light machine gun from a corner of the southwest bunker. Aass was next to him, tucked against a sandbagged wall and talking on the radio, and Queck was close by. A rocket passed right over Beeson's head—the first sergeant was between them and the Crow's Nest—and exploded right near Davis, blowing pieces of shrapnel through his body. It was the second time he had been wounded in several minutes. The first time he refused to be evacuated; now he lay there coughing up blood. Shrapnel blanketed his entire left side. One hunk passed clear through his left arm, a shard was embedded in his left leg, a small piece struck him above his upper lip, and another grazed his right cornea, ruining much of the vision in that eye. Bogar's SAW gun was destroyed.

Staff Sergeant Queck, from the mortar team, was bleeding from his shoulder and lower right leg. Aass was shocked to see that he himself had come through without a scratch. Another explosion nearby wounded Shelke, the medic. He was left with a badly hemorrhaging wound to his right leg. Comrades quickly moved to treat the three of them.

The 1st Platoon medic, Jonathan Kaderli, started working on Davis. Scantlin bandaged Queck. Marine Corporal Jones used his belt as a tourniquet for Shelke, with Grimm arriving to assist. Grimm reached under Shelke's right leg and it felt like someone had popped a balloon full of warm water, there was so much blood.

Shelke told them they should start an IV on him. Grimm went to work on it, but the medic kept offering backseat-driver directions for his own medical care until Grimm finally lost patience.

"Doc, just shut up. I know what to do."

→ ←

For Matt Myer down at the command post it had been an exhausting three hours or more since the battle began, and the enemy was still tearing up his men at Topside—even after sending up four waves of reinforcements. He wanted the Apaches to come in and stop this once and for all and asked them to fire as close as ten meters—or thirty feet—from the outpost.

He gave his initials to approve another danger-close mission.

"I know it's high risk. But we need to get these guys off of us," the Chosen captain told Jimmy Morrow in the Apache attack helicopter overhead.

Morrow and his pilot, John Gavreau, were very uncomfortable about it.

"Ten meters?" Morrow said to his pilot.

"You got to be kidding me."

Morrow gave Gavreau explicit directions on where to fly, keying off the big boulder at the north end of the sleeping terrace.

"Just to the left of that from our position is a tree line. If you go right, that's where the friendlies are. So you need to go slightly left of that."

They did three consecutive runs, their cannon fire churning the earth just along the draw. The soldiers inside Topside hugged the ground and could hear shrapnel from the attack landing just outside their sandbagged walls.

→ ←

Down below in the village Silvernale's two trucks had pushed all the way through to the north side of town. The paratroopers could see up the draw where enemy fighters had filtered down in the days or hours before the attack to close in on Topside. They could see structures several hundred yards up on the terraces from where gunmen had raked the outpost. Silvernale spotted muzzle flashes coming from the far east end of the hotel. He pulled out a grenade Scott Derry had given him. It was Derry's "lucky grenade," the one he had carried around for months after it was damaged by rifle fire during the ambush the previous November. Derry had bequeathed it to Silvernale when he left for home, and now the staff sergeant decided to put it to good use. He pulled the pin and lobbed it in the direction of the enemy gunman.

It was a dud.

The fighters in the draw and up in the structures on the hill began focusing their gunfire and RPGs on Silvernale and his men. The soldiers were shocked at how the insurgents seemed to absorb the Apache helicopter attacks and keep fighting.

In the turret of Silvernale's Humvee was Specialist Ananthachai Nantakul, the soldier they called Nanny, who had fought in the ambush of Lieutenant Colonel Ostlund's convoy as it left Wanat on May 26. In the other turret was Staff Sergeant Joshua Salazar, who had led the paratroopers up at OP1 during the November 9 ambush of Lieutenant Ferrara's patrol. Soldiers poured out of the trucks and took up firing positions with their light machine guns and M4 rifles as Nantakul chugged away with his automatic grenade launcher and Salazar opened up with the .50-caliber in the other truck.

Even as the Americans poured fire into the draw, a ravine, and the buildings up on the terraces, enemy fire was stemmed only momentarily. Paratroopers stepped out from behind cover to unleash rockets from shoulder-fired launchers, and still it didn't finish the fight. Over and over enemy gunmen dressed in battle gear or man-jammies, their heads swathed in scarves, rose up to fire at the Americans.

Nantakul switched to his M4 at one point, holding the gun steady for two minutes, putting a bead on a point along the trench where he'd seen a militant pop up to take shots. His patience paid off. The man showed himself again, and Nantakul put a bullet right over his right eye, throwing him back into the trench. Two Army specialists, Shane Burton and Tyler Kuhlman, ran all the way through the bazaar back to Kahler to retrieve ammunition for Nantakul's grenade launcher. The ammo cans were heavy and unwieldy, and Nantakul had to climb outside the turret to load the gun, each time with Silvernale screaming at him to get back inside.

Desperate to bring in the Apaches, first Silvernale and then Burton ran out into the open far enough to lob yellow smoke grenades toward the enemy, marking targets. The Apaches followed the smoke and started lighting up enemy fighting positions.

It finally gave Silvernale a chance, with Burton and Kuhlman, to clear the bazaar and the hotel room by room, using a shotgun to blow off hinges and then an axe Silvernale had found. They saw plenty of evidence the enemy had used the hotel as a fighting center.

But the militants had fled.

→ ←

The battle was finally beginning to wind down. It was 8:30 A.M. The fighting had raged for more than four hours.

The two Apache helicopters had flown twice back to Blessing during the fight to rearm and refuel. Each of the aircraft had four radios going at all times, and snatches of communications from all quadrants of the battlefield flowed in continuously. The crews caught a piece of one report on efforts to recover all the American dead from Wanat.

"Nine KIA," the voice over the radio said.

Townsend absorbed this news for a moment.

"Goddamn it."

The bodies of seven of the eight Americans killed at Topside had been lined up on a terrace in preparation to be airlifted out. Soldiers ran a grim gauntlet to deliver ammunition to Topside during the latter stages of the fight, among them Sergeant Brian Hissong, Specialist Tyler Hanson, Specialist John Hayes, and even Chris McKaig for one trip before he was medevacked out. They tried to avert their eyes when they passed the dead, but it was hard to do. Many recognized Hovater only by his name tag. Hissong for a while mistook Brostrom's body for a soldier on his team, Mike Denton. It was a terribly emotional blow for Hissong to think he'd lost one of his own men; it wasn't until later that someone finally corrected him.

They couldn't find Gunnar Zwilling until after the fighting eased up and Sergeant Zaccery Johnston located the body down about three terraces from Topside in the direction of the hotel. Some thought he might have fought his way down there. Others, like Scott Beeson, believed the enemy might have tried to drag his body away and gave up because of the Apache gun-runs or maybe Silvernale's counterattack through the village. There was a wound in Zwilling's left side, and his left leg was horribly mangled from his thigh to the top of his boot.

A medevac finally evacuated Zwilling's remains late in the morning. Justin Madill had switched helicopters earlier and was aboard the Blackhawk that touched down near Topside for the last of the fallen.

At the 3rd Squad fighting position during the battle, from where Israel Garcia and Jacob Sones had headed off to save Ryan Pitts, the two soldiers who remained there fighting were Sergeant Mike Santiago and Specialist James Schmidt. They had no idea what happened to their comrades until Specialist John Hayes—who had seemingly been all over the battlefield directing air cover, carrying casualties, delivering ammunition, and marking helicopter landing zones with smoke grenades—showed up looking for supplies. He told them Sones was hurt badly but would likely pull through. When asked about Garcia, Hayes just shook his head.

Santiago couldn't believe it. He never expected that when his friend suddenly took off running in the middle of the battle, he was heading to his death. The two were like brothers, and now Garcia was gone. Just like that. Santiago had hated this mission, coming so near the end of the deployment. He had hated the location, so exposed at the bottom of the valley. He had even hated the hard, rocky ground that made it impossible to dig a decent foxhole.

When the shooting died down and they started cleaning up their site, they found bullet holes in everything. The truck tires were flat. The soldiers' rucksacks were riddled. Sleeping bags were shredded. Someone even found a nearly pristine AK47 bullet resting inside his packed underwear. The aluminum poles for a sun shade were shot through, and for one mad moment all the hardship came crashing down on Santiago. He picked up one of the baseball-bat-sized poles and just started whaling on things. It was a commotion. Heads turned. People stared.

The US military that could only manage a reinforced platoon for the mission to Wanat now had resources to spare just as the battlefield grew quiet. In addition to the fleet of aircraft overhead, a convoy of six Humvees carrying thirty soldiers arrived from Able Company; another thirty-three soldiers, most of them from Battle Company, flew in by helicopter; and later one hundred Afghan National Army commandoes came in along with twenty-one US Special Forces troops. The Special Forces commander wanted to seize the village of Qal'eh-ye Gal two miles east from where many of the attackers had infiltrated into Wanat. His plan would cut their means of escape. But Rock Battalion operations officer Major Scott Himes, who had arrived to assume overall command at Wanat, rejected the plan as too risky.

Battle analysts would later conclude that the attacking enemy forces under the control of Mullah Maulawi Muhammad Osman numbered as many as three hundred fighters. But they were not all on hand when the fight started early that morning; rather, they kept flowing into the area as the morning progressed, and these fresh fighters loaded with rockets and automatic weapons were fed into the battle as wounded and slain militants were carried away. As Americans were re-reinforcing their defenders, the insurgents were doing the same from their side of the battlefield.

As the soldiers from Battle and Able companies entered Wanat on Sunday, their leaders were astonished at Combat Outpost Kahler's location and how valley ridgelines rose above it, with many buildings at higher elevations. Platoon Sergeant Jeremiah Smith of Able Company, drafting a report five days later, said the base "was being built in the worst of locations. The OP provided no tactical advantage in that area."

It seemed painfully clear that if the US Army was going to stay in Wanat, they would need to move the entire base to a higher, more defensible location. Matt Myer would start the process. Eighteen elite Army Pathfinders, kind of super-combat engineers trained to drop into enemy territory to set up landing zones, were brought in to begin clearing trees. They worked in an area high on the eastern ridge. Some heavy construction equipment finally arrived late on Sunday and was put to use building a road up to that higher ground.

That same day soldiers eventually made their way down to the district police station northwest of the village center along the Waigal River. There they found clear evidence of collusion. For a twenty-man police force, the Americans found a trove of six dozen AK47s, fourteen machine guns, and a half-dozen RPGs—far more weaponry than a department this size would ever need. Most of the weapons appeared to have been recently fired. There were spent shell casings on the grounds. The twenty police officers at the station raised even more suspicions; they had on clean uniforms, and many of them looked like they had just shaved. Some even had razor cuts as if they'd been in a hurry to look like clean-cut policemen. The paratroopers were seething. They knew they were looking at men who had just been shooting at them. It was all they could do not to gun them down. The district police chief was later arrested and his police force disbanded.

As scores of additional troops arrived and fanned out into the hills to secure a large area around Wanat, Sergeant Brian Hissong felt for the first time in hours that he could finally relax. He sat down in the bunker and smoked a cigarette as the depth of the tragedy washed over him. Hissong started to weep. Company First Sergeant Scott Beeson walked over and sat down beside him.

"You know, it's all right, Brother Hissong," Beeson said to him, "You've done well."

→ ←

The battle was already shaping up as among the bloodiest engagements in the history of the Afghanistan War. In addition to nine soldiers killed in action, sixteen wounded were airlifted off the battlefield. The last of them was Marine Corporal Jason Oakes, who insisted on remaining at Topside until the fighting died down. There were eleven other wounded who were either not evacuated by medevac or refused to go, among them Company 1st Sergeant Beeson, who had shrapnel injuries to the left side of his neck and his left knee.

The original forty-nine Americans at Kahler when the fight started had suffered an astonishing casualty rate of 67 percent.

Army investigators found at least thirteen enemy fighting positions scattered around Kahler when the battle began. How many of the enemy were killed was anybody's guess. Just one body was found on the battlefield, the fighter who died in the concertina wire up at Topside when Chris McKaig detonated a Claymore mine. The Afghan National Army troops thought he might have been an Arab. Intelligence officers sifting through intercepted messages and talking with their contacts in the field felt certain that at least twenty-one fighters died, perhaps as many as fifty-two. They concluded that the artillery bombardment called in by Myer killed fifteen militants, gun-runs by the Apache helicopters and AC130 gunship killed six more and one of the $70,000, laser-guided Hellfire missiles launched from a Predator drone that showed up in the early afternoon of July 13 left three more fighters dead. Intel officers also estimated that forty-five of the enemy had been wounded, possibly including Osman, although that could not be confirmed. They intercepted communications that some of the aid stations set up by the enemy were "overwhelmed" with casualties. And there was even a report that a suicide bomber who was to be used in the attack was wounded before he could try to detonate himself among the Americans.

→ ←

On the evening of the day of the battle Ostlund and Myer walked the grounds of the base Chosen Company had defended. They could see the ruined bazaar, scorched and collapsed in places. Fires still burned in some of the stalls, and the aluminum garage-style doors covering them were twisted and glistening in the sun. The hotel was riddled with damage from the intense fighting. A mud hut high up on a northeast ridge had been reduced—just as Stockard had demanded—to a single-story hulk by relentless Apache attacks with rockets and Hellfire missiles. Trees near Topside were sheered open. The mulberry bore scars up and down its trunk. At the center of the military base, like the smoking remains of some religious sacrificial pyre, was the blackened, crushed metal skeleton of the TOW truck that burned all the way to the ground. Other Humvees used as part of the defenses for each squad sat lopsided because shrapnel or bullets had flattened some of the tires. A bright red Kellogg's Fruit Loops cereal box lay on the floor of one shot-up bunker, a strange flash of color amid brown detritus. Here and there exhausted paratroopers, each face a mask of sweat-caked dirt, were curled up in deep slumber in whatever piece of shade they could find.

Myer and Ostlund discussed where all of this would go from here. Moving the physical footprint of the base to higher ground would help to defend it. But the whole point had been to connect with the people there. The Americans had intended to lavish $1.4 million in infrastructure improvements—much of it for road building—from Wanat northward as a way of securing alliances with the Afghan central government and alienating the insurgency. But as Ostlund and Myer surveyed the damage around them, they realized that exactly the opposite had taken place. The people of Wanat, even the local police and district governor, had apparently sold their souls to the enemy, allowing them to use their homes and businesses, their fields and creek beds, as fighting positions to utterly surprise the paratroopers and kill them in record numbers.

Setting up a new base on higher ground farther from the village would leave the Americans isolated and looking more like an occupation force than a cooperative partner with the local population—a population that gave no hint that it wanted to cooperate.

Moreover, it was clear to Matt Myer that defending the base would require more people—an entire company rather than just a reinforced platoon. It was unlikely that the unit replacing the Rock—the 1st Battalion, 26th Infantry Regiment out of Fort Hood, Texas—could spare the troops. The Texas unit actually had fewer soldiers than the Rock Battalion.

"You know, sir, this totally changes things," Myer said to his commander.

Ostlund absolutely agreed. Myer said it might be better if they simply closed this operation down and gave up on Wanat for now and tried their best to influence the Waigal Valley from outside of it—from Blessing.

It would be a controversial recommendation to take up to Chip Preysler, commander of the 173rd. They had just lost nine men defending this ground, and now they wanted to leave it. Asked about the decision three days later during the Army's initial investigation into the battle, Ostlund tried to articulate how a war that defies traditional goals of capturing territory can be fraught with ambiguity.

"What is the calculus used to determine what is worth the lives of one or nine troopers? How is that determined?" Ostlund wrote. "I don't know if I can articulate or justify anything at the tactical level worth risking nine paratroopers' lives."

That same evening Ostlund got an e-mailed response to the state-of-the-war assessment memorandum he had drafted and sent to General Petraeus just the day before. By this time Petraeus had heard about the heavy losses at Wanat and acknowledged the "tough fight" Ostlund just had. He offered solace by quoting Ulysses Grant in 1862 after the Union commander suffered massive casualties during the battle of Shiloh. General William Tecumseh Sherman had remarked to Grant how it was a bad day.

"Yep," Grant responded, "lick 'em tomorrow though."

At about 4 A.M. that morning at the US base in Bagram, Amanda Wilson was jarred awake by an intense feeling of dread. A few hours later, when word spread across the base about major US casualties in Wanat, she raced to the brigade office and pressed an officer there to show her the list of dead. Brostrom was on it. The man she thought might have been a future for her was suddenly gone. In shock, Wilson made her way back to her tent, sat down, and tapped out an e-mail to her lost friend.

She called him Jon Boy and asked for a message, a sign, anything at all.

Over the next three days, as if to deliver a final insult, all the reinforcements left. Everyone was allowed to go except 2nd Platoon. They stayed there in the heat on that miserable battlefield where so many of their brothers had died until the base was completely shut down. Santiago, who had mourned his friend Garcia so deeply when the fighting stopped, was seething; sometimes he would just sit alone in the truck at the 3rd Squad position with the door open. Someone even snapped a picture, a shadowy figure in battle gear consumed with grief and rage.

Chosen Company finally finished packing up the remaining gear, and on the evening of Tuesday, July 15, headed down the road back to Blessing.

→ ←

In the years to come there would be extensive investigations into the battle. But in the first routine Army probe, 2nd Platoon sergeant David Dzwik said he never anticipated the scale of the attack.

"I did not think the village itself would let the AAF [anti-Afghanistan forces or the enemy] turn their village into a battle zone," he wrote.

"My men fought heroically," Dzwik wrote on. "The closeness of the members of the platoon caused them to act in ways that would seem above and beyond that required of a soldier. They defended each other and fought with honor."

Erich Phillips went back to the base called Michigan where the Dragon Platoon of Destined Company was located. He would be there for two weeks before heading home. Phillips had just finished fifteen grueling months—the Ranch House and Wanat battles and then crushing news that his wife had met someone else and the marriage was headed for divorce.

He was more than ready to leave Afghanistan and was inside the headquarters at Michigan, sitting at a computer, when a conversation behind him caught his attention. A noncommissioned officer with the replacement unit, 1st Battalion, had walked in and was talking about Combat Outpost Kahler.

"So whatever happened with this Wanat thing?" the soldier asked. "I heard they came in and everybody was asleep, and that's why they got their asses handed to them."

Phillips couldn't listen to another word. He spun his swivel chair around.

"Look, motherfucker, I was there! That was not the fucking case. We were at stand-to," Phillips said. "And I'll put that group of men up against any other fucking group in the rest of the whole god-damned Army."

→ ←

For his actions during the battle of Wanat Sergeant Ryan Pitts, in a 2015 White House ceremony, became the ninth living recipient of the Medal of Honor from the Afghanistan War. Fourteen Silver Stars were awarded for actions in that battle. The recipients were Specialist Aaron Davis, Specialist Michael Denton, Sergeant Jared Gilmore, Staff Sergeant Justin Grimm, Specialist John Hayes, Marine Corporal Jason Jones, Captain Matthew Myer, Staff Sergeant Erich Phillips, Staff Sergeant Sean Samaroo, and Specialist Jeffrey Scantlin; they were posthumously awarded to Specialist Jonathan Ayers, Lieutenant Jonathan Brostrom, Sergeant Israel Garcia, and Specialist Jason Hovater. Sixteen Bronze Stars for valor were awarded. The recipients were Sergeant Erik Aass, Sergeant Hector Chavez, Sergeant Matthew Gobble, Specialist Adam Hamby, Specialist Tyler Hanson, Sergeant Brian Hissong, Specialist

Chris McKaig, Marine Corporal Jason Oakes, Staff Sergeant Kyle Silvernale, Specialist Tyler Stafford, Private First Class Jacob Sones, Private First Class Scott Stenoski, and Lieutenant Aaron Thurman; they were posthumously awarded to Specialist Jason Bogar, Specialist Matthew Phillips, and Specialist Pruitt Rainey. A Distinguished Flying Cross was awarded to Chief Warrant Officer 3 James Morrow III and another to Chief Warrant Officer 3 Brian Townsend.

# 13

> > > **COMING HOME**

*Lesly Garcia was hysterical* back in Long Beach, California, when news arrived that Israel was dead. She was angry. Angry at the world. Angry at God. When Israel's leave had ended in February and she was still not pregnant, that was supposed to be a divine signal that her husband would return safely to her.

*What happened? Did you not hear me!? I had a pact. I got down on my knees and I prayed.*

Lesly ultimately would come to peace with her faith and strengthen her connection with God. But she would remain single, mourning Israel for many years to come.

When David and Mary Jo Brostrom learned of their son's death, they quietly grieved. But Brostrom grew distressed and ultimately consumed with questions after Preysler came to Hawaii to brief his old friend about the battle. It was the beginning of a slow burn as Brostrom pored through the Army's initial investigation and read all of the after-action reports. He wasn't angry at the world or with God—he was angry at the United States Army. He launched his own determined insurgency to bring to justice those he felt were truly responsible for the death of his son and the other soldiers in Wanat, plying a career's worth of contacts to achieve his ends. He argued to reporters who would eventually write his story that he worried about the lives of other young American soldiers fighting in Afghanistan who might suffer the same fate as his son.

There may have been deep guilt there as well. David Brostrom had helped engineer Jonathan's assignment to the 173rd Airborne Brigade. But he said he had acted out of trust in the institution and faith that commanders in the field would take care of their troops. All of that trust drained away the more he examined the facts of the battle, and Brostrom concluded that the Army's official examination was nothing more than a whitewash to cover up mistakes. He enlisted one of his old friends to help. Lieutenant General William Caldwell IV commanded the Army's training centers and schools and, at Brostrom's urging, directed the Combat Studies Institute at Fort Leavenworth, Kansas, to research the battle. A draft of an investigative study by contract historian Douglas Cubbison—leaked to the media—laid blame squarely on feckless leadership that left the 2nd Platoon dangerously exposed to an enemy assault. By the summer of 2009 Brostrom filed a complaint with the Inspector General's Office of the Defense Department, accusing commanders who led the troops in the field—his old friend, Chip Preysler, and Lieutenant Colonel Bill Ostlund—of negligence.

"I didn't start out looking to go after anyone's career," Brostrom told reporter Greg Jaffe of the *Washington Post* that year, but the Cubbison draft report and the Army's handling of the investigation "made it personal." Other family members of those Chosen Few killed in Wanat began to share Brostrom's anger and coalesced around him and the case he was making. The most crucial ally Brostrom enlisted was US Senator James Webb, a decorated Vietnam veteran, who took the issue before Admiral Mike Mullen, chairman of the Joint Chiefs of Staff. Mullen urged that action be taken by General David Petraeus, the head of Central Command that oversees operations in Afghanistan and Iraq. In September of 2009 Petraeus appointed Marine Lieutenant General Richard Natonski to investigate Wanat. Natonski was a veteran field commander who had led troops during fierce fighting in the Iraqi city of Fallujah in December 2004. After nearly four months of investigation Natonski and his team sent findings to General Petraeus, who recommended letters of reprimand for Captain Matthew Myer, Lieutenant Colonel William Ostlund, and Colonel Chip Preysler, commander of the 173rd Airborne Brigade.

Army Secretary Pete Geren appointed one of his most senior commanders, General Charles "Hondo" Campbell, the head of US Army's Forces Command at Fort Bragg, North Carolina, to review the entire case and take appropriate action. By March Campbell had issued letters of reprimand for Preysler, Ostlund, and Myer. The findings were devastating: poor planning and execution for the construction of Kahler and inattentiveness to a lack of resources that left 2nd Platoon ill-equipped to build adequate defenses and send out monitoring patrols.

"Your actions fell below the high standard expected," Campbell wrote in letters to the officers that went out in March of 2010.

If the reprimands were made final, they would destroy the three officers' careers. Myer had been promoted to major and was facing allegations of dereliction for the same battle where he had been singled out for heroism with a Silver Star. Ostlund had since been promoted to colonel and would lose that rank if the findings stood. Before directing that the reprimands be made a permanent part of personnel records, Campbell said he would consider any additional information the officers wanted to provide him. All three responded, but Ostlund's defense was exhaustive. He assembled thick, spiral-bound binders stuffed with PowerPoint slides, data tables and graphs, diagrams, maps, and a multitude of other military records. It was persuasive. Campbell would write in his final analysis that with the additional contextual information provided by the three officers he came to a broader understanding of challenges faced by the brigade, the battalion, and Chosen Company.

Campbell drew some fine distinctions between how he chose to handle the examination versus what Natonski did.

"[Natonski] focused principally on specific actions directly related to the movement to and occupation of" Wanat, Campbell wrote in his findings letter to Ostlund on May 13, 2010. "My review focused on the totality of circumstances that included and affected actions at Wanat."

Far from being feckless, the officers had been burdened with operating in a large and busy war sector with limited resources. The decisions they made under those conditions were reasonable, Campbell said.

"You, Captain Myer and Colonel Preysler were neither negligent or dereliction [sic] in the performance of their duties, exercising a degree of care that a reasonably prudent person would have exercised under the same or similar circumstances. To criminalize command decisions in a theater of complex combat operations is a grave step indeed."

Campbell was also clearly impressed by the two-, three-, and four-star generals who wrote letters of endorsement and support for Ostlund.

Brostrom and other family members assembled for what turned out to be an emotional and widely reported meeting where Natonski laid out his condemnations and the reasons behind them. Then Campbell stunned the families, telling them that after reviewing the evidence, he was revoking the letters of reprimand and clearing the officers.

In a 2011 *Vanity Fair* article writer Mark Bowden quoted Campbell as telling the families: "[They] exercised due care in the performance of their duties. These officers did not kill your sons. The Taliban did."

Brostrom became angry and loud, and other family members applauded when he challenged Campbell's remarks. He repeated Natonski's findings that there had not been enough resources, troops, and supervision for the mission to Wanat.

"Nobody had the balls to say, 'Don't do it!'" Brostrom shouted. "There is no excuse. Things were going wrong. Nobody took any action. ... They left those kids out there to be slaughtered!"

"I can absolutely understand your emotion," Campbell said.

"You can't. You didn't lose a son."

Later that year the Army's Combat Studies Institute came out with its final report on the Wanat battle, and key conclusions had changed from the Cubbison draft version that was leaked the year before.

Nevertheless, there were still career casualties from the controversy. Colonel Chip Preysler, who was commander of the 173rd Airborne Brigade and Ostlund's boss, opted to retire and left the Army on July 31, 2010. Major General Jeffrey Schloesser, one level above Preysler as overall commander for US forces in eastern Afghanistan, saw his nomination to receive a third star placed on hold pending the investigation. He too chose to retire, taking full responsibility for what happened in Wanat, adding that he didn't think Preysler, Ostlund, or Myer should be found guilty of negligence or dereliction of duty. When the reprimands were reversed, Schloesser said he was contacted by the office of Defense Secretary Robert Gates about reconsidering his retirement decision. But Schloesser declined, hoping that by accepting responsibility he might deflect lasting damage to the careers of Ostlund and Myer.

"I'm a man of integrity," he later explained. "I'm a guy who when he says, 'I'm going to do something,' I'm going to do it."

→ ←

As the drama played out in the media many of the Chosen Few were busy reassembling their lives, and the controversy was little more than white noise. Some were recovering from wounds both physical and emotional. A few were wrestling with substance abuse. Many were just moving on. The investigation did manage, however, to divide some of the men, particularly those from 2nd Platoon. There were soldiers angered by the Army's decision to abandon Wanat after so much loss of life. They hadn't wanted to go there in the first place. But they went. They fought desperately for that ground and, at the end of the day, held it, and then commanders gave it up. It was galling for paratroopers like Jared Gilmore who had earned a Silver Star for defending Topside.

"We lose all these people. All these guys wounded. All this, two weeks before going home. All for nothing. Those guys should be sitting at home, drinking beers with their families," Gilmore said years later.

There were those who felt officers might have made poor decisions, but very few believed they were derelict and deserved reprimands. Many disagreed entirely with the decision to investigate Ostlund and Myer. They felt it diminished them all. Chief among those in this camp was Ryan Pitts.

"I don't like the narrative it created that we were victims, that we had incompetent or negligent leadership, because that wasn't the case. I didn't want it framed like that."

He and others who agreed with him, like Michael Denton, said they understood the grief of the families and what motivated them to want reprimands. But the soldiers didn't see the facts the way Natonski did. Both Pitts and Denton wrote letters of endorsement for Ostlund and Myer.

After retaining his rank as colonel, Ostlund eventually rose to become an executive officer on the staff of General Joseph Votel, appointed head of Special Operations Command in 2014. Votel had been a deputy commanding general for the Army task force overseeing operations in eastern Afghanistan when the Rock Battalion was fighting there.

In the years following the Wanat battle Ostlund came to the conclusion that despite his success in tamping down the insurgency in the Korengal Valley, safeguarding the villages, and growing commercial activity in the Pech Valley, the enemy had beaten him in the Waigal Valley. It was not a defeat that would influence the course of the war in any way, but Ostlund knew that when he left, the valley was in the hands of the insurgency.

"At the end of the day we held the ground. But at the end of the deployment they held the valley," Ostlund said. He had offered to improve the lives of the valley people with new roads and other infrastructure improvements, but they had rejected it all. As he saw it, they were no longer worthy of further sacrifice.

"The definition of defeat is either you destroy the enemy or influence them to no longer carry on their objectives," Ostlund said years later. "Well, they influenced me to no longer carry on with my objectives because I was done with them."

At the time of this book's publication, the Waigal River Valley remains in the hands of the insurgency.

Ostlund came to believe the legacy of Chosen Company's war in the Waigal Valley would not be about who controlled it in the end but rather about the heroism of soldiers who repeatedly held their ground against overwhelming odds at Ranch House, during the November ambush, and in Wanat. The way Chosen Company fought always reminded him of a line from the movie *Gladiator* when the Roman general-turned-slave told his fellow combatants before entering the arena, "Brothers, what we do in life echoes in eternity."

"Chosen Company did everything I asked, and much more. The greatest honor is to be called a brother and share, in some small way, in their legacy which will truly echo in eternity."

→ ←

Tyler Stafford spent a month at Walter Reed Army Medical Center in Washington, DC, recovering from shrapnel wounds to both legs and arms. His index finger had to be stitched back together and his bottom teeth capped. In the years that followed, he switched from infantry to Army aviation and achieved his dream of flying. He became an Apache helicopter pilot.

What lingered for Stafford, who is married with two children, was a feeling similar to what many Chosen Company brethren share—that they should have done more when the bullets were flying. "I carry a lot of guilt for leaving Pitts up there," Stafford said years after the battle. "It beat me up for a long, long time."

Guilt is a wound like any other. Chosen Company 1st Sergeant Scott Beeson could see it in the men years after they came home. It showed itself when they gathered to unwind stories at the Sheraton Hotel near the Pentagon during the Medal of Honor ceremonies for Kyle White and, later, Ryan Pitts.

Beeson could almost smell guilt, like some kind of feral beast prowling the hotel, living and breathing inside the young veterans whose only crime had been to volunteer for war. Despite the courage they showed through all the months of unimaginable violence, for most of them it would all boil down to some decision they made in a moment of chaos, frozen forever in a recurring memory.

Among the guilt stricken was Matthew Gobble, who also refused to forgive himself for leaving Pitts. Ever since he was a child Gobble had been fascinated by stories of heroism and wanted to serve in the military. But when his time came in the battle of Wanat, Gobble believed he had failed to measure up.

"I'm not saying that I'm looking for glory," Gobble said long after that battle. "But the one chance that comes for me to actually be a hero, I don't feel that I did everything I could have done. I didn't realize that my wounds were as superficial as they were."

He would later apologize to Pitts for leaving him behind, and the response Gobble received was gracious. "He said, I'll go to war with you any day." It made Gobble feel better in the moment, but it didn't cure his shame in the long run. "I didn't react the same way he did. I didn't react the same way that Sergeant Samaroo, that Sergeant Phillips, that Sergeant Garcia did," Gobble said. "I felt that I had failed everybody and to, I guess, a certain extent secretly, I still kind of feel that way."

As the years passed, a single point in time—some decision made reflexively in the heat of battle—took on so much meaning, it became the sum total of everything they had lived to that moment and colored everything they would be from then on. Beeson saw how this guilt made them weep when they talked about their experiences. It was unjust, and more importantly, it was unhealthy. But it was undeniable.

Brian Hissong—who would leave the Army, marry, have two children, and become a police officer in his home state of Illinois—never stopped thinking that if he had agreed to go along with Matt Kahler that January night, he could have changed the outcome and the platoon sergeant would be alive today. And when so many of his friends died at Wanat months later, Hissong regretted that he survived.

"For years after Wanat I wished I would have died there," he said. "I just wished that while I was there I would have been one of those killed so I wouldn't have to live with the fact that I lived through it."

→ ←

Through his stature as a Medal of Honor recipient, Ryan Pitts became a kind of ad hoc leader for Chosen Few veterans. ("If it's okay with Ryan, it's okay with the rest of us," Stafford once said about discussing the battle.) Pitts also saw in his friends the burden of surviving.

"We talk about it. There's nothing I can do to take that away," Pitts said. "I tell them hopefully we'll see them again someday, and they'll say, 'Hey, don't worry about it.'"

Jason Baldwin, who earned a Silver Star at the Ranch House battle, regretted for years that he left Chosen Company searching for more glory in the Korengal, only to miss the biggest fight of the deployment.

Mike Santiago left the Army shortly after returning home from war. But the one moment he can never forget was when he watched Garcia and Sones head up to Topside. He has replayed it countless times, always with himself going in place of Sones. That's how it should have been, Santiago believes. Maybe it would have ended differently, he keeps thinking. Maybe Garcia would be alive.

Beeson himself is tormented by what he saw as his failure to protect his men at Wanat. "I let them die," he said. "You don't know how many times I went over this in my mind. Why I did not focus 100 percent on security for that location and getting the right equipment out there. . . . We asked them to go do it, and we told them we'd protect them. And we didn't."

→ ←

When the broken body of Joe Lancour—so terribly damaged after being dropped from the medevac helicopter after the November 9 ambush—arrived home in Michigan in the fall of 2007, his family settled for a private viewing with the soldier's remains wrapped almost entirely in gauze. His mother, Starla Owens, was able to identify him only by two tattoos on his right arm. But she faithfully followed the explicit directions Joe had provided for his burial, right down to the white rose placed in his hand.

Sergio Abad's girlfriend, Christina Parra, gave birth to a baby girl. The child Abad called his gummy bear was named Lorilei. The death benefits from the US government—a sum routinely in the six figures—were placed in a special fund for her to use when she comes of age. As Abad had asked, his body was cremated and interred in the location he requested when he was still a boy and told his aunt about how he would die young—Arlington National Cemetery.

Jonathan Brostrom also had made special requests in the event of his death. He was buried at the Hawaii State Veterans Cemetery in Kaneohe in his favorite board shorts, T-shirt, and flip-flops.

Dave Brostrom would eventually launch an effort to have his son's Silver Star upgraded to a Medal of Honor, employing a sworn statement by Tyler Stafford, who believes that his platoon leader died fighting the enemy in hand-to-hand combat, although acknowledging that he could not witness any of this from his vantage point lying in the southern bunker of Topside. As of the fall of 2016, the effort to upgrade the medal was still pending.

In the intervening years after Chosen Company came home, children in the United States were named after men killed or wounded thousands of miles away virtually in another world. Chuck Bell, who fought to stay alive at the battle of Ranch House, named his son Sean Albert Bell after Sean Langevin and Jon Albert. Erich Phillips's firstborn child, a boy, was also named Sean in honor of Langevin. Kyle Silvernale gave his firstborn son the middle name of Lancour.

Jeddah Deloria, who had been left behind in the wreckage of Post Three during the Ranch House battle, remained at Walter Reed Army Medical Center for two years in recovery. He later became an account manager and works with veterans for Oracle Corporation, the multinational computer technology company.

Jon Albert, wounded in the November 9 ambush, was at Walter Reed for a year and a half. His mother, Chele Albert, stayed in Washington, DC, for three months helping her son learn to walk again. When she finally had to return home, he fell into a depression and eventually became addicted to narcotic pain relievers. He moved back home to Iowa, where the drug abuse continued until he was admitted to a detoxification center for twenty-eight days in 2010 and broke the abuse cycle. He eventually took a security job with Kyle Schilling at a nuclear power plant.

Schilling, who Kyle White worked so desperately to save during the ambush, recovered slowly from wounds to his right arm and left leg. He lost muscle mass in his arm and had limited movement. His leg injury left him unable to run. He got married in a 2015 ceremony with Kyle White as his best man and many of the Chosen Few in attendance.

Justin Kalenits, who waved at all of his comrades and told them he loved them as he was hoisted from the ambush battlefield, recovered from his wounds. To help deal with the emotional aftermath of war and at the urging of a therapist, Kalenits started a band back in Cleveland, a heavy metal group called Sykosis. The members wear big, gruesome horror masks and have built an underground following, making enough money to pay travel fare for concert tours.

Aaron Davis, the Destined Company paratrooper who was twice wounded at Topside, was left with only peripheral vision in his right eye. He was diagnosed with posttraumatic stress disorder and has only a spotty memory of the actions he took that earned him a Silver Star. He received a medical retirement from the Army and lost his dream of becoming a Texas state trooper. He decided to become a firefighter.

Mike Johnson, who volunteered for the ambush mission to calm the fears of his friend, Sean Langevin, recovered in a period of weeks from being shot three times and struck by shrapnel. The tough sergeant actually returned to Afghanistan to finish out the deployment with 1st Platoon, and his team provided security at Blessing during the Wanat battle. He stayed in the Army and has five children. He became a sergeant first class and was put in charge of the sexual assault and prevention office at Joint Base Elmendorf-Richardson in Alaska.

Many other members of Chosen Company or those who fought with them forged on to fulfill old aspirations or find new ones.

Brian Townsend, whose nickname was Tizzle, left the Army in 2010 and joined the family business at Townsend Aviation in Monticello, Indiana, with his father, John, and does crop-dusting from a Bell helicopter. James Morrow III, or Jimmy Jam, as Townsend called him, became a chief warrant officer 4 and instructs pilots in a master gunnery course at Fort Rucker, Alabama, where he still flies Apaches.

Chris Ryan, the medevac pilot who fought the buffeting rotor wash of another helicopter while he hovered to pick up Chosen Few casualties at the ambush, saw his life change for the better. Five months before the ambush battle Ryan had flown a mission to recover the remains of an Able Company soldier who was killed in combat, Specialist Christopher Honaker. A forward operating base built by the Rock Battalion was named after Honaker and Specialist Joseph Miracle, another Able Company soldier who was killed. In 2011, when Chris Ryan returned to Afghanistan on another medevac tour, a flight medic with the Army who was Honaker's sister, Charlene, was serving in-country and was eager to visit the base named in honor of her brother and talk with the medevac crew who recovered his body. She met Chris Ryan at Bagram Air Base. They stayed in touch through Facebook and fell in love, marrying in 2013.

Erik Aass, the Chosen Company clerk who fought at Wanat, left the Army on his birthday in 2008 and spent two years in the Maryland National Guard. More recently he has been working for the global professional services giant KPMG as a consultant in their Chicago office. Matt Myer attended Aass's wedding in April 2012. That same year Aass legally changed his name to Haass.

James Takes, who received a Distinguished Service Cross for his valor at the ambush, nearly lost his life in a motorcycle accident after coming home. He recovered and got married on the anniversary of the ambush, November 9, 2013. He and his wife, Lauren, who had two children from a previous marriage, live in South Carolina, where James runs his own heating and air conditioning service company. He and Lauren had their first child together in 2013, a boy they named Sullivan Joseph Takes. The child's middle name, Joseph, is for the second name of Jeddah Joseph Pama Deloria.

Chris McKaig, a survivor of Topside, and Jeffrey Scantlin, the ad hoc medic who treated so many wounded at Wanat, remained with Chosen Company through another deployment to Afghanistan. McKaig stayed on in the Army after that and took a job training snipers at Fort Benning. Scantlin transferred to the Army Reserve in 2011 and became a medic and later a nurse. In 2014 he joined the Texas National Guard, where he trains soldiers to become medics.

David Dzwik, still in the Army, became a senior military instructor for ROTC students at the University of Akron.

Shane Stockard graduated from the Army's sergeant major academy at Fort Bliss, Texas, in the spring of 2016 and became the senior non-commissioned officer for 2nd Battalion of the 504th Parachute Infantry Regiment at Fort Bragg, North Carolina. He wanted to stay with paratroopers.

Sean Samaroo, who led the relief team that saved Ryan Pitts, suffered physically and emotionally in the years after Wanat. He lives with bits of shrapnel embedded throughout his lower body and his arms and legs. There's a piece of metal buried in his right temple. He developed depression, and the posttraumatic stress disorder that had begun after an earlier deployment grew more intense after Wanat. Like others of the Chosen Few, Samaroo turned to alcohol and ultimately wound up in a rehabilitation center. He finally received a medical discharge from the Army in 2012. His marriage to Natasha fell on hard times, but the two have tried to work through it. Only in early 2016 could Samaroo begin to talk about his combat experience in Wanat.

"It's been a rocky road," he said.

Mike Denton, who was part of Samaroo's team, recovered well from his wounds at Wanat. His relationship with the young woman he took on a date during his leave from that deployment blossomed into a romance, and Mike and Christina married in 2009. The couple had a daughter, and Denton works today as a police officer in Florida.

"I try to live each day so that the guys who didn't come home would be proud of me," he said.

While the shrapnel wounds Jacob Sones suffered up at Topside healed, his marriage to Nicole struggled and they separated. Sones was in a dark place suffering from posttraumatic stress disorder and abusing alcohol. But then he spent three months in an Army detoxification program and began to pull his life together. He and his wife reunited. They had a son, Gavin, and Sones began working on a degree in instrumentation and electrical programming at Texas State Technical College.

He remembers his time with Chosen Company as the best period of his life.

"I'm absolutely and completely humbled that I can say that I was one of them," Sones said. "I never laughed harder in my life than I did with them. Just this feeling that life was right. I was where I wanted to be, where I was supposed to be."

Staff Sergeant Kyle Silvernale, who led soldiers in driving militants out of the center of Wanat, left the Army to become a ship captain up in Alaska in 2011. He owns a boat and works with a marine company managing the dispensing of seismic devices on the ocean floor for oil companies searching for new reserves under the sea.

"Anybody who asks me about what I did in the Army, the first thing I'm going to say is, 'I was part of Chosen Company,'" Silvernale said.

"I'm very proud of it, to the point where I put it on my side. I tattooed it on my side. I put crosses for every guy we lost. I'm proud of that. I wouldn't change that for nothing. . . . It's a humbling experience to be part of that group of men, to me some of the greatest, the best men of their generation, and some of the greatest in our country's history."

Erich Phillips, who received a Distinguished Service Cross in the Ranch House battle and a Silver Star at Wanat, stayed in the Army and became a platoon sergeant, serving another tour of duty in Afghanistan. His first marriage did indeed end, but while on leave with a couple of buddies traveling to Barcelona he met and fell in love with a hotel clerk, Sonia Barrioneuvo. They married in 2010 and have a boy and a girl. Phillips rose to the rank of sergeant first class and joined the elite Army Green Berets in 2011.

Phillips said that when he served in Chosen Company he finally found the family he never had growing up.

"There are grown-ass men and I tell them I love them. And I got no problem with it. And I got no problem saying I do. I'll do anything for them. Call me right now and say I need you here, I'd jump in my damn car and drive away," Phillips said. "If it's in the middle of the night, call me, man. I'm here for you."

Scott Beeson also remained in uniform. In December of 2014 he lost his only son, Todd, who idolized his father and followed him into the Army and the airborne. Todd was stabbed to death trying to help a woman who was being beaten by her boyfriend. The tragedy nearly destroyed Beeson's marriage to his wife, Giselle. But they pulled through. Three of their daughters also followed their father into the service; the fourth planned to do the same.

In the fall of 2015 Scott and Giselle drove from Anchorage, Alaska, to Washington, DC, where Beeson became command sergeant major of the Old Guard the following spring. They guard the Tomb of the Unknowns at Arlington National Cemetery and carry out the ceremonial burials on that sacred ground.

Kyle White, who would receive the nation's highest honor for bravery, eventually realized that he'd had enough of war.

"Something changed that day," he said about the ambush.

White was allowed to go back to the United States for several weeks to attend the funerals of his friends Langevin and Lancour. Returning to Afghanistan, he served with 1st Platoon at Bella. But before the siege of Bella he was sent to Blessing for a promotion board to become a sergeant. The command declined to send him back to Bella because the operation to abandon that base was already in the works. Soon he was rotating out of the war zone and did not deploy again, leaving the Army in 2011.

"I didn't feel like I had my whole life in it anymore. I had passed the board and was chosen to be a team leader. But actually after that day I didn't have the drive to keep doing that," he said, referring to the ambush where he earned the Medal of Honor. "I figured if I didn't have my entire head in the game, it's not very fair for the mission or for the guys that would be following me. So I made the decision to move on."

Doctors at the Department of Veterans Affairs later diagnosed White with mild traumatic brain injury and posttraumatic stress disorder from his combat experiences. For a time he considered going into business with James Takes selling outdoor power equipment, but decided against that. Instead he went to school, earning a degree in finance from the University of North Carolina. He took a job as an investment analyst for a bank in Charlotte and later as a vice president for fixed-income sales and trading at a Merrill Lynch, also in Charlotte. White married and divorced and then married again in November of 2015.

Ryan Pitts had a scary moment at the military hospital in Bagram after the Wanat battle when doctors thought they might have to amputate his right leg below the knee. But they managed to save it, and he eventually regained use of both legs. Pitts spent a month as an inpatient at Walter Reed and then another ten months in physical therapy. He started seeing a young woman he knew from his youth back in New

Hampshire, Amy Guilbeault. They married in 2012 and have two children. After being medically retired from the Army, Pitts earned a business degree from the University of New Hampshire.

Pitts said he reached a level of personal fulfillment serving with Chosen Company that he will never know again. "It's crazy to say, but I had some of the best times in my life with those guys in Afghanistan."

It was a feeling shared by many of the Chosen Few.

"It's a struggle to not be living in the past anymore and accept that this was a great thing, but it's gone. It's hard to let go. But you need to move on," Ryan said. "I still struggle with it. You want to find it again. You know you won't. But that's also what made it so special. If we could find that all over the place, then it wouldn't be any different than any other part of my life."

Matt Myer saw the foundations of his belief in God and Christianity shaken to the core after the horrors of Wanat. He had been raised with the faith that Jesus died for everyone's sins and believing in Him was an avenue to paradise. There was a contract with God which held that a good person doing good deeds would see blessing and favor. But he knew that Jason Hovater lived this kind of life, and Myer could not forget the image of that young soldier's destruction. It would be years of thought and contemplation, part of that time spent working with an Army chaplain, before Myer began to reconcile those religious contradictions. He found solace in the book *When God Weeps*, by Joni Eareckson Tada, a woman confined for decades to a wheelchair who discusses how a loving God allows suffering and the opportunity to appreciate unexpected blessings. Myer decided the silver lining from the Waigal Valley ordeal was the indestructible, self-sustaining bonds built with those who survived—Ryan Pitts, Scott Beeson, Erik Haass, Brian Hissong, and others.

"We've gone through this shared hardship, and now we have this really deep, caring interest in one another," Myer said.

Bill Ostlund is hoping that many of the veterans come together again during a Rock Battalion ten-year reunion in 2017, which he believes will offer not only a chance to reconnect but also a tonic for long-term emotional health. He worried that the difficult feelings so many still carry—not being there when the worst happened or surviving when others didn't—don't get better with time. They get worse.

"The reunion will be important. The message is clear: Hey, don't go crazy on us," Ostlund said.

→   ←

Conrad Begaye, who fought in the Ranch House battle, never came back to Chosen Company after he was medically evacuated to Europe for wounds he suffered during the ambush. He struggled emotionally with the experience, with his ambivalence about returning to his unit, and with alcohol. An Army counselor eventually helped him. He went on to become an instructor for the mountain training phase of the Army's Ranger School. More recently he was named a company first sergeant for 101st Airborne Division, heading back to Afghanistan, his first time there since the ambush of November 9, 2007.

For all the years since, Conrad Begaye has felt certain that the medicine pouch he kept in the front pocket of his shirt saved his life that day. He believed it provided some kind of shield against the volley of bullets that killed or gravely wounded so many of his comrades. He also believed the spirits of his Navajo ancestors watched over him and that he was spared for a reason—to train other soldiers in the best practices of war.

After the battle, when Begaye was delivered to a forward surgical hospital and his shirt was removed so doctors could treat him, his medicine pouch went missing. Somehow his platoon sergeant, Shane Stockard, found it, knew it was important, and returned it to Begaye.

It was just another way of bringing his men home.

> > > **SOURCES**

Core material for this book came from a series of interviews with forty-one former members of Chosen Company along with twenty-five family and friends of those who did not come home. Eleven Army and Air Force aviators who flew over the battles also spoke about their experiences. Additional material for this book, particularly for the Wanat battle on July 13, 2008, was drawn from a series of investigations and studies beginning with an initial Army review of the fight, known as an Army Regulation 15-6 investigation, and followed by a voluminous Central Command probe examining actions by the chain of command. Useful material was also provided by the US Army Combat Studies Institute's review of the battle, both a draft and final version. Army 15-6 investigations of the Ranch House fight on August 22, 2007; the ambush of First Lieutenant Matthew Ferrara's patrol on November 9, 2007; the killing of Sergeant First Class Matthew Kahler on January 26, 2008; and the Apache attack on militants on July 4, 2008, were valuable sources.

The book would not have been possible without an extensive file of material graciously provided by Bill Ostlund. The paper and digital records he made available to me were rich with firsthand accounts, including all after-action reports filed by Chosen Company soldiers following the Wanat battle and the entire volume of transcribed testimonies taken during the Central Command investigation. Other material included daily intelligence briefings that were excellent sources for understanding day-to-day enemy activity, and briefings on intercepted enemy radio traffic. Additional material included academic articles on the Kunar and Nuristan culture and insurgencies, PowerPoint briefings on counterinsurgency methodology and operation plans, a bevy of maps and award citations, photographs, and memorials to the fallen.

Erik Haass, who served as radio operator and company clerk for Chosen Company, generously provided a host of material, including copies of rosters that were always evolving because of casualties and replacement arrivals. Erik also provided name spellings, citation narratives, promotion records, stop-loss lists, and a diagram of the Ranch House outpost.

Enemy-filmed videos of the Ranch House, ambush, and Wanat battles offereded valuable insight, as did footage shot from Air Force jets during the Ranch House fight and Apache helicopters over Wanat.

Many live quotes were reconstructed from the memories of those who said or heard them, with the wording cross-checked whenever possible by others who were present. Other quotes were collected from after-action reports where statements were cited with quotation marks.

A large number of direct quotes were drawn from recordings made during Chosen Company's 2007–2008 deployment, including from gun cameras and the many videos shot by individual Chosen Company soldiers during the deployment. Transcribed interviews with Matt Ferrara and Jonathan Brostrom conducted by Army historians who visited the Waigal Valley during their combat tour captured the sentiments of two men who would later be killed. More direct quotes were drawn from letters, e-mails, and journals.

Some intrepid soldier left a digital recorder running for seven hours in Observation Post One or OP1 above Bella combat outpost during the ambush of Lieutenant Ferrara's patrol, capturing the radio discussions between soldiers who were pinned down, those up at the observation post relaying communications, and leaders down at the Bella headquarters. The recording was a rich source of direct quotes and allowed for creation of a timeline of events.

Experts at the US Army Combat Studies Institute at Fort Leavenworth used satellite imagery to create a virtual tour of the Waigal Valley from Wanat north to Bella and the Ranch House outpost. They offer "staff ride" tours of historical battlefields for military academy students, and as of the writing of this book their most requested class was the virtual tour and explanation of the Wanat battle. Instructors kindly allowed me to take this tour of the Waigal Valley to better understand the physical terrain where Chosen Company fought.

Army Captain Jesse Sheehan provided details on the inner workings of parachute training at Fort Benning. Paul Stevenson, director of public affairs at the US Army Garrison Italy in Vicenza, offered a primer on Camp Ederle and the surrounding area.

Diaries provided by Matt Myer contained details of Chosen Company training.

Chris Cavoli, who commanded the unit that preceded Rock Battalion in Kunar and Nuristan provinces, generously shared an unpublished manuscript he wrote that was an invaluable source for understanding his efforts to set up military bases in the Waigal Valley near Aranas and at Bella. The published writings of irregular warfare expert David Kilcullen were also helpful.

Some details about the combat experience of Chosen's sister unit, Battle Company, fighting in the Korengal Valley, were derived from excellent accounts written by Medal of Honor recipient Salvatore Giunta in his book *Living with Honor* and Sebastian Junger in his book *War*. The videos shot by Jason Bogar and others provided a colorful understanding of off-hours life for Chosen Company paratroopers.

Battalion intelligence briefings and transcripts of intercepted enemy radio communications were important for describing the siege of Bella.

Perhaps the most difficult challenge in writing this book was reconstructing, with as much precision as possible, the movements and actions of individual soldiers during the fighting. In trying to get as close to the truth as possible, I studied official written accounts by each soldier; pored over maps, photographs, and video footage; and interviewed the participants. In many cases I reinterviewed subjects and checked back with them repeatedly to reconfirm facts and discuss discrepancies or conflicting accounts, all with an eye toward understanding events as accurately as possible. Many of those interviewed showed incomparable patience with my repetitive questions about details that in some cases bordered on minutia.

That said, I take full responsibility for any errors in this book.

> > > **ACKNOWLEDGMENTS**

This book was possible only because of the generosity and support of so many. First and foremost were those members of the Chosen Few who gave unsparingly of their time and energies, inviting me into their homes, sharing lunches and dinners, and spending long periods on the telephone, trying their best to remember joys and sorrows from their pasts. I thank Jon Albert, Jason Baldwin, Scott Beeson, Conrad Begaye, Charles Bell, Jonathan Benton, Aaron Davis, Adam Delaney, Jeddah Deloria, Michael Denton, Scott Derry, David Dzwik, Ian Eads, Jared Gilmore, Gabriel Green, Matthew Gobble, Justin Grimm, Brian Guttersen, Erik Haass, Tyler Hanson, Brian Hissong, Michael Johnson, Justin Kalenits, Will Krupa, Chris McKaig, Matt Myer, Erich Phillips, Ryan Pitts, Sean Samaroo, Mike Santiago, Jeffrey Scantlin, Adam Schick, Kain Schilling, Kyle Silvernale, Jacob Sones, Tyler Stafford, Shane Stockard, James Takes, Jake Walker, Kyle White, and Nathan Wright.

Family and friends of the fallen were especially kind and gracious sharing details about lost loved ones, along with photographs, videos, letters, diaries, and personal e-mails. I'm grateful to Sergio Abad's great aunt, Sorangel Herrara; Jonathan Ayers's parents, Bill and Suzanne Ayers; Jason Bogar's mother, Carlene Cross; Phil Bocks's mother, Peggy Bocks; Jonathan Brostrom's parents, David and Mary Jo Brostrom, and his friend, Amanda Wilson; Matthew Ferrara's mother, Linda Ferrara, and his brothers, Andrew and Damon; Israel Garcia's widow, Lesly Garcia; Jason Hovater's sister, Jessica Davis; Matthew Kahler's widow, Vicki Patterson, and his mother, Colleen Kahler; Joe Lancour's mother, Starla Owens, and his father, Rob Lancour; Sean Langevin's widow, Jessica Langevin, and his mother, Roxane Langevin; Jeff Mersman's father, Robert Mersman, and his uncle, Mark Mersman; Matthew Phillips's widow, Eve Phillips; Pruitt Rainey's father, Frankie Gay; and Gunnar Zwilling's brother, Alexander Zwilling.

I'm grateful for the help of the medevac crew members who rescued the wounded at the ambush and Wanat, including Eric Doe, Clayton Horney,

Justin Madill, John Morales, Peter Rohrs, Chris Ryan, and Ben Seipel, as well as A-10 pilots Andrew Wood and the late Dan Cruz, who contributed selflessly of his time and memories and, tragically, died before publication. My gratitude also goes out to the Apache pilots Jimmy Morrow and Brian Townsend who fought at Wanat.

Bill Ostlund's support in providing a mountain of documents and ready access for any questions was unparalleled and absolutely critical to writing this book. Other current and former officers and officials to whom I'm indebted include Chris Cavoli, Erik Malmstrom, Jeffrey Schloesser, Jesse Sheehan, and Paul Stevenson. Don Wright, deputy director of Army Press at Fort Leavenworth, which includes the Combat Studies Institute, graciously invited me to Kansas to see a virtual tour of the Waigal Valley and learn more about what happened to Chosen Company. I also wish to thank Frank Shirer, chief of the Historical Resources Branch of the US Army Center of Military History. Researcher John Beckham's generous and kind assistance was indispensable. Professional arborist Tim DeCoste willingly assisted me with identifying trees populating the Ranch House battle site and the mulberry that was a magnet for rocket-propelled grenades over Topside.

USA Today allowed me to work part time in order to research and write this book, and for that I'm grateful. I would also like to thank my editor at the newspaper, Owen Ullmann, for his valuable support; my book editor, Robert Pigeon, for his steady guidance and many kindnesses; and my agent, Jill Marr, for her eternal optimism. For their encouragement and willingness to listen, I want to thank Ray Locker, Jim Michaels, Rick Paddock, Doug and Kathie Ross, Dana Theus, Liz Szabo, Greg Toppo, and Tom Vanden Brook.

Absolutely crucial to the completion of this book was the assistance of my good friend, Denise Kostbar, who selflessly gave of her time and energy to transcribe interviews, proofread transcripts, and share her thoughts, feelings, and tears of compassion for the Chosen Few.

More than anyone I am indebted and fortunate for the love and support of my wife, Faye Fiore. She carefully read the manuscript more than once, offering brilliant writing insights, thoughtful editing, and boundless encouragement. She alone saw my dream of writing this book and helped make it happen. I will cherish her forever.

# >>> INDEX